Panpsychism
and
the Religious Attitude

The Happiness of Fish

Chuang Tzu and Hui Tzu were taking a leisurely walk along the dam of the Hao River. Chuang Tzu said,

"The white fish are swimming at ease. This is the happiness of the fish."

"You are not fish," said Hui Tzu. "How do you know its happiness?"

"You are not I," said Chuang Tzu. "How do you know that I do not know the happiness of the fish?"

Hui Tzu said, "Of course I do not know, since I am not you. But you are not the fish, and it is perfectly clear that you do not know the happiness of the fish."

"Let us get at the bottom of the matter," said Chuang Tzu. "When you asked how I knew the happiness of the fish, you already knew that I knew the happiness of the fish but asked how. I knew it along the river."

—The Chuang Tzu

Panpsychism
and
the Religious Attitude

D. S. Clarke

State University of New York Press

Published by
State University of New York Press, Albany

© 2003 State University of New York

For information, address State University of New York Press, Albany, NY
www.sunypress.edu

Production by Judith Block
Marketing by Fran Keneston

Library of Cataloging-in-Publication Data

Clarke, D. S. (David S.), 1936–
    Panpsychism and the religious attitude / D. S. Clarke.
        p. cm.
    Includes bibliographical references and index.
    ISBN 0-7914-5685-4 (alk. paper)—ISBN 0-7914-5686-2
    (pbk. : alk. paper)
      1. Panpsychism.   I. Title.

B823 .C55   2003
141—dc21   2002070715

10 9 8 7 6 5 4 3 2 1

Contents

Preface

This work is an essay in defense of panpsychism, the view affirming the presence throughout nature of mentality in the form of a qualitative perspective on an environment. Panpsychism has had a long history marked by a variety of formulations and much controversy. It has had its advocates in the nineteenth and twentieth centuries, but weakness in certain formulations of the doctrine have left it vulnerable to criticisms. Those by Paul Edwards and Karl Popper have been especially effective in discouraging its widespread acceptance and in promoting the view that panpsychism offers its advocates an emotionally satisfying view at the expense of sacrificing minimal standards of rationality.[1] It is this view that I want to challenge after outlining a defensible version.

Panpsychism was extensively discussed at the end of the nineteenth century under the influence of Charles Darwin's theory of evolution. One of the most sensible discussions is provided by William James in chapter VI of his *Principles of Psychology*. James thinks that panpsychism in the form of what he refers to as the "mind-stuff" theory can only be established for psychology if simple units of experiencing can be identified whose compounding results in the consciousness of which we are aware. Since there is no experimental evidence for such compounding, panpsychism has no place in psychology. He does acknowledge, however, that evolutionary theory provides grounds for the doctrine because the introduction of mentality of consciousness from matter represents a radical discontinuity in evolution. We ought, he says, "sincerely to try every possible mode of conceiving the dawn of consciousness so that it may not appear equivalent to the irruption into the universe of a new nature, non-existent until then." The most plausible solution, he indicates, is to conceive of consciousness as always being present:

> If evolution is to work smoothly, consciousness in some shape must have been present at the very origin of things. Accordingly we find that the more clear-sighted evolutionary philosophers are beginning to posit it there. Each atom of the nebula, they suppose, must have had an aboriginal atom of consciousness linked with it. . . . Some such doctrine . . . is an indispensable part of a thorough-going philosophy of evolution. According to it there must be an infinite number of degrees of consciousness, following the degrees of complication and aggregation of the primordial mind-dust.[2]

Our conceptions of cosmology and evolution have changed since the nineteenth century. The Big Bang theory has replaced the earlier view that stars and planets evolved from an original gaseous nebula. Also, we now recognize the discontinuities in evolution represented by such events as the relatively sudden extinction of the dinosaurs and the corresponding rapid development of land mammals. Nevertheless, despite these changes in theory, the transition from bare matter to material systems with a mental perspective on things remains an unexplained puzzle, and panpsychism of a kind related to the speculations of the nineteenth century provides—so I will argue—a plausible alternative solution.

To say it is plausible is not to claim either conclusive arguments in its favor or experimental confirmation. Panpsychism represents one of what James describes as those "great traditional objects of belief" which we "cannot afford to despise." Whether we realize it or not," he notes, "there is always a great drift of reasons, positive and negative, towing us in their direction."[3] The chapters that follow are an extended argument that "the drift of reasons" favors the panpsychist alternative. Forced with a choice, this alternative should be preferred over its competitors, but we cannot expect the reasoning used to arrive at this conclusion to have the finality we find in some areas of philosophy. For many philosophers, this in itself is good reason to avoid discussing it, preferring to restrict themselves to more tractable questions about uses of language and areas where there seems to be realistic hope of eventual agreement on answers. Better to be cautious, they think, than to run the risk of repeating the frustrating failures of the past. I sympathize with this preference. But the effect of following it has not been to eliminate metaphysics from contemporary intellectual life. Instead, we find two competing metaphysical dogmas enshrined. One is that of universal mechanism whose proponents note continuity between infrahuman and human levels, and use this continuity to argue from what seems to be our ability to give mechanical explanations of infrahuman behavior to the conclusion that human behavior can be similarly explained. The other is a humanistic bias that elevates capacities specific to the human species into metaphysical differences between ourselves and other forms of life. Both deserve to be challenged, because to sit back and refuse to accept the challenge is, in effect, to contribute to the continuance of their reign.

This requires more than expressing biases and exchanging invectives with those of differing views, however. To be a responsible participant in the debate over metaphysical alternatives is to be aware of epistemological issues of a sort that appear as early as Chuang Tzu's discussion in the frontispiece of knowing about the happiness of fish. The methodological and linguistic considerations we are now able to bring to bear mark an advance over nineteenth century discussions, and are a prerequisite to any decision by us in the twenty-first century whether to accept or reject the panpsychist thesis.

This book consists of two parts. The first four chapters outline panpsychism as represented by some of its early and more recent advocates, and then redefine it and contrast it with the alternatives of humanism and universal mechanism. This survey is a highly selective one that seeks to isolate issues raised in more recent discussions of panpsychism. One of the central problems of this first part is the methodological one of extending the language with which we report and express sensations, feelings, and attitudes to organisms with which we have no social interactions.

In the last three chapters, the focus shifts to larger questions associated with the religious attitude. Daniel Dennett's mechanistic view of evolution and the problem of the evolutionary origins of mentality are the topics of chapter 5. Here we consider an "Origination Argument" derived from the earlier continuity argument outlined by James, and note the apparent conflict between this argument and the analogies initially used to justify panpsychism. Although the version of panpsychism I offer for considering here is atheistic, and disavows any relations to theology, it has religious aspects. Chapter 6 contrasts atheistic panpsychism's solution to the problem of explaining the origination of mentality with that of traditional theism, while the final chapter argues for the consistency of panpsychism with a religious attitude shared by the world's religions.

An important stimulus for this work was a reading group organized by Pat Manfredi of Southern Illinois University (SIU) to discuss Dennett's *Darwin's Dangerous Idea.* Manfredi and David King of SIU's Anatomy Department championed Dennett's views during our discussions, and I found myself quickly in opposition. This work evolved as my way of laying the foundations for opposition to both Dennett and to some influential humanistic views. I did the bulk of writing while on a temporary teaching assignment at Kansai Gaidai University in Osaka, Japan during the period 1997–1999, with versions of its guiding ideas tried out to audiences at Kyoto University and Tokyo University. I am grateful to President Sadato Tanimoto, Dean Nobuhiro Adachi, Dean Takeo Fujii, and Professor Seisaku Yamamoto of Kansai Gaidai for providing a wonderfully hospitable environment, to Professor Yamamoto for lunch-time discussions that helped clarify issues, and to Professor Kunitake Ito of Kyoto University, Professor Michio Kobayashi of Osaka City University, and Professor Junichi Murata of Tokyo University and their colleagues and students for valuable comments and criticisms. Jane Bunker, Katy Leonard, and Judith Block of the State University of New York Press helped shepherd this project through its various states, and three anonymous readers provided helpful comments. A & B Typesetters and Editorial Services, Inc., provided capable copyediting assistance. Most of all, I am grateful to my wife Sadako for the support that made this work possible.

CHAPTER ONE

Introduction

Panpsychism has been developed in a variety of ways through the course of philosophy. In the first section of this chapter, I offer an introductory sketch that abstracts some common features within this variety. In very general terms, panpsychism is the view that mentality is present in all natural bodies with unified and persisting organization. Its principal advocates have excluded from its scope aggregates lacking this naturally occurring organization such as rocks, trees, and human artifacts. One of the central problems for such a view is that of specifying the range of natural bodies to which this thesis applies, and for this there are a number of alternative solutions. After surveying some of them, I outline the form of the analogical inference that constitutes the doctrine's initial rational basis. Finally, the epistemological status of panpsychism as a thesis of metaphysics is examined in a preliminary way.

What is Panpsychism?

The etymology of "panpsychism" provides us some suggestions of its meaning. *Pan* is the word in ancient Greek for "all," and *psyche* means "soul," which the early Greek philosophers understood to be the principle of life, that whose presence distinguishes the living from the dead and inanimate. Thus, panpsychism can initially be understood as the thesis that throughout nature there are forms of life. This animistic version of the doctrine is commonly referred to as *hylozoism*.

After Gottfried Wilhelm von Leibniz, panpsychism was reformulated in psychological terms as the claim that we can justifiably attribute mentality to all natural forms. Such attribution is justified, we would say, when its object can be said to have an interested point of view, a perspective from which things around it are encountered. Such a perspective has a qualitative aspect in at least some minimal degree. It is this psychological version that is our topic.

It should be noted that we use the term "mentality" in this formulation of the panpsychist thesis, and avoid the term "consciousness" that has been commonly used. If the term "consciousness" is defined as having a qualitative perspective on an environment, there can be no objection to its use. But the term is typically used in a way that implies either self-awareness of a kind that seems unique to the human species or a type of experiencing restricted to animals. Thus, someone can be said to have not only a certain feeling (a pain in his foot), but also to be conscious of having this feeling; or of not only seeing a tree, but of being consciously aware of seeing it. Such second-order reflective awareness would seem to require the use of language, and thus cannot be attributed to lower animals (We return to this topic later). In contrast to this use of "consciousness," Nicholas Humphrey understands it as applying to having sensations, and this seems to be the sense used by those who inquire about the evolutionary origins of consciousness.[1] Such a use has the effect of automatically ruling out the panpsychist thesis, however, for having sensations requires sense receptors of a kind only observed for animals. Only organisms with pain or pleasure receptors can experience pain or pleasure. At levels more primitive than the organic, mentality, if indeed present, would seem to be the capacity within certain natural bodies lacking sense receptors for a type of protoexperiencing with a qualitative aspect. Exercises of mentality as a capacity may be intermittent, as is the case for our own wakefulness interrupted by sleep. It is conceivable that there are bodies in which this capacity is exercised for only one infinitesimally brief moment during their entire careers as a type of qualitative blip. If so, they would qualify for attribution of mentality as understood here, although they would not be said to be conscious in either the sense of being aware of the exercise of their mental capacity or of having a sensation.

In addition to the capacity for consciousness, experiencing, and protoexperiencing, more recent advocates of panpsychism such as Alfred North Whitehead and Charles Hartshorne have added the characteristic of having at least a minimal degree of spontaneity of behavior that we associate with some form of self-determination as a prerequisite for mentality. From the standpoint of an outside observer, this behavior can be described as probabilistic or "chance" behavior, but mental spontaneity is to be distinguished from indeterminacy as such. The claim that all organized natural bodies have a qualitative perspective is logically independent of the claim that they also possess spontaneity of behavior; indeed determinists might concede the first but would deny the second. Because of its association with Whitehead and Hartshorne, panpsychism will be understood here as endorsing both claims, and I shall not consider a deterministic version.

Understood as claiming that all natural bodies have a qualitative perspective, panpsychism is so vague that it is effectively meaningless; in one sense it would seem to be trivially true, in another obviously false. We attribute mentality to a variety of sentient forms, including mammals, reptiles, and insects. If panpsychism were to require only that mentality be present wherever there is sentient life, then none could question it: it becomes tautologously true by simply stipulating that sentience is a form of mentality. But if the doctrine is taken as holding that to everything we see around us we can attribute mentality—if *pan* is to be interpreted as literally everything—it would seem to be absurd. Objects in our environment include rocks and human artifacts like bottles, chairs, and tennis balls, and these we would judge to lack a qualitative perspective as the requisite of mentality. Some thinkers to whom the "panpsychism" label is applied have extended the thesis to such objects, and in so doing have contributed to the disrepute into which the doctrine has generally fallen. But as we shall see in the next chapter, the principal figures in the panpsychist tradition have been careful to exclude such aggregate objects as planets, rocks, and artifacts.

To avoid the opposites of triviality and absurdity, advocates of panpsychism must both extend the term "natural form" beyond what we recognize as sentient and at the same time restrict the doctrine's application in a way that excludes rocks and bottles. An initial specification would require a subject with mental attributes to be a unified natural body sharing our evolutionary past and with an appropriate level of structure and internal organization.

The requirement that there be a natural body excludes all artifacts, including those with functional organization. We shall be considering a version of panpsychism that does not make this exclusion and considers the possibility of extending mentality to all information processing devices, including thermostats and computers. Biological organisms with a shared evolutionary past do indeed process information, but it does not at all follow that information processors with very different origins have the same characteristics as these organisms. Such objects as thermostats and computers have functional organizations that introduce regularities into their reactions to their environments, but they certainly lack a perspective or interested point of view in terms of how these environments are encountered. Lacking an evolutionary past, they should not be included under the heading of "natural body" as used in the formulation of panpsychism.

Quarks and leptons, as the fundamental particles of physics, are by definition elements that are themselves not wholes consisting of parts, and therefore lack organizational structure. It would seem, therefore, that, like rocks and bottles, they should be excluded from panpsychism's scope. Nevertheless, we find its principal advocates extending the scope of their doctrine to fundamental particles, and there are indeed difficulties in excluding them, difficulties which we shall postpone considering until chapter 5. For now, it is sufficient to note that because by definition they lack internal structure, fundamental particles fail to satisfy what seems to be an essential feature of the natural bodies to which the panpsychist thesis is extended.

It is also difficult to exclude crystals such as a piece of quartz because their lattice arrangements of atoms exhibit structure and a type of organization, and they certainly do have an evolutionary past. Similar considerations hold of metals like gold, silver, and iron. We would not judge such forms of organization to qualify for mental attribution: a nugget of gold certainly can't be said to have a point of view. But on what grounds can they be excluded? An answer can be provided by requiring a structure and organization in which there is functional specialization of parts within a unified whole. Such specialization is exhibited by the organelles and macromolecules making up the cells of the human body and plants, and thus cells would meet the condition of a "unified body with an appropriate level of structure and internal organization." It may be exhibited in certain molecules, perhaps in atoms, and even by certain particles that are the constituents of atoms. Because of its relatively large mass, there is speculation that the so-called "top quark" recently identified in the laboratory may have some internal structure, and hence not be a fundamental particle.[2] If so, it would qualify as a possible subject of mental attribution in a way that crystals and lumps of gold do not.

How do we determine whether an object exhibits the appropriate unity of structure and organization? How do we distinguish between a cell-like body with unity and a crystal-like object that lacks the appropriate type of organization? Here we again risk trivialization, this time in the form of circularity, for we can't say that there is "appropriate unity" only when we are able to ascribe mentality. This must be recognized as a problem for panpsychism because the nature of the "appropriate level" of organization remains unspecified. But the problem does not seem to be an insuperable one. The distinction between a unified whole with specialization of parts and an organized collection of elements is one that seems capable of extension from the cell–crystal contrast to other natural forms. Although there admittedly will be difficult borderline cases, the distinction itself seems one that we can apply to a wide range of examples.

There is an immediate qualification we must introduce, however. A dead animal is a body with a unified organization of specialized parts, and thus qualifies for mental attribution by the account just given. But it is subject to the tendency toward the increase of entropy to which all nature is subject, and over time makes the transition from organization to disorganization and degradation of structure. We must therefore add the condition that to be a possible subject of mental attribution, a natural body must maintain itself through homeostasis against the forces of the environment in which it is placed. A necessary condition for an object to be a subject of mental attribution would thus seem to be that it both exhibit unity of organization as a whole relative to specialized parts and maintain itself through homeostasis.

Are these two necessary conditions of unity and homeostasis also sufficient conditions for mental attribution? The answer would seem to depend on the version of panpsychism being defended. For what we can refer to as *restricted panpsychism*, further conditions are imposed. These typically have the effect of restricting mental attribution to organic living forms capable of metabolism and either asexual or bisexual reproduction. As we shall presently see, Aristotle's extension of the term "soul" to plants seems to represent a special form of such restricted panpsychism. Other possible forms of this version may restrict mental attributions to those organisms exhibiting learning, as for the single-celled amoeba or a primitive organism such as a protozoa. Such forms of restricted panpsychism are by no means trivial, and indeed are controversial—metabolism and reproduction themselves don't seem to require the attribution of mentality. And even if we grant that where there is learning there is a qualitative perspective, there are many who would describe learning, even that exhibited by relatively advanced mammals, in mechanical terms that exclude mentality as understood in terms of spontaneity.

Restrictions of this kind, however, are inconsistent with panspsychism's first syllable "pan," which implies universality of scope. Far more interesting, controversial, and removed from triviality is *unrestricted panpsychism*, the version that sets no further conditions on mental attribution beyond those of unity of organization and homeostasis, and it is this version that we will be considering here, because this version of mental attribution can be extended from multicellular organisms with central nervous systems to single-celled organisms such as protozoa, to certain molecules with internal specialization, and even to atoms and certain subatomic particles. For understandable reasons, such extensions strain the credulity of many, striking some as bizarre and as an example of that fatal tendency to overgeneralize that so often marks philosophy. But cogent reasons can be given for unrestricted panpsychism, as I hope to be able to show in this chapter's next section, the historical survey of chapter 2, and in chapter 5 where the topic is the role of mentality in evolution. And as we shall see in the final two chapters, with unrestricted panpsychism rests the most plausible justification that can be given of religious belief in the eternality of mentality.

In this preliminary account of conditions for attributing mentality I have made no mention of the problem of describing the nature of mentality. As we shall presently see, it is ascribed to natural forms by analogically extending features of our own experience that include the presence of a qualitative aspect and spontaneity of behavior. But to claim *that* mentality is present in a given natural body is not to claim to know *what* this mentality is, in particular whether it is the same as or different from the physical state of this body—that is, to make a choice between materialism and dualism. As I have argued elsewhere,[3] both metaphysical alternatives mistakenly assume that there is a meaningful sense of identity and difference employed when we say either that the mental is the same as the physical or that it is different. There is no need for panspsychism to involve itself in a debate that is due to imposing on the very special subject matter of the mental logical categories derived from language used to refer to spatially locatable objects.[4] The question before us is simply whether mentality as qualitative and spontaneous—whatever this might happen to be—is present in all self-sustaining, organized natural forms.

At this introductory stage, we should mention differences between advocates of panpsychism and philosophical humanists arguing for radical discontinuities between the mentality characteristic of humans and that of infrahuman species. Human mentality is claimed by these humanists to be marked by self-consciousness and freedom of choice, while infrahuman mentality, including that of the higher primates, at best exhibits unreflective consciousness, and as a result simply accompanies behavior that is the effect of antecedent mechanical causes. Most recent advocates of panpsychism agree with philosophical humanists in rejecting deterministic theories of human behavior. But they extend this denial also to infrahuman species of organisms, and finally to all unified, self-maintaining bodies to which we attribute mentality. Mentality, wherever it is present, is claimed to be accompanied by spontaneity with at least some degree of similarity to the freedom of choice with which we humans think we are endowed. Everyone must acknowledge the sharp discontinuities that mark the various stages in the evolution of mentality. But for panpsychism as we are understanding it here, no one stage introduces metaphysical distinctions between the free and the determined of the kind advocated by philosophical humanism. Besides distinguishing the doctrine from humanism, the claim that mentality has a spontaneous aspect distinguishes it from a view we can label *universal mechanism*, the view that the behavior of all natural forms, including members of the human species, is the effect of determining antecedent causes.

Analogical Inferences

Throughout this introductory discussion, I have been referring vaguely to "mental attributions" without attempting to specify the forms they might take. We attribute to others beliefs, desires, and hopes, and say of them that they see, hear, smell, etc. various kinds of objects. Pleasures and pains, as well as such feelings as itches, are also attributed. One major problem we face is deciding the extent to which such attributions of mentality can be extended to other natural forms. Can we say of a dog that it believes that there is a bone under the ground, or simply that it expects to find it? Does the dog desire the bone, or simply want it? And what will be the form of mental attributions applied to primitive organisms without sense receptors for seeing, hearing, smelling, and so forth? Is there some form of attribution that will apply to all levels of complexity of organization, or does each level have its unique form? Such questions demand that panpsychism develop some theory of mental attributions that will provide grounds for answers. It must also develop some method of extending mental terms beyond their normal applications to attribute mentality to primitive natural forms. In chapter 4 I shall be examining the nature of specific forms of mental attributions and problems related to their extension. For now we must try to understand, at least in a preliminary way, the logical basis for attributing mentality in any form to members of other species.

This logical basis is provided by what is known as an *analogical inference*. An analogical inference begins with two populations, *A* and *B*, whose members are respectively $a_1, a_2, \ldots, a_n$ and $b_1, b_2, \ldots, b_n$. There may be only a single individual in each population. We assume that both *A* and *B* share some attributes $P_1, P_2, \ldots, P_n$ in common and that *A* has the further attribute *Q*. We then infer that population *B* has *Q* also. The form of inference is thus

$$A \text{ and } B \text{ are } P_1, P_2, \ldots, P_n$$
$$\underline{A \text{ is } Q}$$
$$\text{Therefore, } B \text{ is } Q$$

The attributes predicated of the populations *A* and *B* by $P_1, P_2, \ldots, P_n$ we can refer to as the *base* of the analogy, while *Q* expresses the *projected attribute*. Alternatively, an analogical inference can be described as the *analogical extension* of the predicate *Q* from *A* to a population *B* sharing a common base with it.

To illustrate this form of inference, suppose we have a barrel of apples all of which are red and ripe and come from the same orchard (the base P_1, P_2, P_3). We cut open half of them (the population *A*) and find they are rotten inside. We may then infer by analogy that the other half of the barrel of apples (*B*) are also rotten inside—that the adjective *rotten* (the projected *Q*) can be extended from *A* to *B*. The larger the number *n* of attributes $P_1, P_2, \ldots, P_n$ that are shared by *A* and *B*, the stronger the inference, provided the shared attributes are relevant to the possession of *Q* by *B*. Size and shape of apples do not seem relevant to their rottenness in the way that coloration, ripeness, and common origin are. Therefore, if the only attributes shared by the apples were their being all large and round, the inference to rottenness would be extremely weak.

It should be noted that while the number of attributes shared by A and B is relevant to the strength of the analogical inference, the sizes of the populations A and B are not. Very strong analogical inferences can be formed where both A and B consist of single individuals. If astronomers discover that our planet Earth and a planet orbiting a distant star are similar in mineral composition and evolutionary history, they would infer with some confidence that because water is present on Earth it is also present on the other planet. To introduce the size of A and B is to confuse analogical with inductive inferences.[5] For an inductive inference, the size of the sample $a_1, a_2, \ldots, a_n$ sharing attributes P and Q is relevant to the conclusion that the next individual a_{n+1} of kind P sampled is also a Q. An inductive inference from 3,000 crows being black to the conclusion that the next crow will be black is certainly stronger than an inference to the same conclusion based on a sample of 15 black crows because the increase of sample size usually is accompanied by variation within the sample and makes it more representative of the total population. We could infer from the fact that members of a selected sample of apples in our barrel are rotten to the conclusion that all of them are rotten, and in this case the size of the sample would be relevant to the strength of the inference. But this inductive inference is very different in form from the analogical inference of the previous paragraph. Analogical inferences, unlike inductive inferences, rely on similarities between populations, which may consist of single individuals, not on representativeness of samples produced by variation.

Besides strengthening an analogical inference by increasing the relevant attributes of the base shared by A and B, we can also achieve the same effect by making the projected Q more indefinite. The conclusion that members of B are all rotten is fairly specific, and needs the support of a reasonably large number of relevant attributes. But we could choose the much more indefinite attribute of having some defect or other as our Q. The conclusion that B is a Q would then require much weaker premises, perhaps only the observation that both A and B are from the same barrel. In this way, making a more indefinite Q allows reducing the inference's base. We thus have two ways of strengthening an analogical inference: either increase its base or make the projected attribute more indefinite.

In the 19th century, John Stuart Mill argued that we can justify our mental attributions to another person on the basis of an analogical inference that starts with the observation that when we have a certain experience, it is combined with a characteristic form of behavior. For example, when I have a sharp pain in my foot I may commonly grimace, hold my foot, and hop around. I then notice that another person is exhibiting similar behavior, and infer by analogy that this person is also experiencing pain. Here I am a, the other person is b, and the base $P_1, P_2, \ldots, P_n$ are the observed behavioral similarities between the two of us. The inference is then made that because I experience pain (Q), b does also. Mill's analogical inference has since been proposed as a solution to the "problem of other minds," the problem each individual faces of justifying the belief that other minds exist other than his or her own. We may be aware only of our own sensations and feelings, but because these are accompanied by behavior that we also observe in others, we are justified in attributing these experiences to them.

Mill's account seems mistaken for those mental ascriptions we apply to members of our own species because inferences seem irrelevant to them. Often we base our ascriptions to another of a certain belief or desire directly on the basis of what he or she says, as when someone says "It will rain" and we attribute to this person the belief that it will rain. We do this without comparison to a belief state of which we are aware. But as Ludwig Wittgenstein and Gilbert Ryle have noted, even where behavior is the basis for our ascriptions, there seems to be a direct, noninferential judgment. I see a man on the balcony of a tenth-floor apartment cautiously staying away from the railing, and judge he is afraid of heights. But this does not seem to be the result of an inference in which I notice similarities between my behavior and his, know that I am experiencing fear when I behave in such a way, and conclude he does also. I don't regard his cautious behavior as *evidence* of some unseen fear. Instead, his behavior would seem to constitute *criteria* for ascribing fear. The term *fear* means for us, at least in part, what I see before me.

For infrahuman creatures, however, the situation is very different. I see a recently caught fish flopping around on the deck of a boat. Is it experiencing pain? The fact that we can raise this question and have some initial uncertainty of its answer indicates that the flopping does not constitute a criterion for applying the word "pain." We may conclude that the fish is in pain, but this seems to be only after an analogical inference in which we compare the flopping to the writhing behavior of those humans we describe as being in pain and judge that they are sufficiently similar to warrant the analogical extension of pain. Our inference seems to have the following form: Both humans and fish exhibit behavior that is similar in relevant respects. Humans exhibiting this behavior are in pain. Therefore, the fish is also. Clearly, the greater the anatomical and behavioral similarities between members of infrahuman species and our own species, the stronger the analogical inference. We are thus more confident about ascribing pain to a yelping dog that has just had its foot stepped on than we are to the flopping fish.

Thus there seems to be a common form of analogical inference applied both in extending "rotten" to apples in a barrel and "pain" to fish. But we should not be misled into overlooking differences between the extension of standard descriptive predicates and mental predicates. An obvious one is that there is always the possibility of independent confirmation of conclusions reached in the standard cases. We can, after all, cut open the unexamined apples to determine whether they are in fact rotten, and we may eventually determine through later space exploration whether water in fact exists on the planet similar to our own. In contrast, the *only* possible basis for concluding that the fish experiences pain is to be found in the similarities of anatomy and behavior. There can be no independent confirmation.

Another contrast exists for the meaning of the predicates being projected. We have been assuming that the term used to express the projected Q of an analogical inference has a meaning fixed by agreed-on criteria of application. This is certainly true of the adjective "rotten" when applied to the populations of apples. But this assumption does not seem to apply to "pain" as extended from human applications to attributions for dogs and fish; here we lack agreement on criteria of application. Our uncertainty about applying "pain" to the flopping fish seems not only to be due to the tentativeness of the analogical inference being employed, but includes also the lack of a fixed meaning for "pain." Whether the term should be applied seems to be as much a matter of a *practical decision* on our part about the term's application as the acceptance of a warranted descriptive conclusion. This feature seems to be shared by the mental ascriptions of the far-reaching kind advocated by panpsychism. As we shall see when considering religious implications of the doctrine, its thesis is to be judged as much on the basis of practical as well as theoretical considerations.

It is important to remind ourselves of the difference between the thesis of panpsychism and specific extensions of mental predicates. Panpsychism as a philosophical doctrine does not attribute any specific experiences to members of this or that species. Its claim is instead that mentality in general, that is, having a point of view, a perspective on things with qualitative and spontaneous aspects, can be attributed to all natural forms having an appropriate level of unified structural organization that maintain themselves over a period of time against their environments. The basis for this extended claim would seem to be an analogical inference generalized beyond applications to creatures such as dogs and fish for which there are behavioral and anatomical similarities to ourselves. Insects such as beetles, wasps, and bees have sense receptors and exhibit exploratory, communicative, and aggressive behavior. Even amoebas and protozoa exhibit learning behavior that we seem to be able to use as the basis for attributing sensitivity in the form of primitive tactile sensations. But for extensions of mentality to the molecular and atomic level we have only unity of structural organization and homeostasis as a feature shared by our bodies, those of infrahuman species, including mammals, fish, insects, and protozoa, and finally the suborganic forms to which unrestricted panpsychism attributes mentality. The persisting unity of these natural bodies constitutes by itself the base for the analogical inference to the presence of mentality.

How strong is this inference? Rather weak is the quite obvious reply. This is seen by considering our barrel of apples where we are attempting to determine the rottenness of unexamined apples. Suppose the only attribute the apples share is simply that they are apples in the same barrel, with variation in color, ripeness, and origin. Then if we find that the half we examine are rotten, we would have a very weak analogical inference to the conclusion that the remainder are also. We have seen how in attributing mentality we start with ascriptions we make to others of our species on the basis of behavioral and anatomical criteria. The fewer the respects in which behavior and anatomy of other species is similar to ours the more tentative the inference, as for our more confident attribution of pain to the yelping dog than to the flopping fish. Where we lack sense receptors and behavior, such as in inanimate suborganic forms, we are left with only unity of organization and homeostasis as common features, and at this stage the inference falters. Moreover, we are given no convincing reasons for thinking that these remaining features are in themselves relevant to the attribution of mentality. They may be, but why they are remains to be explained.

In defense of panpsychism, it must be emphasized again that weakness due to an inference's limited base can be offset by making the projected attribute more indefinite. As we saw, by changing the projected attribute from rottenness to simply having some defect or other, with nicks and bruises as well as rottenness qualifying as defects, we offset decreases in similarity between the apples. In this way we generate a considerably stronger analogical inference, even if we continue to begin with the premiss that the only shared feature is being an apple in the barrel. Panpsychism does not claim that macromolecules with the appropriate unity of organization have pains or pleasures, nor indeed that they have any sensations whatsoever. The claim is only to the very indefinite conclusion that they have some form of mentality or other, that they have their individual perspectives on things marked by *some* qualitative aspects and *some* spontaneity over *some* duration of time, however brief. This perspective may include only minimal and intermittent traces of feeling and the presence of only infinitesimally brief spontaneity interrupting long periods of causally explained movements. The indefiniteness of this conclusion helps to offset the lower number of relevant similarities in the inference's first premiss.

Given this indefiniteness of the projected mentality, the question arises as to whether panpsychism's conclusion could be justified if the base were weakened further. Can extension of mentality to fundamental particles without structural organization be justified? How such a question should be answered is a puzzle we postpone until chapter 5. At this stage we need to pause to raise some questions about the epistemological status of the panpsychist thesis itself.

Epistemological Questions

First of all, is the thesis intelligible? Or, in stating it, have we robbed its central term "mentality" of any meaning specific enough for us to evaluate the thesis as true or false? We have seen how in descending to more primitive natural bodies the base of the analogical inference being used is progressively weakened. As compensation, panpsychism must progressively make more indefinite the form of mentality being attributed to natural bodies lacking observable sense receptors. Does this progressive indefiniteness eventually convert "mentality" into a vacuously general term whose only meaning is derived from the inference to the panpsychist conclusion? The answer seems that it does not. We cannot, of course, *imagine* what having a qualitative perspective might be at very primitive levels, but we can certainly *conceive* such a state. The contrast between a natural body such as a molecule having such a perspective and a stone lacking it would also seem to be one that we can conceptualize. Some might claim that mentality is present at the molecular level; others might disagree, claiming that molecules are aggregates like stones; and still others might decide to suspend judgment. Whatever our views, this disagreement seems to presuppose prior understanding of the question being posed.

Michael Dummett has defined *realism* relative to the applicability of the law of excluded middle. One is a realist about a certain subject matter if one believes that propositions about this subject matter are true or false independently of whether we possess means of confirming this judgment.[6] Most would probably agree that the proposition that Cleopatra wore gold earrings with embedded gems when she first met Caesar is either true or false, although we may have no relevant evidence for or against it, and may never acquire such evidence. We are therefore realists regarding propositions about the past. Should we also be realists for the panpsychist thesis? Let's assume that we never have any means of determining whether a certain molecule has or lacks a qualitative perspective on things. Is the proposition that it has this perspective nevertheless true or false? The answer seems to be, I think, yes. If this is correct, then the general claim that every natural body with unity of organization and homeostasis has a qualitative perspective and spontaneity is a realist thesis in Dummett's sense.

Realism has many forms, however, and we must be careful not to read into panpsychism's special version features of standard descriptive language. In particular, to describe a natural body as having a qualitative perspective is not to describe some special matter of fact about that body. The mental ascription simply functions to compare that natural body with ourselves and establish the appropriateness of attitudes toward it that differ from those for stones and bottles. Exactly how mental language performs these functions will be examined in chapter 4 where we discuss its interactive aspects.

This leads us to another and more difficult question. How do we determine whether the realist panpsychist thesis is true or false? The contrast between the typical use of an analogical inference and the special use of it described in the previous section shows the difficulty of answering this. Normally, we have some means of independently confirming or falsifying the conclusion of such an inference. The apples we infer by analogy to be rotten can be split open and checked; the planet we infer by analogy to have water can be probed by some future space vehicle. Analogical inferences are typically used within science to provide some initial plausibility to a hypothesis as a candidate for further testing. Their conclusions are rarely accepted until this later testing is carried out. In contrast, the conclusions of the analogical inferences in which mentality is attributed to infrahuman creatures can *never* be independently confirmed. The *only* basis for concluding that mentality of any form is present are the behavioral and anatomical similarities used as the first premisses of the inferences. In this respect the panpsychist thesis does not qualify as an empirical hypothesis.

It is, instead, properly classified as a thesis of metaphysics. Through the influence of Immanuel Kant and the logical positivists, the term "metaphysics" has been applied to the discipline investigating what "transcends the world of experience." Any sentence purporting to describe this special domain was by that very fact not testable by any observation, and was thus excluded as meaningless by the positivists. This sense of metaphysics obviously has no application to panpsychism, because the panpsychist thesis makes no claims that the mentality it ascribes to natural bodies constitutes a special domain distinct from the subject matter of the natural sciences. To be sure, some of the historical advocates of panpsychism I will be presently discussing also held dualistic views that postulated such a distinct subject matter, but others did not. In general, panpsychism is consistent with a naturalistic view that denies the existence of special types of objects or activities beyond the scope of the sciences. Its thesis is therefore not metaphysical in this Kantian sense.

There is a second sense of metaphysics derived from Aristotle that applies instead. Metaphysics in this sense is the discipline that describes observable phenomena in one domain and analogically extends these descriptions to a more inclusive domain, just as Aristotle developed a conception of a substance derived from objects such as statues and animals and extended it to all of nature. Analogical extensions can take the form of generalizing from features of human experiences and language use to infrahuman natural bodies, and panpsychism represents one such project. But they can also take the form of generalizing from mechanical forms of behavior at infrahuman levels to reach conclusions about human behavior. The alternative of universal mechanism introduced in chapter 3 represents this latter project. What distinguishes metaphysics in this Aristotelian sense from the empirical sciences is not that it has a special subject matter. Nor is it distinguished by reaching conclusions independently of experience by a priori reasoning. What distinguishes it, rather, is its use of analogical inferences with observational premisses but with very general conclusions that cannot in principle be independently confirmed or falsified.

Some may argue that this distinction between metaphysics and the empirical sciences cannot be maintained in the light of W. V. O. Quine's criticisms of the analytic–synthetic distinction. Quine argued that individual sentences cannot be classified as either analytic (true or false by virtue of meanings of constituent terms) or synthetic (true or false by virtue of observational tests). All sentences of any empirical theory are instead more or less vulnerable to falsification. Some, such as the logical law of excluded middle and physics' principle of the conservation of energy, are relatively invulnerable, while others such as observational reports of data are easily revised. An empirical theory consists of an indefinite number of sentences with varying remoteness from observation, including background assumptions often not made explicit. When anomalous results occur, the revision of a theory requires choices between those parts relatively close to observations and central assumptions that may be very remote. If Quine's account is correct, the fact that the panpsychist thesis cannot be directly tested by observation should not lead us to exclude it from the domain of the sciences, since this is a feature shared by many sentences of a scientific theory.

This attempt to assimilate metaphysics into science should be rejected, however. Quine's criticisms of the analytic–synthetic distinction has the effect only of showing that it cannot be applied to individual sentences. But it can be applied to blocks of discourse as combinations of sentences about some topic and with accepted methods for gaining consensus. We can easily distinguish a theory of pure mathematics with its questions of whether theorems can be proven from its axioms from a scientific theory whose acceptance by the scientific community is dependent on empirical testing. The panpsychist thesis should not be regarded as a single sentence to which the traditional epistemological classifications are applied; these classifications have no application to sentences as such. The thesis should instead be regarded as a part of a general metaphysical theory formulated in a form of discourse governed by a methodology of comparing features of human experience and language use to what is observed in primitive natural forms. It is distinguished from science in its use of analogical inferences in which its premisses include descriptions of our experience and language use and a conclusion that cannot be independently tested.

The use by metaphysics of analogical inferences without independent confirmation helps explain the persistence of controversies throughout its history. As has often been remarked, everything is in certain respects both similar to and different from everything else. Analogical reasoning requires the selection of attributes that are relevant to the conclusion being inferred, but what is relevant to some may be judged as irrelevant by others. Indeed, if the sole basis for panpsychism were the analogical inference used as its initial rational basis, this metaphysical view should rightfully be looked on with suspicion. To earn our support it requires supplementation derived from the requirement for continuity in evolution and practical needs derived from the religious attitude. This supplementation will be provided in later chapters.

CHAPTER TWO

Versions of Panpsychism

Panpsychism has its origins in Greek philosophy, but its formulation as a comprehensive metaphysical theory came only much later in the writings of Leibniz. Its contemporary version is commonly identified with that developed in the twentieth century by Whitehead and Hartshorne. The next four sections trace the central stages of this development. More recently, Thomas Nagel has formulated a version of panpsychism designed to explain the relationship between mental events of which each individual is directly aware and physical states of the brain known about by others. This version is examined and rejected later in this chapter. Finally, we consider a defense of panpsychism used in the nineteenth century and reformulated recently by David Chalmers in a way borrowed from information theory.[1]

Greek Origins

The origins of the Greek term *psyche* that was to be translated by the Latin *anima* and *spiritus* and then by "soul" or "spirit" are obscure. At some early stage the term seems to have become associated through the influence of Eastern mystery religions with the concept of an immortal substance surviving after death. This association is clear in the doctrines of Pythagoras and his followers. Death is acknowledged by the Pythagoreans to be the decay of the body. But for certain practitioners of the mystery religions, those leading exemplary lives of temperance, engaged in the study of theoretical matters, and having privileged knowledge of the secret rituals of their religious sects, Pythagorean doctrines held out the hope for a "purification" from the body. These special few practitioners were believed to have cultivated souls that could survive the death of the body.

This religious concept of a soul somehow separable from the body was borrowed from Pythagoras by Socrates and Plato, and is defended by Socrates in the dialogue *Phaedo* in which he argues for his belief in his own immortality.[2] It is also the basis for Socrates' use of the doctrine of recollection to explain the possibility of a priori knowledge. If the soul had a disembodied existence prior to birth, this would explain, Socrates reasons in the *Meno*, our ability to comprehend the proof, independent of any past or present experience, that the length of the hypotenuse of a right-angled triangle with equal sides is not a rational number. In following the proof, we are simply recollecting what in disembodied form we had previously known.

This concept of an immortal soul existing before birth, joining temporarily with the body, and then existing after death was specific to humanity for the Greeks. There is no suggestion that a cow or pig had the remotest chance of immortality. In the sacred writings of the Hindu religion, the belief is expressed that the souls of humans can inhabit the bodies of lower animals in some afterlife, or that what in a previous life was at the animal level could be elevated to the human. This has the effect of endowing immortal souls to the animals to and from which the souls migrate. In Buddhism we find similar notions, along with the mysterious assertion that all things can be regarded as having in them the Buddha nature. But no such religious beliefs seem to have found their way westward to Greece, nor can they be found in the later Christian theology that based itself in large part on the writings of Plato. For this theology, members of our species were accorded a very special status that elevated them far above all other living creatures. In this way, Pythagoras, Socrates, Plato, and Christian theology introduced a humanistic bias that has tended to predominate in Western philosophy from René Descartes to the present.

This religious use of the term *psyche* is in stark contrast to uses found in the surviving writings of the early cosmologists who predated Socrates. The soul was defined in these writings as the life principle, that which distinguishes the living from the dead and inanimate. A person is at one time alive, at another time dead, and the difference between the two conditions the early cosmologists regarded as explicable in terms of the presence or absence of a soul. But clearly the living–dead contrast can be applied to cattle, dogs, and even plants, and hence the definition seems to require attributing souls to living things of all kinds, both human and nonhuman.

This continuity of application can easily be recognized in the characterizations of the soul by the early cosmologists in their formulations of a materialist metaphysics. Heraclitus identifies the soul with a rarefied form of fire, which as an element present throughout nature is at least potentially in everything. Democritus identifies the soul with a sheath enclosing spherical atoms that are in motion during waking life. Because on death the sheaths disintegrate, there can be no immortality of souls, although the atoms formerly enclosed in the sheaths are eternal. Again, this is a conception easily extended to the infrahuman. Perhaps the clearest acknowledgment of this continuity can be found in the surviving fragments of Empedocles' writings. In them, Empedocles describes the evolutionary development from relatively simple life forms to the human species, and in such development there is an implied continuity between advanced and primitive.

Aristotle's *De Anima* shows the influence of these early cosmologists. Aristotle defines the soul as "the second grade of actuality of a body with life potentially in it." [3] By the "first grade of actuality" Aristotle means the actual exercise of a capacity, as when someone thinks or perceives on a given occasion. The "second grade of actuality" is the capacity for a certain form of activity. By defining the soul as this second grade of actuality, Aristotle is not forced to say (as was Descartes later) that our souls (for Descartes, our minds) go out of existence when we sleep; during sleep we may not be actually exercising psychological capacities of thinking or perceiving, but the capacities themselves remain. Exactly which capacities are present in a living thing depends for Aristotle on its position in a hierarchy. There are, he says, three basic types of souls, with the capacities at lower levels included in those at the higher. The most basic capacity for living things is that of nutrition as a natural body's capacity for ingestion of nourishment and excretion of wastes. This is a capacity present in plants as well as in animals and humans. Besides this capacity, animals have a capacity that Aristotle thought was plainly lacking in plants. This is the capacity for sensation and self-locomotion, the capacity to respond to objects in the environment and move in response to them. At the top of the hierarchy are humans, who share with all animals the capacity for nutrition, sensation, and self-locomotion. In addition, they have the capacity for rational thought, which for Aristotle is the capacity to use language and formulate arguments in which conclusions are inferred from premises.

Aristotle thus advances a form of restricted panpsychism that extends to plants, but not to any natural bodies more primitive than they. The soul is defined as the principle of life, and all other natural forms other than plants, lower animals, and humans are relegated to the realm of inanimate nature as material elements of their combination.[4] His *Metaphysics* expresses a generalized contrast between form and matter that is applied to all substances, and this might seem to suggest a generalization of panpsychism to more primitive forms. (As we shall see in the next section, this was a generalization Leibniz was willing to make.) The form of a substance, or its substantial form, is the actuality of the substance, as contrasted with the potentiality of matter, and because the soul is identified with a thing's actuality, it would seem to follow that every substance with a form has a soul. But the examples Aristotle gives clearly indicate that he would want to withhold the term *psyche* from substances that are neither plants nor animals. One commonly used example of a substance is a statue with a form as its actuality that is distinguishable from the bronze as the matter from which it is made. But this actuality is not of a thing "with life potentially in it," nor is it intrinsic to the substance itself. Rather, as for all artifacts, it is a form externally imposed by the artisan who created the statue out of the bronze, what Aristotle describes as the definition or formula we give to a thing. There are thus for Aristotle substances with forms, namely artifacts, which lack souls.

So far we have been describing Aristotle as advocating a form of restricted panpsychism. But even for this restricted version, we must be careful not to attribute to him the modern doctrine that dates from Leibniz. The modern doctrine, as we shall see, insists in applying mental attributions to various natural forms. Aristotle, however, only states that we can attribute the capacity for characteristic forms of activity to selected natural forms. For animals, this includes the capacity for having sensations, which are clearly mental, and for self-locomotion as a form of spontaneity.

For plants, however, the description of the characteristic "second grade of actuality" is not formulated in mental terms. The capacity for ingesting selective nutrients and excreting wastes may require mental sensations of some kind, but there is no suggestion in *De*

Anima that Aristotle thought that this is essential to plants' level of soul. Exercise of the capacity for nutrition is necessary for a plant to stay alive, that is, to maintain itself in equilibrium with its environment against potentially destructive elements. Loss of this capacity brings about the withering and death of the plant. But for a plant to exhibit such self-maintenance is only for it to demonstrate a capacity for homeostasis, a capacity that is at least logically independent of a mental capacity of any kind. Of course, Aristotle was unaware of the invisible elements involved in nutrition—the cells that compose a plant, their cell walls, the transport of molecules through these cell walls, the conversion of these molecules into usable forms of energy. If he had shared our knowledge of these elements, would he then have attributed mentality to cells in their selection of molecules to ingest? Perhaps, but this is only the wildest speculation. The macrobehavior of homeostasis of plants that he was aware of provided no grounds for the attribution of mentality in any form.

The version of panpsychism put forward by Aristotle we can refer to as *classical panpsychism*, as contrasted with the later modern form. For classical panpsychism, as we have just seen, things with souls have a capacity for homeostasis and/or mental activity. In animals both are combined; in plants only the capacity for homeostasis is present. Of the two capacities, homeostasis is the more basic because it is shared at all levels of life, and we can perhaps regard the advanced capacities for sensation, self-locomotion, and rational thought as the means by which homeostasis is maintained at the higher levels, what for later evolutionary theory was to be understood as their adaptation necessary for survival. Understanding nutrition as a form of homeostasis allows us to extend classical panpsychism in a way not found in Aristotle's writings. No matter how primitive the organization of a natural body may be, if homeostasis is present, it can be said to have a soul in a sense generalized from what we find in Aristotle's *De Anima*. We shall consider a contemporary version of this functionalist conception in chapter 3.

Aristotle's conception of a soul as the capacity for activities that vary with level of life has much more in common with conceptions of early cosmologists such as Heraclitus and Empedocles than with the religious conceptions of Pythagoras, Socrates, and Plato. And yet in a curious concession to this religious conception, Aristotle argues for a sharp discontinuity between human and infrahuman souls with respect to immortality.[5] The capacity for rational thought, he claims, brings with it the capacity for philosophical contemplation as a kind of thinking by the soul about itself and its own activities, and for the apprehension of the necessary truths of mathematics. The self-directed activity of contemplation he regards as similar to the activity of the Prime Mover, the Eternal Actuality whose activities are directed to itself alone, and which is in this respect self-sufficient. Aristotle believes that we gain future immortality for ourselves after the death of our bodies through the similarity of our contemplation to the activity of the eternal Prime Mover. Contemplation, a type of mental operation that includes what was later to be termed "self-consciousness," is thus regarded by him as a very special form of human activity, one that creates a sharp metaphysical distinction between humans (or at least those capable of philosophic contemplation) and all other living natural forms. Similarly, necessary truths are timeless truths, and when humans apprehend them they also somehow participate in the eternality of the Prime Mover. Because other creatures lack this capacity, their souls are fated to perish with their bodies.

Although it is understandable in human terms why Aristotle would seek to justify belief in immortality and provide special status to human lives, especially to those of philosophers like himself as professional contemplators, these claims inserted at the end of *De Anima* are clearly inconsistent with the definition of the soul with which this work opens and with his description of the hierarchy of souls. If a human soul were simply the capacity for an activity in a living body, then when that body perished so would the soul as its capacity. The fundamental fact of the finality of death for plants and animals would seem to apply to humans also, even granted their special capacities for discursive thought and the possibilities this opens up for the species. Aristotle's metaphysical system posits an unobserved Prime Mover as a means of satisfying human aspirations for immortality. His classification of levels of souls, in contrast, is based on observed similarities and differences between the macrobehavior of plants, animals, and humans. Thus it has a more secure observational basis than the speculative framework used to justify the belief in immortality.

Leibniz's Monadology

Leibniz wrote his *Monadology* some twenty-five years after his *Discourse on Metaphysics* and his letters to Arnauld in defense of the

Discourse. In the *Monadology* we find a dogmatic statement of panpsychism as understood in modern times, free from the qualifications and doubts expressed in his earlier writings. The soul of a thing is alternatively referred to in the latter work as its "monad," its principle of indivisible unity, and its "entelechy," its vital, self-sustaining principle. There is, he writes,

> a world of created things, or living beings, of animals, of ente-
> lechies, of souls, in the minutest particle of matter.
> Every portion of matter may be conceived as like a garden full
> of plants and like a pond full of fish. But every branch of a plant,
> every member of an animal, and every drop of the fluids within it,
> is also such a garden or such a pond.[6]

Every appropriately organized body has what Leibniz calls a "dominant monad" or "dominating entelechy," and the parts of this body in turn have their dominant monads: "It is evident, then, that every living body has a dominating entelechy, which in animals is the soul. The parts, however, of this living body are full of other living beings, plants and animals, which in turn have each one its entelechy or dominating soul." [7]

Leibniz thus claims a regress of parts within wholes, which in turn are wholes relative to other parts that are themselves composed of parts, as an animal is described in modern biology as composed of cells, which are composed of molecules, which are composed of atoms, which are composed of particles. If continued, this obviously leads to an infinite regress. For Leibniz, matter constitutes a continuum, and is infinitely divisible; he denies the existence of absolutely simple material elements without parts, what in his day were called "atoms," what we refer to now as "fundamental particles." To avoid the irrationality of an infinite regress, he resorts to the concept of a monad as a "simple substance," a constituent of other substances but itself without parts and hence not a "composite." These simple monads are immaterial elements, the most primitive of souls, without extension or form, and are described as the "true atoms of nature" that can neither be created nor destroyed.[8]

This is obviously an impossible solution to the problem of an infinite regress, for it is utterly mysterious how monads without extension can combine to form an extended body. Only elements with extension can combine to form an extended whole of which they are parts, just as from the juxtaposition of any finite number of unextended points it is impossible to form a line with extension. Indeed, there are only two plausible solutions to the problem of an infinite regress. One is to admit the existence of material elements without parts, and claim these material elements to have associated monads. The other solution is to either deny the existence of such indivisible elements, or refuse to ascribe to them mentality on the grounds that only bodies with parts qualify for such ascription. In either case, this second solution leads to what seems to be the most plausible alternative remaining for us. This is to concede that the regress terminates at some level at which there are organized bodies with dominant monads, and that the parts of these wholes do not themselves have dominant monads. But this is in effect to abandon a doctrine of unrestricted panpsychism of the kind Leibniz is advocating.

Indeed, in letters to Arnauld in defense of his earlier *Discourse*, Leibniz indicates doubts about the truth of unrestricted panpsychism. Here only bodies with dominant monads or souls are said to be true substances, that is, bodies that constitute unities. Regarding bodies such as blocks of marble and machines, in a draft of a letter to Arnauld he writes,

> they might perhaps be units by aggregation, like a pile of stones,
> but . . . they are not substances. The same can be said of the sun,
> of the earth, of machines; and with the exception of man, there is
> no body, of which I can be sure that it is a substance rather than an
> aggregate of several substances. . . .[9]

In the final version of this letter he expresses doubts only about attributing mentality to nonliving things, saying "I cannot tell exactly whether there are other true corporeal substances beside those which have life. But souls serve to give us a certain knowledge of others at least by analogy."[10]

In the *Discourse* and accompanying correspondence, the problem of mental attribution is stated in terms of a concept of substantial form originating with Aristotle. What distinguishes an individual substance such as a particular human or a cow from a mere aggregate such as a pile of rocks, block of marble, or machine is the presence of a substantial form. Such a form provides the individuating criteria that distinguish the man or cow from all others of the same kinds. It also seems to provide a principle of organization that preserves the identity of a thing through changes in its parts. A human body can replace its cells and still remain the same body, but if the individual rocks of a pile were to be replaced, we would seem to have a different pile. Leibniz seems to be saying that it is only to organized bodies with substantial forms that mentality can be attributed, or in his terms, it is only to them that we can assign a dominant monad. But if the substantial form of a substance is its soul—its actuality— then he is claiming, in effect, that what has a soul can be said to have a soul.[11] This is not very helpful in providing us with a guide in identifying those things to which we should attribute mentality.

Later critics of panpsychism interpreted the doctrine as requiring the extension of mentality to all bodies, including planets and trees. Paul Edwards, for example, concludes that this extension is a defining characteristic of the view: "To qualify as a panpsychist a person must claim that all bodies *actually* have an inner or psychological nature of aspect."[12] Edwards then argues that because it is obvious that such objects as tennis balls lack this aspect, the doctrine is absurd. Indeed, it is absurd under such a formulation, but this is not the standard formulation in the panpsychist tradition. Leibniz carefully distinguished aggregates from organized wholes, and would have distinguished rocks, planets, and trees from those bodies to which mentality can be ascribed. In this he was to be followed by Whitehead and Hartshorne. But he did bequeath to us the problem of determining the kinds of things to which we attribute mentality, because it is tautological to say, as he does, that those things with souls (what he calls things with "substantial forms") are those to which we attribute mentality.

Leibniz is more successful in his descriptions of the levels of mentality found among natural forms, and provides some useful hints for conceiving its occurrence in lower forms. At the highest level are human beings endowed with desires and perceptions accompanied by conscious awareness, or what he calls "apperception." Not only do we see a tree or smell a rose, but at the same time we are aware of our seeing and smelling. This capacity for this type of awareness, or what is often called "self-consciousness," is thought by Leibniz to be derived from the capacity to grasp necessary truths: "it is . . . through the knowledge of necessary truths and through abstractions from them that we come to perform Reflective Acts, which cause us to think of what is called the I, and to decide that this or that is within us." This capacity, he says, "is called in us the Rational Soul or the Mind," and is "that which distinguishes us from mere animals and gives us reason and the sciences, thus raising us to a knowledge of ourselves and of God."[13] The human capacity for discursive thought and reflection thus gives us a special status. But unlike Aristotle, Leibniz does not elevate this into a contrast between the mortal and the immortal. In his view, every monad, no matter how simple, cannot be destroyed, and is thus eternal.[14]

At the next lower level in Leibniz's hierarchy are those natural forms with a capacity for appetition and perception accompanied by memory but not reflection. This level would seem to be occupied by lower animals and perhaps other natural forms with a capacity for learning. Descartes' "I think; therefore, I am" required an identification between self-conscious thought and mental activity, and committed the Cartesians to the view that when we are unconscious in deep dreamless sleep, we lapse out of existence, only to recontinue existing on waking. The error of the Cartesians, Leibniz claims, is in their regarding "as non-existent those perceptions of which we are not conscious. It is this also which has led them to believe that spirits [or Rational Souls] alone are Monads and that there are no souls of animals or other Entelechies, and it has led them to make the common confusion between a protracted period of unconsciousness and actual death."[15] Leibniz has no argument against the Cartesian view. He simply rejects it out of hand, apparently because he regards it as obvious that we do in fact attribute mentality to lower animals when we say of a dog that it is in pain, and it is even more obvious that a person continues to exist during sleep. Any conclusion that conflicts with these obvious facts must rest on false premises, he seems to be claiming, and the false premiss is the Cartesian claim that all perceptions must be accompanied by conscious awareness, or that all perceptions must also be apperceptions. He may also be appealing to our experience of often sensing something without this being accompanied by any awareness that it is we who are doing the sensing. I remember having heard a sound last night, but the original hearing may not have been accompanied by any self-awareness. In cases such as this there seems to be perception and memory without self-consciousness or reflection.

Recall that Aristotle described the souls of plants in a way very different from that for lower animals and humans, for he characterized the capacity of plants in terms of an activity of nutrition that was not itself psychological. Leibniz rejects such a differentiation, choosing instead to describe in psychological terms a level more primitive than that at which perception is accompanied by memory. Often he uses the term "monad" with reference to this more primitive level, in contrast to the more generalized use in which every natural form has a dominant monad. In this more restricted use, monads are said to be "simple substances which have only perception, while we may reserve the term Soul for those whose perception is more distinct and is accompanied by memory."[16] At this primitive level, appetition accompanies perception, but his descriptions are exclusively directed toward the special type of perception that is present. It is said to be like those we have when we are in a dreamless sleep or in a stupor, and he suggests that our experience of such states makes it possible to conceive the experiences characteristic of this level. When we have perceptions in which there is "nothing distinctive, or so to speak prominent, and of a higher flavor of our perceptions, we should be in a continual state of stupor. This is the condition of Monads which are wholly bare [*toutes nues*]."[17] Although our perceptions are typically distinct and accompanied by self-awareness and memory, in special situations they are not, and from these we are led to conceive of "wholly bare" monads that constitute the most basic level of mentality.

Leibniz thus suggests a method for describing the forms of mentality present in primitive natural forms. We can describe the basic features of our own mental life: the fact that we can reason discursively by means of language, reach conclusions through reflection on our mental operations, perceive objects and be aware of what we are perceiving, and remember what has been perceived in the past. By successively excluding certain of these features, we can reach conclusions about the mentality characteristic of forms more primitive than ourselves. By excluding discursive reasoning, reflection, and self-awareness, we are able to isolate certain features of our own experience, for instance, sensations of which we may not have been aware when we had them, and use these as a means of describing the mentality of lower animals. By further excluding memory, remembering the nature of the vague stupor of just awakening, and conceiving of a type of experiencing had during dreamless sleep, we are able to describe still more primitive forms of mentality at a protoexperiential level, although as noted previously, for nonliving forms he seems to concede this is a conjecture by means of a remote analogy. At all stages, our own experience is thus the starting point for mental ascriptions.

How do such descriptions of the various levels of mentality relate to the descriptions of the natural sciences? During Leibniz's time, physics was emerging as a special science employing its own distinctive methods and freeing itself from all vestiges of Aristotelian metaphysics. As a leader in this development, Leibniz is careful to state in a letter to Arnauld that "consideration of forms or souls is useless for special physics," although "it is, nevertheless, important in metaphysics."[18] Unfortunately, he fails to also explicitly exclude biology from being an application of the doctrine. His concept of an entelechy or vital principle in all organisms that directed their development through some preformed "seed" proved useless in biology, and was to be rejected in the nineteenth century when embryonic development began to be explained in the same mechanistic terms as was used in physics. For such a method, the concept of a monad or entelechy represented only a block to inquiry, a postulated psychic entity with no explanatory value whose elimination was an essential step in the development of biology as an empirical science. Through guilt by association, Leibniz's more general doctrine of panpsychism, which for him was important only for metaphysics, was to be understood by many in the nineteenth and twentieth centuries as a fanciful speculative project that was in competition with the explanations of the natural world provided by the empirical sciences.

The Panpsychism of Whitehead's **Process and Reality**

The revival and reformulation of panpsychism in the twentieth century by Whitehead and Hartshorne seems to have been motivated by a rejection of alternatives presented to philosophers at the end of the nineteenth century. Biology had by then succeeded in establishing an empirical method for explaining evolutionary and embryonic development and patterns of animal and plant behavior, and it had done so against a conservative reaction that appealed to Leibniz's entelechy and other legacies of Aristotle's metaphysics. Its explanations now postulated causal mechanisms in terms of which interactions between material elements constituting the parts of an organism determined the behavior of the whole. Thus, interactions between atoms determined the behavior of molecules, and molecular interactions determined cellular behavior, which in turn determined the behavior of the organism of which the cells were constituents. The success of these explanatory models suggested universal mechanism as the view that the behavior of all natural forms, whether of submolecular elements, single-celled organisms, or multicellular organisms of the complexity of humans, can be explained in terms of both causal mechanisms that regulate interactions between their constituent parts and interactions between the natural form and its environment. Mentality was excluded from a role in such explanations.

The alternative to the universal mechanism developed during the nineteenth century was humanism as derived from the Greek philosophers and Descartes. As noted in the outline of Leibniz's panpsychism, most philosophers after Descartes regarded us humans as unique by virtue of our capacity for self-awareness or "self-consciousness." Not only do we perceive objects, but we are aware that we perceive, and by means of this we have a conception of the "I" as the subject of such perceptions. Not only do we have desires, but we are aware that we have desires, and this self-awareness allows us to control these desires in a way impossible for subhuman forms of life. The phenomena of nature, including our own bodies, may be explained by mechanical laws that determine behavior, but as possessed with self-awareness and as controllers of our own desires, we are the grand exception to their operation. We shall consider universal mechanism and humanism as the principal alternatives to panpsychism in some detail in the next chapter.

Whitehead refers to the humanist distinction between the human and subhuman as the "bifurcation of nature," created by the Cartesian philosophic method. It seems to him as unreasonable as its rival, universal mechanism. Mechanism seems inconsistent with what seems to be the self-evident fact that our decisions do make a difference in the way that things come out and with our sense that when I make a decision it is "my" decision to make. But the humanistic alternative seems equally inconsistent with our ascriptions of mentality in daily life to lower animals. Why is the dog digging a hole? Because it wants a bone, and expects to find it there, we reply. In this reply we attribute mentality to the dog just as naturally as we would to another human. The humanists' denial of our right to make such an ascription seems unreasonable because in effect it would prohibit, or at least explain away, a very useful practice for which we seem to have no viable alternative.

Whitehead regarded the two alternatives just described as unacceptable, and proposed replacing them with a version of unrestricted panpsychism derived from Leibniz. But he was aware of Bertrand Russell's criticisms of Leibniz's metaphysics,[19] and set out to correct its defects. For Leibniz, monads as subjects of appetition and perception were self-contained unities locked in their own sensory fields and isolated from their surroundings. Accompanying the sequence of images experienced by each "windowless monad," there were parallel events and processes in their associated bodies and physical world, with the coincidence of image sequences and physical events due to God's action in establishing a "pre-established harmony." But there was no interaction between the physical and the mental. Russell attributed this isolation of monads to the limitations of the Aristotelian logic used by Leibniz. If he had been aware of the modern logic of relations, Russell argued, he would have been able to formulate relationships between the mental and physical and develop a more adequate metaphysical system.

Whitehead set out to construct such an improved system in his *Process and Reality*. In this system, the basic psychic elements are not souls or monads as subjects of experiences, but instead psychic events called "actual entities" or "actual occasions." These events had two components or "poles": a physical pole in terms of which they are related to an environment, and a conceptual pole enabling anticipation of the future.[20] What had been regarded as a subsisting subject of perceptions and appetitions by Leibniz now were conceived as an ordered sequence of these psychic events in which later events selectively inherited the contents of antecedent events in the sequence and at the same time were related to the environment by what Whitehead terms "physical prehensions." Complex causal sequences of events, both of selective inheritance and physical interaction, are thus postulated as a means of adapting the new logic of relations to the requirements of metaphysics. By virtue of its conceptual pole, each actual entity is said to have what is termed "conceptual prehensions" of ideal objects called "eternal objects," and this apprehension of the ideal enables what Whitehead terms its "subjective aim," the equivalent of Leibniz's appetition. Eternal objects function as what he calls "lures of feeling" that impel all self-movement.[21]

For Whitehead, actual entities as psychic events with physical and conceptual poles occur at all levels of nature, from humans to protozoa, molecules, atoms, and subatomic particles. A major problem for panpsychism is extending a mental terminology designed for use at the human level to subhuman levels at which it seems clearly inappropriate. We, along with mammals such as cats and mice, can be said to see objects, but what sense can be given to ascriptions applied to a molecule without distinguishable distance receptors? Can the molecule be said to "perceive" its environment? Whitehead attempts to solve this problem by adopting a totally novel technical vocabulary designed to be neutral between levels, one that substitutes, for example, "prehension" as a term of art for our ordinary language term "perception." Free from misleading associations with our ordinary language, Whitehead thinks the metaphysician can construct a description of the processes undergone by any actual entity, no matter what its level of development, and then detail the specific forms these processes take at different levels of mentality.

The resulting system must be regarded as unsatisfactory in many respects, however. One problem arises from the basis used to construct the system. As David Hume noted, our sense impressions are discrete and fleeting, and in this sense event-like. But it does not follow that whatever has these impressions is an event and that we need a causal relation of inheritance to explain the relation of our experiencing in the present to the past. Few philosophers today accept the substance conception of the soul or mind of Descartes and Leibniz. But rejection of this conception does not at all require us to adopt an event conception and employ a causal terminology that mirrors our descriptions of causally related natural events. Philosophers seem much more successful in describing the phenomena of human experience and uses of language than they are in specifying what it is that is having experiences or using language—whether this is a mental substance, mental event, or a material body, as for the materialists. With regard to all these alternatives, we find ourselves agreeing with Ralph Waldo Emerson's Sphinx in her reply to the poet's attempt to answer her riddle:

> "Who taught thee me to name?
> I am thy spirit, yoke-fellow,
> Of thine eye I am eyebeam.
> Thou art the unanswered question;
> Couldst see thy proper eye,
> Always it asketh, asketh;
> And each answer is a lie." [22]

Another difficulty in Whitehead's project arises from the technical terminology with which it is formulated. First of all, the replacement of our ordinary-language mental vocabulary by technical terms in *Process and Reality* is not thoroughgoing; for instance, the familiar word "feeling" is used to describe experiences at the most primitive of levels. But second, where technical terms do occur, in our struggle to understand them we invariably find ourselves forced to translate them into familiar terminology. Thus, a technical term such as "prehension" tends to be interpreted by the ordinary term "perception." And finally, the difficulties and uncertainties of such interpretation serve to obscure the analogies that are the basis for ascribing mentality to subhuman forms in a way required by panpsychism. We must start with what we know best, and this is surely the familiar facts of experience and language use that have been central to the philosophic tradition. As Leibniz acknowledged, it is only by analogical reasoning that we use these familiar facts to reach conclusions about the mentality of primitive natural forms. For Leibniz the extension from the familiar human case to other forms is by successive subtractions from human capacities for discursive reasoning and reflective thought, arriving finally at wholly "bare" monads whose experiences are compared to those we have in a stupor or in dreamless sleep. But the effect of Whitehead's direct descriptions in a technical vocabulary of the components of the experiences of actual entities in general is to leave us uncertain about what method he is using in generalizing from the human case.[23] The more or less explicit method of Leibniz is replaced by one marked by obscurity.

Despite these difficulties, Whitehead has much of value to say about basic problems inherited from Leibniz that confront any version of panpsychism. One central problem is that of terminating the regress from wholes relative to parts, which in turn are wholes relative to other parts. In *Science and the Modern World*, Whitehead states that events constitute the final termination.

> The organisms of biology include as ingredients the smaller organisms of physics; but there is at present no evidence that the smaller of the physical organisms can be analyzed into component organisms. It may be so. But anyhow we are faced with the question as to whether there are not primary organisms which are incapable of further analysis. It seems very unlikely that there should be any infinite regress in nature. Accordingly, a theory of science which discards materialism must answer the question as to the character of these primary entities. There can be only one answer on this basis. We must start with the event as the ultimate unity of natural occurrence.[24]

To deny materialism for Whitehead requires postulating psychic events as the "primary entities," events that were later to become the "actual entities" of *Process and Reality*. The "root doctrine of materialism," he tells us in this later work, is the view that the material enduring substance "is the ultimate actual entity."[25] The panpsychist alternative is to postulate mental events as the ultimate parts. But just as for Leibniz, it is difficult to conceive how such parts can serve as "ingredients" in the formation of physical bodies such as atoms or in organisms such as cells as the constituents of plants and animals. How can mental elements, whether events or monads, combine to form the natural forms we observe around us? The reply may be that actual entities are described by Whitehead as having both physical and mental aspects, their physical and conceptual poles, and that such entities are eligible candidates for the formation of observable things. But it would seem that only their physical aspects would be relevant to their combination into observable wholes, and this is to deny to the mental status of actual entities any role in their functioning as primary parts.

Perhaps more tractable is the problem of determining which things we are justified in ascribing mentality to, or in Whitehead's terms, which material bodies that we observe will have an associated causally ordered sequence of actual entities. An electromagnetic field by itself, he says, is not the proper object of such ascription. What is required is that there be structured wholes with a degree of persisting organization, or what he refers to as "structured societies." He gives some examples: "Molecules are structured societies, and so in all probability are separate electrons and protons. Crystals are structured societies. But gases are not structured societies in any important sense of that term; although their individual molecules are structured societies."[26] What of the physicists' fundamental particles, those elements that by definition lack parts and structure? Whitehead may be claiming that what is substantialized by the noun "particle" should be conceived instead as what he refers to as "electromagnetic occasions," events that simply occur in an electromagnetic field without any association of an ordered sequence of actual entities.

His inclusion of crystals as structured societies suggests that although organization may be a necessary condition for mental ascription for him, it is not sufficient by itself. Indeed, he claims that even at the level of multicellular organisms, there can be organized wholes that lack what he calls a "center of experience" of a dominating sequence of actual entities.

> There are centres of reaction and control which cannot be identified with the centre of experience. . . . For example, worms and jellyfish seem to be merely harmonized cells, very little centralized; when cut in two, their parts go on performing their functions independently.[27]

Insects are said to have "some central control," but clearly plants, like worms and jellyfish, do not, and for such organisms we would attribute mentality to their cells, but not to the wholes of which these cells are parts. In Leibniz's terms, for the purposes of ascribing mentality they are "mere aggregates," though with a minimal form of organization. It is even more obvious that crystals as ordered arrays of atoms would not qualify as appropriate objects of mental ascription, although their constituent atoms might.

Finally, in this brief survey of Whitehead's version of panpsychism, mention should be made of his very cursory descriptions of primitive levels of mentality. All actual entities, he says, are characterized by subjective aims driven by ideal "lures of feeling" for which there is a striving for satisfaction. At different levels of complexity of organization, there are "gradations of intensity in the satisfactions of actual entities," ranging (at least on this planet during this current epoch) from near-zero intensity at the most primitive levels to the joys and sorrows, the senses of fulfillment and frustration, experienced by humans. The "lure of feeling" is said to be "the germ of mind," with the suggestion being made that this "germ" might be present at very primitive levels in the absence of a capacity for anything remotely related to animal perception.[28]

How are we to conceive of such primitive feeling? For Whitehead it is a type of experiencing not accompanied by consciousness—"consciousness presupposes experience, and not experience consciousness."[29] In the previous chapter we noted how "consciousness" is used with different senses. Sometimes it is used for what is more commonly called in philosophy "self-consciousness" (Leibniz's "apperception"), a capacity for reflection that seems characteristically human. It is unlikely that when Whitehead describes experiencing at primitive levels he has this sense in mind because absence of consciousness in this sense is too obvious to bear mention. It is more likely he has in mind one or both of two other senses. In one of them, experiencing accompanied by consciousness is understood as standing for a condition of wakefulness, as when a person is said to become conscious after recovering from being knocked out by a severe blow to the head. In still another sense, a person awake is said to be conscious of something in the sense of being aware of some item of his experience or having that experience as the focus of attention, as when someone is said to become conscious of a burning sensation in his leg of which previously he had been unaware because of his attention being drawn to some task at hand. In the sense of consciousness as wakefulness, Whitehead could be comparing primitive experiences without consciousness to those he apparently thinks we have in dreamless sleep, as Leibniz did in his *Monadology*. In the sense of consciousness as a focus of attention, he may be comparing preconscious experiences to subliminal experiences. But because Whitehead fails to make explicit the analogies from our own experience he is appealing to, we can only guess at his intentions.

Hartshorne's Reformulation

To his undying credit, no such guessing is necessary when we consider Hartshorne's reformulation of panpsychism. He retains Whitehead's conception of mentality as an ordered sequence of psychic events or experiential occasions, but eliminates Whitehead's technical terminology and those elements of his system that can't be related to what we encounter in our own experience. In particular, he does not mention physical and conceptual poles of an actual entity, and rejects the conception of an eternal object.[30] By mercifully sweeping away this metaphysical dust that serves only to obscure the grounds for the generalizations necessary for panpsychism, Hartshorne is free to concentrate on descriptions of our experience on which such generalizations can be based. The ascriptions of mentality required for panpsychism are then justified, not by the demands of a comprehensive speculative system as for Whitehead, but by a method that analogically extends certain features of our own experience to other natural forms that are judged to be similar to us in certain relevant respects.[31]

Exactly how such analogical extension is to be achieved is not spelled out in detail by Hartshorne, but he does offer many valuable suggestions. Following Whitehead, the term that he singles out for the most general extension is "feeling," which seems to represent for him an immediate qualitative experience with affective tone of a kind characteristic of aesthetic experiences. This affective tone can be either positive or negative. We see a flaming red sunset or hear a resolving chord in a Mozart symphony, and enjoy the beauty of what we see or hear. Its effect is attractive: we linger to enjoy the sunset or listen for the remainder of the symphony. We may then attempt to describe to another what we have seen or heard, but the experience itself is absorbing and sufficient in itself, not dependent on linguistic interpretation. For negative affective tone, we have examples of offensive odors and discordant sounds, again with an immediate, repelling qualitative aspect. Writing in another tradition, the Japanese philosopher Kitaro Nishida describes such experiences as "pure experiences," experiences where "the subject and object become one," that is, where there is at least temporary suspension of interpretation in which we apply the subject–predicate structures of language.[32] For Hartshorne these aesthetic experiences, described simply as "feelings," are those aspects of our own experience that can be generalized to other natural forms in the way required by panpsychism.

His most detailed attempts to analogically extend such aesthetic experiences to infrahuman species can be found in his studies of bird songs. Such songs, he argues, illustrate basic aesthetic principles that are evident in our aesthetic experiences. Experiences with positive affective tone are marked by a balance between order and variety. Too much order is dull and monotonous; too much variety is chaotic and discordant. The successful work of art, whether literary, pictorial, or musical achieves a delicate balance between the two, a balance that can change with the sensibilities of the century or decade in which the works are created. Hartshorne finds a similar balance between order and variety in bird songs, and reasons by analogy that they experience enjoyment similar to our own in response to such balance, and frustrations when it fails to occur. How such enjoyment and frustrations and the attractions, and repulsions that accompany them, may have influenced the evolution of these songs will be discussed in chapter 5.

For panpsychism, birds are organisms of a relatively high level of complexity. The basis for analogically extending the term "feeling" from our own aesthetic experiences and applying it to them would seem to be the similarity of anatomical structures—the fact that birds have distance receptors and a neurophysiology with some similarity to ours—and the fact that they exhibit learning behavior. But in advancing his version of unrestricted panpsychism, Hartshorne extends "feeling" to a wide range of natural forms at the protoexperiential level that fail to exhibit such similarities, including cells, molecules, atoms, and subatomic particles. On what basis is the extension made to such forms?

The question can be made more precise by use of some examples. Let's say that we agree to attribute mentality to single-celled organisms such as amoebas, which have been shown to learn to reject pieces of glass that they have previously ingested, and protozoa, which learn to orient themselves away from a toxic liquid environment. With reference to this learning behavior we then agree to justify the attribution of tactile feelings that serve to attract and repel. Then by analogy we extend mental attributions to the cells of a plant whose location is fixed, unlike the mobile amoeba and protozoa. Perhaps we attribute this mentality to stationary cells in the form of tactile feelings of nutrients and some selection among those passing through their cell walls. So far we have specific analogies as the basis for attribution. But now we proceed to attribute mentality to macromolecules such as viruses that exhibit no learning behavior, or at least none that we are presently aware of, and then to their molecular constituents, to their atomic constituents, and finally to some bodies that terminate the regress. At these progressively more primitive stages, we attribute feelings of a more attenuated kind that asymptotically approach zero as we reach the terminating stage. But what now is the basis for such attribution? There is no observed learning behavior at these more primitive levels, nor are there detectable sense receptors. In the absence of any of the behavioral and anatomical similarities that provide some plausibility to the analogical extension of feelings to amoebas and protozoa, mental attribution to these primitive forms seems unwarranted on any rational grounds. It can, of course, be argued that we have no evidence showing that mentality is not present at these primitive levels. But this plainly commits the fallacy of arguing *ad ignoratium*. Because we don't know that mentality is absent, it does not at all follow that we have any grounds for asserting that it is present.

Hartshorne has two replies to such criticisms, one of which seems very weak, the other, which is derived from Leibniz, considerably stronger, though inconclusive. Often in his writings we find appeal being made to the indeterminacy principle of quantum mechanics, the principle asserting that unique values cannot be simultaneously assigned to both the position and momentum of a particle such as an electron or photon, or that if a unique value is assigned to one variable, a probability of less than 1 and greater than 0 for a given value of the other must be assigned. Hartshorne interprets this principle as asserting that there is spontaneity of behavior at the subatomic level, and this he attributes this spontaneity to the presence of faint degrees of feeling that are present.[33]

Now such spontaneity may very well be present, but to appeal to quantum mechanics to establish it is surely suspect. The indeterminacy principle is usually interpreted by physicists as demonstrating the impossibility at the microlevel of isolating the influence of the human observer from the bodies she is observing. In order to observe the position of a particle, the observer must interfere in such a way as to impart momentum to it; to observe momentum requires interfering in such a way to yield only a probability of its location. On this interpretation—the one most widely accepted within the scientific community—indeterminacy is not attributable to anything internal to the particle itself, but is the result of an external observing process.

Another factor leading us to reject Hartshorne's use of quantum indeterminacy is the level at which it is employed. The indeterminacy principle is applied to fundamental particles, but these by definition lack organizational structure, and thus are totally unlike our own bodies as the basis for an analogical extension of mentality to primitive natural bodies. Further, even if we could attribute mentality to fundamental particles, we would expect them as the most primitive of all bodies to exhibit least spontaneity because they would have minimal mentality. Yet they are employed here as the basis for an analogical extension of feeling. Macromolecules such as viruses, with their more complex forms of organization, would be expected to exhibit considerably more spontaneity, but at this level quantum indeterminacy has no observable applications, and no other form of indeterminacy of behavior is appealed to. We are thus left with an enormous gap in levels, one representing at least one billion years of evolution, between particles to which spontaneity is attributed by Hartshorne and relatively complex macromolecules for which such attribution cannot be based on quantum indeterminacy.

More plausible is Hartshorne's appeal to unity of organization as a basis of mental attribution, an appeal that has the effect of excluding fundamental particles. "From man to molecules and atoms we have a series of modes of organization," he says, and for each level in the series there is a distinctive "mode of experiencing."[34] Like Leibniz, he distinguishes between aggregates such as a heap of stones or a crystal as an ordered array of atoms and unified wholes with specialization of parts. Only to the latter can mentality be attributed. All individuals, he claims, have a degree of mentality in the form of what he sometimes refers to as "sentience," but "of course aggregates of individuals need not themselves be sentient individuals."[35] The presence of internal organization thus seems to provide, for Hartshorne, the principal grounds for attributing mentality to primitive natural bodies. They may fail to exhibit behavior similar to our own and may lack sense receptors. Because of this, we have no basis for attributing sensations to them, which we regard as specific to animal, reptile, and insect species. Nevertheless, they at least have—in common with these organisms and ourselves—an internal organization with diversified parts that persists through environmental changes, and this similarity becomes the basis for attributing "sentience" to them and analogically extending feelings to them as what Whitehead had earlier called the "germ of mind."

Such, then, is a brief summary of the version of panpsychism formulated by its most forceful advocate in recent American philosophy. How persuasive is it? There does seem to be much merit in his use of feelings with affective tone as the basis for analogical extensions to primitive natural forms. The amygdala as the portion of the brain associated with emotions is located at the base of the brain and close to the centers of proprioceptive sensation. At more peripheral locations in the cortex are the centers of perception in the various modalities of vision, hearing, taste, touch, and smell, and even more remote from the brain's base in the neocortex are areas of memory and cognition. In embryonic development the cells for these emotional centers are laid down earlier than for portions of the brain associated with these other capacities. There is a measure of truth in the saying, "Ontogeny recapitulates phylogeny," that from the progressive stages in the development of an organism, both physiological and behavioral, we can trace its evolutionary origins. Where mentality of the protoexperiential variety exists, we would expect it to be in the form of feelings associated with systems of cells in the brain's base in us. This is perhaps the wisdom behind the popular notion that the "heart," located more to the center of the human body and associated with the emotions, is more central to us than the "head" with its more peripheral location because such location is the means by which we trace our evolutionary lineage. In this sense, then, Hartshorne seems correct in singling out "feeling" as the most appropriate term for attributing mentality to natural bodies existing in the early stages of evolution.

Despite the apparent appropriateness of his selection of a term for widest extension, however, Hartshorne, like his predecessors, leaves us with a speculative doctrine whose rational grounds for acceptance seem very uncertain. The search for stronger grounds will lead us to considering the nature of competing alternatives and the bases for mental attributions in the next four chapters.

Nagel on Mentality in Wholes and Parts

Thomas Nagel should be credited with being chiefly responsible for reviving interest in panpsychism within recent philosophy. He proposes the doctrine as a means of solving a problem posed by attempts to explain the relationship between physical and mental states.

Observed uniform correlations between events occurring in some whole, Nagel notes, are regarded by us as evidence of underlying processes within component parts of this whole that provide a necessary explanation of the correlations. When we light the fire under the kettle, the water in it regularly boils within a restricted temporal interval. This correlation calls for an explanation, and physics provides it by citing the motions of H_2O molecules as the constituent parts of the water. Given the increase of kinetic energy imparted by the lighting of the fire under the kettle, the water must as a matter of natural necessity exhibit the observed motions that we describe as boiling. An underlying process within water molecules as the liquid's constituent parts thus provides an explanation of the necessity of increase in heat being followed by boiling in the water as the whole.[36]

Nagel reasons that correlations we observe between physical and mental events or states should also be regarded as evidence of some underlying necessity. Psychologists observe a uniform correlation between pains experienced by us and patterns of neurophysiological activity in our brains. We tend to accept these correlations as a matter of brute fact, and hence content ourselves with the existence of a contingent relation between brain event and mental event. But as for the case of boiling water, we should regard the physical–mental correlations as presupposing, Nagel contends, some underlying processes that confer on them necessity. Thus, there is a requirement to postulate some explanation in terms of component parts that will convert the contingent relation between the physical and mental into a necessary one.

Nagel argues that such an explanation cannot be provided simply in terms of physical processes within component parts. The brain is composed of neurons as its constituent brain cells. Processes within these cells may explain the particular pattern of brain activity that we correlate with the experience of pain. But they cannot explain the correlation of this activity with the experienced pain, and thus the physical–mental correlation remains a contingent one. The only explanation of the correlation that can convey necessity, he argues, must be one that ascribes mentality to the brain's component neurons, for this alone avoids an inexplicable physical–mental correlation. Nagel declines to tell us what form this explanation takes, but at least we know that the mentality of parts must be somehow included in whatever explanation that might be given, and this is sufficient to establish a form of restricted panpsychism that extends mentality to component cells.

Advocates of physicalism will object to the way Nagel formulates his argument. The heating of the water and its subsequent boiling are independent events whose correlation does require an explanation. But a particular brain process is not correlated with an experience of pain in the same way, they will say. The two are instead identical. The process that is open to public observation is described in one way; the felt pain is described in another. But the two descriptions refer to the same item, namely, the brain process. Now an identity does not itself require an explanation in terms of some underlying processes of component parts, and hence there is no need to postulate the type of explanation Nagel appeals to.

There is a ready reply to this objection. Let's concede that a particular pain experienced on a given occasion is identical with a particular brain process.[37] Nevertheless, the correlations Nagel is referring to are between types of events, between a type of pain that regularly occurs and a type or pattern of brain activity. Most philosophers nowadays concede that there are no such type-type identities, preferring to describe the relation as a functional relationship, as the pain being somehow a function of brain activity that can take very dissimilar forms. With this concession, contingent relations still remain between physical types of events, for example, a type of brain process that can recur on different occasions, and mental types of events such as a recurring type of pain. These would seem to require an explanation of the kind Nagel calls for.

There is, however, a more serious objection to Nagel's view. Let's grant that physical–mental correlations within a whole presuppose some underlying explanation in terms of component parts, and that in order to convert the contingent correlation to a necessary one we must postulate mentality as present in the parts. Nevertheless, there must always remain contingent physical–mental correlations for which no such explanation can be given. This follows from the fact that at some stage we must terminate the potentially infinite regress of wholes and parts. Let's suppose that the mentality of component neurons provides an explanatory basis for the necessity of correlations between brain activity and pains. This requires us to suppose there exists a correlation between mental items associated with the neurons and physical events occurring at these sites, and this by Nagel's argument requires an explanation in terms of component parts of the neurons, say their constituent molecules. We then ascribe mentality to these molecules to provide necessity for physical–mental correlations supposed to exist for the neurons. This now introduces other physical–mental correlations that must be explained at the lower level of constituent atoms, and with this explanation come correlations at a still lower level. Eventually this regression from wholes to parts to subparts must terminate and where it does we will have physical–mental correlations that from the nature of the termination must be accepted as contingent and inexplicable.[38]

In general, a whole W_1 at a level L_1 at which there are physical–mental correlations will have parts with a mental aspect in terms of which the L_1 level correlation is to be explained. But each such part will be a whole W_2 at level L_2 relative to which there will be parts explaining other physical–mental correlations, and each of these parts will in turn be a whole W_3 at level L_3. This regress must eventually terminate at some level L_k at which there will be a whole W_k for which there are mental correlations for which no parts exist that provide an explanation. But to admit such a level L_k violates Nagel's assumption that we must presuppose every physical–mental correlation as having an explanation for its necessity. One exception invalidates the reasoning that led from wholes to parts, and leads us to simply accept our beginning point, the mental–physical correlations at the human level, as inexplicably contingent.

Reasoning similar to Nagel's has been used by Hartshorne and David Griffin in defense of panpsychism, although unlike Nagel, they specify the form of explanation appropriate for the mental.[39] Both accept Whitehead's view that there is a kind of psychic causation between wholes and parts in which experiences of wholes directly interact with experiences of parts. Thus, the feelings of pain by a person are regarded as the direct effect of feelings of pain in constituent cells. The existence of such direct psychic causation, they claim, enables panpsychism to provide a solution to the otherwise insoluble mind–body problem.[40] But it is clear that it faces the same difficulty of terminating the regress as confronted Nagel. At some stage the regress must terminate, and then we will be confronted with the same mind–body problem for which psychic causation between wholes and parts is being proposed as the solution.

All versions of panpsychism, with the exception of Aristotle's, have historically attributed mentality to parts of wholes, and cells seem the appropriate level for such attributions relative to a human person as a whole. If Nagel's argument is not adequate to justify such attributions, is there another that is? The most plausible seems to be one that analogically extends mental terms to single-celled, mobile organisms such as amoebas exhibiting learning, and then further extends these terms to cells as fixed, specialized constituents of multicellular organisms. An amoeba presented with small fragments of glass will ingest the fragments and then eject them. As this is repeated, the temporal interval between ingestion and ejection is reduced, until finally there is no ingestion. Such behavior seems similar to how more complex organisms, including ourselves, learn to reject irritating substances, and on the basis of this comparison it seems plausible to attribute irritation to the amoeba. Now cells within multicellular organisms don't exhibit learning behavior because of their lack of mobility. But their structures are very similar to single-celled organisms such as amoebas and protozoa that do exhibit such behavior, and this similarity of structure leads us by another analogical inference to conclude that in some manner they can select for ingestion or reject substances as potential nutrients to which they are exposed in their environments. Where there is rejection, we can now analogically extend the term "irritation" as originally applied to the amoeba.

Using such reasoning, we can arrive at the conclusion that we can attribute mentality to the neurons of the brain as fixed cells with specialized functions. But however this mentality is described, it seems restricted to those specific to the level of cells, namely sensitivity to the potential nutrients and toxic substances that may pass through cell walls. If this is correct, it would seem totally independent of any pains or pleasures of those persons as wholes for which the neurons are constituent parts, contrary to the views of Nagel, Hartshorne, and Griffin. The sensitivity to potential nutrients surely cannot be used as part of the explanation of why brain processes are correlated with certain kinds of experiences. This is precluded by the independence between the two levels with respect to their characteristic forms of mentality.

The Analogical Reasoning of Fechner and Chalmers

Advocates of panpsychism in both the nineteenth century and toward the end of the twentieth on occasion have extended its thesis in what seem to be implausible ways. To conclude this historical survey, I consider the analogical reasoning used by them to reach their conclusions, first with nineteenth century versions and then with the recent version of David Chalmers. Both illustrate the difficulties in arriving at consensus by using this type of reasoning.

The earlier version can be found in Arthur Schopenhauer's declaration that "we shall judge all objects which are not our own body according to the analogy to this body."[41] The analogy used by Schopenhauer begins with the direct awareness we all have of our own experiencing with its qualitative aspects. We know also that we have a body. We know, therefore, that we have two aspects: the experiential one of which we are aware and the bodily one that both we and others can observe. Each individual can then infer by analogy that because he or she has these double aspects, every natural body that can be observed has them also. The aspect of which we are aware in our own case is described as the "phenomenal," "inner," or "subjective" aspect. In contrast, we observe only the "outer" or "objective" form of natural bodies; their "inner" experiences are for us their inaccessible "noumenal" mental aspect that we know of only indirectly by means of an analogical inference. On the basis of this inference, we conclude that all natural bodies have, in addition to that "outer" aspect that we observe, a mental aspect, and this conclusion is now understood to be the thesis of panpsychism. Among those holding this double aspect theory, there was disagreement over what these aspects are aspects of. Idealists held that it is the mental that has inner and outer aspects. Materialists, on the other hand, regarded material bodies as having an inner aspect as a kind of "epiphenomenon." Experiences were regarded by them as epiphenomenal in the sense that they were caused by bodily processes, as when a person feels a pain when stuck with a pin, but these experiences themselves exerted no causal powers. Others, labeled "neutral monists," thought that some "neutral" stuff, neither mental nor physical, constituted the underlying "reality."

Fechner on Plant Souls

The psychologist Gustav Fechner endorsed what is called the "double aspect" view of the relation between the mental and physical. "What will appear to you as your mind from the internal standpoint, where you yourself are this mind," he says in his early *Elements of Psychophysics*, "will, on the other hand, appear from the outside point of view as the material basis of this mind."[42] Toward the end of his career, Fechner took up the task of defending a version of panpsychism based on this double aspect theory.

Fechner assumes that analogical inferences are used for the minds of other humans, for animals, and for extensions beyond animal species. We are certain of our own minds, he thinks, by virtue of Descartes' *cogito, ergo sum* argument, but it is only by what he describes as an act of "faith" that we conclude that other humans and animals have minds or souls. This faith is based on the similarity between our bodies and behavior when we have certain experiences and thoughts and the bodies and behavior of others: "My brother is very much like me and expresses himself like me; I therefore believe most firmly that he is animate."[43] Observed similarities are in this way evidence for what is unseen and in principle incapable of observation. As noted in chapter 1, we now regard this as a misunderstanding of our use of mental language, having been convinced by Wittgenstein and Ryle that anatomical form and behavior constitute criteria for the application of this language, not evidence of the unseen. Fechner himself seems to anticipate this contemporary view in his acknowledgment of the conviction (rather than the tentative faith) with which we ascribe mentality to those around us. We believe, he says, "in the souls of other men and of animals as surely, or almost as surely, as we believe in our own." The basis for this is the "substitute" of observed bodily form and behavior for the unseen. This conviction, he argues, should give us confidence in ascribing souls to other forms of life.

> But if these substitutes are capable of arousing such confident faith in the souls nearest to us that we are not even sensible of the lack of strict proof, and even the most exact scientists do not ask for it,

why not seek out and put to use the same substitutes or others related to them?

This in fact is the fundamental point of view from which I
start: in the whole question about souls I would take into account
no kind of assurance but that which we have for the souls nearest
to us, but also I would employ the means which are available to us
in this case.

The existence of those souls in which we are *compelled* to believe by reasons which lie nearest to hand will have to serve us as
examples, foundation, and support for the further extension of the
realm of souls.[44]

Fechner uses analogical reasoning to then infer that plants have
souls, though they are dissimilar in many respects from ourselves
and other animals. Animals differ from us, he argues, and yet we are
confident they have souls.

It is true that the animals are quite different from us in appearance;
yet like us they move about, seek their food, generate offspring,
even utter cries upon similar provocation—or if all of them do not
do all of these things, they do some of them. Consequently we ascribe to them a somewhat similar soul, subtracting only reason in
view of the differences we observe. But in the case of plants we sub-
tract definitely the whole soul; and if we have a right to do this, we
can justify it only by alleging that in build and behavior the plants
are too dissimilar to us and to the animals analogous to us.[45]

But this denial of souls to plants is mistaken, he concludes, because
of the many similarities they have to animals—the fact that, like animals, they live and die and exhibit regular behavior in maintaining
themselves.

But in addition to the souls [of animals] which run about and cry
and devour might there not be souls which bloom in stillness,
which exhale their fragrance, which satisfy their thirst with the
dew and their impulses by burgeoning? I cannot conceive how run-
ning and crying have a peculiar right, as against blooming and the
emission of fragrance, to be regarded as indications of psychic activity and sensibility, nor why the finely constructed and graceful
form of the cleanly plant should be thought less worthy to contain
a soul than the unshapely form of a dirty earthworm.[46]

How should we reply to such exuberant affirmation? The difficulty lies in the fact that all things are in some respects both similar and different from others. The analogical inference to the conclusion that mentality is present in plants requires selecting those shared features that are *relevant* to this conclusion. But how do we decide what is relevant or irrelevant? Plants live and die, and exhibit tropistic behavior. There is some similarity between the means they have for transporting nutrients to their parts and nutrient transport in animal circulatory systems. Are such features to be relevant similarities? Most of us would probably agree with Whitehead and Hartshorne that there is no justification for attributing mentality to trees as wholes, because they lack the requisite central organization, although we would be willing to concede that plant cells are apt candidates. But are such judgments matters of taste? On what basis do we decide to extend mentality to plant cells but not to plants as wholes? Why is lack of central organization a relevant dissimilarity, while transition from life to death and tropistic behavior are judged irrelevant?

Chalmers on Information Processing

These problems, inherent in analogical reasoning, also arise for David Chalmers' recent reformulation of panpsychism. Like Fechner, Chalmers uses a double-aspect theory of the mental and the physical. Each of us has an observable body that processes information in the form of sensory inputs, including social inputs from speech and writing. This is our fundamental "extrinsic" aspect. We also have an "intrinsic" aspect that is described in terms of phenomenal properties such as having qualitative experiences. This relation between information processing and experiencing in our own case is the basis for what Chalmers describes as the "grander metaphysical speculation concerning the nature of the world." According to this speculation, "information is truly fundamental, and . . . has two basic aspects, corresponding to the physical and phenomenal features of the world." There arises, then, the question

whether *all* information has a phenomenal aspect. One possibility is that we need a further constraint on the fundamental theory, indicating just what *sort* of information has a phenomenal aspect. The other possibility is that there is no such constraint. If not, then experience is much more widespread than we might have believed, as information is everywhere. This is counterintuitive at first, but on reflection I think the position gains a certain plausibility and elegance. Where there is complex information processing, there is complex experience. A mouse has a simpler information-processing structure than a human, and has correspondingly simpler experience; perhaps a thermostat, a maximally simple information-processing structure, might have maximally simple experience?[47]

Besides the possibility of attributing experience to thermostats, Chalmers envisions attributing it to particles described in quantum mechanics on the grounds that the states of these particles can be described in the terminology of information theory.[48]

Chalmers's extension of mentality to mechanical information-processing devices seems to be derived from ambiguities in the term "information," which has three basic senses. "Information" can be understood as *syntactic information* as understood in engineering applications. Here there are sequential or synchronous arrays defined within information spaces for which there are alternative possibilities. For example, a 4-bit information space with two alternative values 1 and 0 defines $2^4=16$ possibilities. A specific sequence such as 1001 would represent a selection from these possibilities, and hence convey information in this syntactic sense. In an 8-bit space with $2^8=256$ possibilities, the sequence 11001100 would be a selection from the greater number of possibilities. It is therefore more improbable and would convey more information than would the 1001 of the 4-bit system. Our auditory system is trained to discriminate the vowels and consonants of our system of spoken language. Within this system there is a certain range of phonemes from which any given sequence of sounds is a selection. Thus, the word "red" is discriminated from "yellow" and conveys less information than the latter, which as the longer sequence of sounds is the more improbable. Information in this syntactic sense is processed within the body at the levels of both sense receptors and the central nervous system, and this information processing is similar to that for mechanical artifacts such as thermostats and computers. There is no evidence of such information processing at the atomic and subatomic levels.

"Information" is also used in the sense of *semantic information*. For this use there are also semantic spaces or fields defining a range of possibilities as *meanings* in relation to an *interpreter* of a sign.

Thus, the word "red" has a meaning for a native speaker of English that excludes the meanings of alternative color words such as "yellow," "green," "blue," and so on. The semantic information conveyed by a word is a function of the number of such alternatives it excludes. Semantic information is not confined to human language systems: the signs interpreted by organisms capable of learning would seem to exclude alternatives and thus convey this type of information for their interpreters. For bodies such as mechanical artifacts, in contrast, such interpretation does not seem present. Thermostats and computers may process information, just as we do, but unlike ourselves and a wide range of animal species, they do not interpret what they process.

Finally, there is a sense of "information" applied to systems that is defined in terms of their degrees of organization. Entropy is the tendency within systems toward increasing disorganization in accordance with the Second Law of Thermodynamics. Any persisting organization is an offsetting of this tendency, and thus we can refer to this organization as negative entropy or *negentropic information*. The constituent molecules within a container of gas tend over time to distribute themselves equally within the container in such a way that there is an equal probability of finding a molecule within any given volume within the container. This equal distribution is the system's most probable state. In contrast, the constituent molecules of a cell have a complex form of organization. We can therefore contrast the high degree of the cell's negentropic information, or alternatively, its highly improbable state, with the absence of this information in the gas container. When the term "information" is applied to the level of subatomic particles, it would seem to be in this third sense. Because of the tendency of signals to lose their cohesion over time, information in the negentropic sense has engineering applications, and these lead to its sometimes being confused with syntactic information. Negentropic information is, of course, not processed by either organisms or machines; it simply exists as a measure of a system's degree of organization.[49]

Chalmers seems to be led to his conclusion that thermostats might be conscious by confusions between these syntactic, semantic, and negentropic varieties of information.[50] We are aware of our ability to discriminate speech sounds, and we can regard this as a form of syntactic information processing. We also understand certain sequences of these sounds in the form of morphemes, sentences, and blocks of discourse, and thus interpret signs with semantic information. We do have bodies that process sensory inputs and that maintain a degree of organization. Having persistent organization, our bodies realize a certain form of negentropic information, and our activities function to maintain this against environmental forces. Information in this organizational sense was used in the preliminary formulation of the panpsychist thesis in chapter 1. All three forms of information thus apply to ourselves as having mental capacities. In contrast, we think that thermostats only process information of the first syntactic kind, and certainly are not themselves active in maintaining information in the organizational sense. Moreover, they differ from us and organisms capable of sign interpretation and learning in their lack of an evolutionary history. Despite the differences, can we plausibly extend mentality to them on the basis of their processing of syntactic information? Here we should judge, I think, that the base for the analogy is too weak to merit the extension because they lack the evolutionary history of a natural body. It seems to be only negentropic information common to all natural bodies sharing this history that can provide a base for analogical reasoning to the unrestricted panpsychist thesis.

The implausible speculations of Fechner and Chalmers illustrate the difficulties inherent in panpsychism's use of analogical reasoning. Both proponents and opponents of its thesis must make judgments about what are relevant and irrelevant to inclusion in the base for the analogies being employed, with differences in these judgments creating the controversies marking this area of philosophy. Before we judge this too harshly, however, we must recognize that analogical reasoning subject to the same indeterminacies is present in *all* philosophy, whether in attempts to extend mechanical models of information processing to human thought or in comparisons and assimilations of one form of language to another. Because philosophy relies so heavily on analogical reasoning, it can never be an exact science with the same standards as those of mathematics and the natural sciences. But it can be judicious and reasonable in its use of analogical reasoning, and to achieve this goal is its continuing challenge.

This concludes this introductory survey of versions of panpsychism and the types of reasoning used to support them. We now consider universal mechanism and humanism as the principal alternatives to panpsychism. Humanism in recent times has been based on the uniqueness of the human linguistic capacity, and this leads us in chapter 4 to investigate the differences between discursive language and more primitive signs. Chapter 5 will consider an application of universal mechanism to evolutionary theory. At the beginning of this fifth chapter, we introduce the principal argument panpsychism employs to offset the weaknesses we have just seen in its analogical reasoning.

CHAPTER THREE

Humanist and Mechanist Alternatives

The dominance of humanism within philosophy since Descartes explains in great measure the incredulity with which panpsychism is usually greeted. Humanism seems to rest on three related considerations. First, there is appeal to the uniqueness of the human linguistic capacity. On the basis of this uniqueness, it is argued that we must provide a very different description of human behavior from that we employ for other species of life. Secondly, appeal is made to our unique capacity for self-consciousness, our capacity to not only have experiences, as do lower animals, but to be aware that we are having them. And finally, it is claimed, often on the basis of the first two considerations, that members of the human species are endowed with the capacity to freely choose between alternative courses of action. This is contrasted with animal behavior that is determined by external stimuli and internal physiological mechanisms. This chapter first outlines the nature of the alternatives posed by humanism and naturalism, and then describes attempts to extend mechanist descriptions of animal behavior to human language use. Finally, I outline the basis for humanist claims for human uniqueness.

Humanism and Naturalism

Humanism can be understood in a variety of ways. Some of them are entirely innocent, and included within them are some that indeed deserve our highest praise: they were the means of freeing humanity from the shackles of religious dogmatism. Not so innocent, however, is a form of humanism we can label as *philosophical humanism*, the view that there exist metaphysical differences between human beings and lower forms of life that create what in chapter 2 we found White-head calling the "bifurcation of nature."

Philosophical humanism is most explicitly stated in Descartes' well known division between humans and other species. The grounds for this division were methodological. We humans are capable of formulating to ourselves the sentence "I think" on the basis of our awareness of our thoughts, sensations, and emotions; we cannot be mistaken about the truth of the proposition expressed by this sentence. On the basis of this, Descartes argued, we postulate a subject of thinking, that which we refer to as our "mind," the referent of the pronoun "I," which is distinguished from the body as the object of public observation. Our minds are the source of our freedom, our capacity to choose between alternatives through acts of will that cause our bodily movements. Our bodies, in contrast, are governed by the mechanical laws investigated by the natural sciences. The awareness we have of our own thoughts and sensations doesn't extend to other animals. For us they are only observed bodies, out there in the natural world, and governed by the laws applying to all bodies. For them we have no basis for thinking that they have minds; hence we must conclude that they are totally lacking in the capacity for choice enjoyed by our species. There is some question whether Descartes was even willing to attribute sensations to lower animals. But even if he had been, these sensations would be regarded by him as mere effects of physical stimuli having no causal powers themselves. Thus, lower animals may experience sensations, but their bodies are machines determining their behavior. With the distinction between what is free and what is determined comes also a distinction with regard to immortality. Although our bodies may perish on death, our minds survive, and immortality is insured for us; no such happy fate awaits the creatures with which we share our planet.

Most contemporary humanists refuse to accept the gift of immortality offered by Descartes, and they reject his substance conception of minds. They do insist, however, on a division that preserves the uniqueness of human freedom. A version of this humanist view of human uniqueness has been recently formulated by John McDowell in terms of a contrast between behavior caused by "biological imperatives" and actions that are freely chosen.

In mere animals, sentience is in the service of a mode of life that is structured exclusively by immediate biological imperatives. . . . We can recognize that a merely animal life is shaped by goals whose control of the animal's behavior at a given moment is an immediate outcome of biological forces. A mere animal does not weigh reasons and decide what to do. . . . When we acquire conceptual powers, our lives come to embrace not just coping with problems and exploiting opportunities, constituted as such by immediate biological imperatives, but exercising spontaneity, deciding what to do.[1]

Thus for McDowell there is a sharp division between "mere animals" (note that "mere" is repeated three times in the above passage) and us privileged humans, at least those of us reaching a certain stage of maturity accompanied by the acquisition of "conceptual powers." Biologists estimate that life has been evolving on this planet for about two billion years. For humanism, somehow during roughly the past 100,000 years—a small fraction of this period—one species became miraculously endowed with very special features that distinguish it from all that has gone on before. Despite the implausibility of this miraculous transition, however, philosophical humanism is not to be casually dismissed. In fact, it is supported by strong linguistic reasons arising from the nature of our attributions of mentality and accountability to others, reasons to be discussed later in this chapter and that to follow.

The general point of view we can label as *naturalism* considers it unreasonable to suppose there was such a miraculous transition in the course of evolution and regards belief in it as a form of human conceit. For naturalism, metaphysically speaking, what applies to one applies to all: if infrahuman creatures lack immortality, so do humans; and if humans are endowed with freedom of choice, it is unreasonable to think that all other organisms are mechanical automata. For all naturalists there are clear and sharp differences between the capacities of different forms of life. Chimpanzees are much more complex than rodents, and rodents have features that sharply distinguish them from insects with their relatively stereotyped forms of behavior. Humans, with their linguistic capacity to form sentences and combine them to form varieties of discourse, are very different from chimpanzees in many respects. But for naturalism there is no basis for claiming that the differences between a human and a chimp, however great they may be, are any greater than the differences between a chimp and a rodent, or between a rodent and an insect. And despite all of these differences, there is general continuity between all natural forms with respect to metaphysical aspects such as the presence of mentality, and the same answer must be given to the question whether behavior is causally determined by antecedent conditions.

Naturalism itself takes two forms. One is the version I have labeled universal mechanism, the view that all natural forms are analogous to mechanisms as human artifacts. Machines are characterized by invariable regularity in their workings and the fact that every one of their processes is the determined effect of some antecedent cause. Universal mechanism extends this determinism to all natural bodies, including humans, chimps, rodents, and insects, all of which are regarded as material systems whose behavior is determined by external environmental and internal physiological causes. Differences between levels arise from differences in weighting external and internal causes as determinants of behavior, because among organisms of increasingly higher complexity internal physiological causes, including innate structures as determinants of motivations, become increasingly prominent. This makes explanation of past behavior and prediction of future behavior increasingly difficult, but this difficulty is due to our incapacities in the face of complexity, and does not reflect any differences in nature.

Universal mechanism can be either *reductive* or *nonreductive*. The reductive version claims that regularities at higher levels of complexity can be deduced from those at lower levels and ultimately to the laws of physics governing fundamental particles. The nonreductive version—the version most widely favored by today's advocates of universal mechanism—admits the possibility of "emergent" properties at the successively higher levels, structural properties or features of behavior that cannot be derived from lower-level laws.[2] For nonreductive mechanism, behavior at every level, including that of humans, is determined, but this determination may in part be due to structures unique to that level, that is, structural properties that cannot be derived from those at lower levels.

Universal mechanism as the claim that all behavior has causal determinants applies to behavior of any kind, whether of the kind we attribute to the anatomical control system of an organism, such as breathing or perspiration in mammals, or more variable behavior such as hunting for prey or avoidance of predators. The two types of behavior differ only in the nature and complexity of their causes. It also applies to the behavior of all natural bodies, from humans to those natural bodies with minimal internal organization. In recent philosophy, universal mechanism is usually formulated as *functionalism*, a theory used for describing behavior in relation to its antecedent causes that abstracts from specific physical causal mechanisms.

It should be noted that universal mechanism employs the same general form of analogical inference as was outlined in chapter 1. The base for the analogy is, as before, the observed behavioral and anatomical similarities between humans and relatively primitive mammals and insects. Mechanists then conclude that because the behavior of these primitive organisms is determined by environmental and physiological causes, we can justifiably conclude that human behavior is also. The inference is thus "bottom up," as contrasted with the "top down" reasoning of panpsychism. The projected attribute for mechanists is determination of behavior, which is extended from the infrahuman to the human. On the basis of this inference, our common sense belief that we can make choices between alternatives is explained away as an illusion.

The other principal version of naturalism is panpsychism. Mechanistic naturalism is inspired by the successes of the natural sciences in explaining a wide variety of observed phenomena, and seeks to extend the methods of the natural sciences to ourselves. It attributes any probabilistic description of behavior at a given level of complexity to human ignorance of the environmental conditions or structural features that cause the behavior. Panpsychism, in contrast, starts with a consensus that has been reached within philosophy, psychology, and linguistics about features of our experience and our uses of language from our common standpoint as participants in social practices. It then attempts to analogically extend these features to natural forms whose origins predate our own. One of the features that it takes to be obvious (or at least has been regarded as obvious through much of the philosophic tradition) is that we do have the capacity to make choices between alternatives, and that this capacity provides the ground for attributing responsibility for what we do. We refer to this as the "freedom" of action that we enjoy. In employing their analogical extensions to the subhuman, panpsychists commonly refer to a corresponding spontaneity of behavior within natural forms. Attributions of spontaneity are assumed to be entailed by attributions of mentality, including attributions of primitive forms of feeling. To the extent that the most infinitesimal degree of feeling is present, according to the panpsychism of Whitehead and Hartshorne, there is at least a trace of spontaneity and hence a degree of indeterminacy of behavior.

Naturalism is commonly identified with universal mechanism, whether of the reductive or nonreductive variety, and in this form is a very influential view within contemporary philosophy. But there are no grounds for this identification because there is no part of the definition of "naturalism" that precludes its extension to panpsychism. It is true that to advocate naturalism is to deny the existence of nonmaterial elements such as substantial minds and Platonic forms. Some panpsychists have been dualists, notably Leibniz, and others such as Whitehead have introduced nonmaterial ideas ("eternal objects") as objects of apprehension (Whitehead's "conceptual pole.") But the doctrine of panpsychism does not itself require the introduction of nonmaterial elements. To say that a dog has a point of view or perspective on its surroundings, that this perspective has a qualitative aspect, and that the dog's behavior is to some extent spontaneous—that is, not determined by antecedent physical conditions—is not to say that it is possessed of a nonmaterial mind or that there are mysterious nonphysical causes of its behavior. We are instead noting the obvious difference between the dog and an unfeeling stone or thermostat. The dualistic framework employed in characterizing mentality of bygone eras does not have to be dragged into a contemporary formulation of panpsychism tempered by an awareness of criticisms of this framework. What is essential to naturalism is its insistence on continuity between human and subhuman nature and its denial of the astounding contrasts claimed by philosophical humanism. In this respect panpsychism has stronger affinities with universal mechanism than it does with philosophical humanism.

In chapter 5 I shall be considering and rejecting universal mechanism as applied to evolutionary theory, arguing that its accounts of evolutionary development are implausible. At this stage I offer a brief outline of attempts to extend mechanism to human language use and the nature of the humanist response.

Behavioral and Functionalist Descriptions of Language Use

Our ability to make judgments, decide, and reason has always been cited, and correctly so, by those seeking to distinguish our species from all others. Since the beginning of this century, there has been a concerted effort to understand these thought processes in terms of the use of language. Often when we think we don't also speak, but it seems reasonable to conceive of private thinking as a kind of "silent speech," a kind of "silent dialogue of the soul with itself," as Plato describes it in the dialogue *Phaedo*. Guided by this conception, it is believed that investigations of language use should lead to an understanding of our thought processes. Speech behavior is, after all, a public phenomenon that can be investigated by the same methods as those employed in all the empirical sciences. The hope is that by applying these methods to speech it will be possible to incorporate thought processes—that mysterious area previously relegated to philosophic speculation—within the domain of the natural sciences.

To demonstrate that human thought does not represent an exception to the order in nature, advocates of universal mechanism have sought to isolate regularities in linguistic behavior, and have devised increasingly sophisticated mechanistic models to explain them. One of the most influential has been B. F. Skinner's behavioral theory of language acquisition.

Instrumental Learning and Language

Skinner starts with the assumption that animal behavior exhibits law-like regularities that can eventually be explained in terms of underlying physiological processes. As a psychologist, he restricts himself to describing the law-like regularities relating environmental stimuli to which animals are exposed and their responses, but as a mechanist he assumes there is some underlying physiological explanation, although we may be unable now to produce it. The laws of animal behavior described by Skinner, and his extension of them to language acquisition in his work *Verbal Behavior,* have been much discussed, and I shall summarize them only very briefly here. In what he calls "instrumental learning," Skinner notes how animals such as rats are observed to modify their behavior in regular ways as the effect of scheduled reinforcements. The simplest of such modification arises when some form of behavior from among random behaviors is selectively reinforced, as when a rat wandering around in a cage eventually presses a bar and is rewarded with a food pellet. Subsequent pressings followed by positive reinforcements will increase the likelihood of the bar-pressing response, until at some stage the response becomes virtually automatic. Absence of the reinforcement has the effect of eventually extinguishing the response.

More complex modifications of behavior occur when a stimulus called the "controlling stimulus" is presented at the same time as the selected response. Let's suppose that the rat is exposed to a flash of red light when the bar is pressed, and is then rewarded with a pellet, but when blue light occurs there is no reward. Then the rat will learn to discriminate red from blue flashes, and will press only when red, the controlling stimulus, occurs.

In *Verbal Behavior* Skinner argues that these models of instrumental learning can be extended to children acquiring use of a language. Commands issued by young children to parents are initially random babblings. Some of them are rewarded by parents' responses (the child says "ice cream" and is rewarded with the dessert), and this shapes the linguistic response. For descriptive language, the model of controlling stimuli followed by reinforcement is applied. If the child says "apple" in the presence of an apple, parents reward with approving sounds and gestures. Gradually these positive reinforcements lead to the child learning to say appropriate words in the presence of kinds of objects. After learning words to both command and describe, the child learns by similar procedures to combine words to form sentences.

Noam Chomsky has offered two different kinds of objections to Skinner's project of extending of mechanistic explanations of animal behavior to verbal behavior. The first is methodological, and is the more basic of the two, while the second is directed toward special features of language that Skinner's model cannot account for. The methodological objection is stated in terms of a contrast between descriptions of verbal behavior as linguistic *performance* on the part of members of a given linguistic community, and descriptions of the rules governing a language by those having a *competence* in the use of a language. Linguistic performance as verbal behavior can be observed, and hypotheses that explain these observations can be formulated. When Skinner applies the methods of behavioral psychology, he is necessarily comparing linguistic performance to animal behavior. For both human performance (e.g., the utterance of "apple") and animal behavior (the bar pressing), the generalizations derived are typically statistical generalizations based on observations of what actually occurs, and normal behavior is simply probable behavior. But unique to language is the fact that it is rule governed and that speakers of a specific language as participants in their linguistic community can be judges of what is correct and incorrect. Native speakers do not simply observe what in fact occurs when they and others speak; they judge what *should* occur, and this is not a judgment about what has a high probability of occurring. Speakers often make mistakes that competent speakers can recognize; in such cases what has a high probability of occurring may be different from what should occur. Consideration of competence is only possible for language use, and introduces a distinction between it and animal learning behavior. This distinction prevents us, Chomsky argues, from extending principles of animal behavior to language learning.

Chomsky's second objection appeals to combinatorial features of language that he claims cannot be accounted for by models derived from instrumental learning. At a very early age, children acquire the capacity to form novel sentences, sentences they have never heard before, nor ever uttered, and hence were never reinforced. This novelty of verbal responses cannot be accounted for by models of learning in which responses are shaped by rewards and punishments. Indeed, it can't be accounted for by any learning theory. Instead, the capacity for mastering the combinatorial rules of a language requires us to postulate, Chomsky argues, an innate linguistic capacity on the part of children to generate and then test hypotheses about the grammar of their community's language on the basis of the limited amount of linguistic data provided by their surroundings. Chomsky agrees with Skinner on the mechanistic nature of animal behavior; here stimulus/response/reinforcement behavioral generalizations do imply mechanical explanations of determined behavior. But the human linguistic capacity is uniquely different, and such explanations cannot be applied. In this respect, Chomsky can be regarded as affirming the thesis of philosophical humanism.

Functionalism and the Teleological Theory

This second criticism by Chomsky has been almost universally accepted by linguists and philosophers, with agreement reached that the earlier learning models of behavioral psychology are inadequate as descriptions of language acquisition. But this has not put an end to attempts to formulate mechanistic accounts of such acquisition and of language use in general. Instead, the criticisms have helped to give rise to a new discipline referred to as "cognitive psychology" or (when applications are extended beyond psychology) "cognitive science." This discipline relies on the fact that many human activities, including what we label as "intelligent" activities, such as checker and chess playing, can be simulated on a computer. Using the analogy of computers, the human brain is conceived as an information-processing device in which the linguistic and environmental data the child receives as inputs are transformed into the utterances of speech as the output data. By simulating these inputs and devising programs that will transform these inputs into ouputs that match speech utterances on a computer, cognitive science hopes to be able to provide a functional description of the brain's processing mechanisms in language acquisition and speech production.

Functional descriptions have been claimed by some as equivalent to the mental ascriptions we make when we say of someone that he is in pain or that he understands a certain sentence. What is important in ascribing a mental state, argue the functionalists, is the correlation between environmental and internal stimulation as inputs and behavior as output. This same correlation can be preserved by many alternative material realizations and causal mechanisms, as occurs when robots are constructed that mimic the behavior of humans, or artificial intelligence devices are constructed that simulate our language-processing capabilities. In such cases, the input–output correlations are preserved by substituting mechanical sensors and silicon chips for organic sense receptors, transducers, and neurons of the brain transmitting electrical and chemical information. Remaining constant are functional relations between inputs, intermediate transitional states, and behavioral outputs. Functionalism thus assumes universal mechanism, but chooses a form a description that leaves indefinite the underlying causal mechanisms.

When applied to language use, functionalism singles out for special attention the lexical items of our language—its nouns, adjectives, and verbs. Within sentence contexts these items have meaning and, at least in the case of nouns, have reference. Thus, the noun "horse" when occurring in the subject position of a sentence such as "This horse is large," is used to refer to a particular horse in the environment of speaker and hearer. The noun can be applied to objects on the basis of meaning criteria—a horse is a four-legged mammal with a characteristic shape, range of color, and behavior— or on the basis of a quick matching with an average shape and color exemplar. Transformations brought about by an information-processing device must operate on these lexical items, which when occurring in thought as internalized speech, are referred to as "mental representations."[3] It then becomes a central challenge for the project of cognitive science to give an account of the role of mental representations with meaning and referential content in functioning as effects of environmental stimuli, as objects of transformation, and as causes of behavior.

A number of attempts have been made to give such an account. Most relevant for our purposes is what has been labeled the "teleological theory of content" because it provides a clear example of how mechanistic naturalism can claim a continuity between the human and infrahuman. Mental representations become defined in terms of their functional role of utilizing information about the environment to regulate behavior in ways advantageous to the survival and flourishing of relatively simple organisms. The use of language within human societies is then understood as a later evolutionary development of what is present in these more primitive organisms. The teleological theory is developed in two stages. First, a causal base is provided by defining the meaning and reference of mental representations in terms of causal relations between them and objects in the environments of organisms. And second, the causal role of the representation is defined relative to responses by organisms that promote their goals.

Two simple examples illustrate how these definitions are derived by those formulating the teleological theory. A person looks at an apple and forms for himself the mental representation "apple." The meaning of the representation would be those properties of apples that would regularly cause such a representation to occur in the brains of speakers of English; the reference of the representation "apple" is to that particular apple which on that occasion is actually causing the particular representation. The apple as the cause of the representation can be regarded as the controlling stimulus of Skinner's model, with the internal mental representation replacing the overt verbal response. Similarly, a toad sees a nearby hover fly, and as a result an image of the insect is formed on its retina. This image can also be regarded as a mental representation, and as a representation can be regarded as having content in the form of meaning and reference. Here the meaning of the image representation is the properties of flies that regularly cause the image in toads, while its reference is to the particular fly causing the image on that occasion.[4]

As Ruth Millikan has argued, such a causal account is inadequate in itself to define the content of a representation; causal relations alone fail to distinguish those events that are internalized signs from other effects of causes. A red face may be the effect of overexertion as its sufficient causal condition in normal situations, and the chemical constitution of blood is the effect of alcohol consumption, but certainly neither is a representation of its cause. Also, there are many causal conditions of what are regarded as representations, as the toad's retinal image of a dark spot may be caused by its eyes being opened, adequate lighting conditions being present, and so on. But then on what basis do we distinguish the fly as what is represented by the dark spot from these other conditions?[5] There is a myriad of sights, sounds, odors, tastes, and feels experienced by organisms as the consequence of decoding mechanisms within their sense receptors and nervous systems, but only a select few would seem endowed with representational content. We lack a means of distinguishing those neural effects with representational content from those without it.

Such considerations require, Millikan argues, the introduction of the goals of the organism and behavioral responses that promote them. For lower animals these goals would include reproduction, obtaining food, and avoiding predators: those responses required to sustain life and continue the existence of the species. Thus, a dark, moving image on the retina of a toad triggers the reflex response of extending its tongue and snapping up the fly. The image as mental representation performs its proper function normally only if it corresponds to the fly that is its cause. This same image on the retina of a male hover fly, in contrast, would evoke a pursuing response, thus performing its proper function of detecting a female fly as a potential mate.[6] Under this conception, the neural mechanisms for forming representations are regarded as goal-promoting detection devices. As before for the causal theory, the content of a particular representation is a combination of the particular object causing it and the distinctive properties of the type of object being selectively responded to. But now we have a way of identifying the representation as such in terms of its functional role in relation to behavior and the promotion of goals.

Although the examples just given are of behavior by relatively complex organisms, the account can be extended to any system that reacts in law-like ways to given inputs, as illustrated by the tropistic behavior of plants orienting toward a light source, or of members of a species of bacteria that orient themselves in water away from a light source.[7] It is also illustrated by mechanical devices such as thermostats and coin detectors in dispensing machines. In all such cases there is an event within the system that is brought about by some cause, for instance, a lowering of temperature or the insertion of a coin, and is in turn the cause of a type of response by the device—the switching on of a furnace or the dispensing of a drink. For each such causal sequence, we can single out this event as a representation in terms of its function of producing such effects only if it reliably detects the presence of a type of cause.

Defenders of such mechanistic accounts concede that there are great differences between images within toads and linguistic representations that occur in humans. Nevertheless, both are regarded as mental representations, and the having of representations is characteristic of the presence of mentality. By understanding the mechanisms that explain the primitive forms of representational behavior, it is hoped that some day we will be able to understand those that might explain our own more complex behavior.

A Generalization of Functionalism

Before turning to criticisms of the functionalist version of universal mechanism just outlined, we should note that it provides a way of interpreting the claim of panpsychism that mentality can be attributed to all natural bodies exhibiting unity of organization and homeostasis. For the teleological theory, the causal sequence of visual stimulus of hover fly, fly image in the brain of the toad, and snapping response is a means for the fly to sustain itself within its environment. The sequence of fly stimulus, fly image in the brain of the male hover fly, and mating response is a means by which the male fly perpetuates its genes and participates in the continuance of its species. In the cases of both the toad and fly, to attribute mentality is, in effect, to claim that within the respective organisms there is an image performing a certain goal-related functional role. And in both cases this attribution is applied to organized natural bodies that are maintaining themselves, either by securing nutrition or reproduction, within their environments. It seems an easy step to generalize this to more primitive organisms. To attribute mentality to them is to simply attribute internal events analogous to the mental representations of the toad and hover fly, that is, events performing the functional role of maintaining the natural body within its environment. In primitive bodies such as atoms or molecules this maintenance of homeostasis may take the form of energy exchanges with the environment.

Functionalism thus has a ready interpretation of panpsychism's thesis. Mentality can be attributed to all natural bodies exhibiting organization and homeostasis simply because mentality just *is* the means by which these bodies maintain internal organization and homeostasis. To attribute mentality is to attribute mental representations whose most generalized function is this maintenance. In human societies this requires complex social transactions made possible through the use of language, and mental representations take the form of internalized linguistic representations. Among other species mental representations can take the form of images such as the visual image of the hover fly for the toad as effects of triggering stimuli and causes of goal-related behavioral responses. For the most primitive of natural bodies we extend the term "mental representation" to those internal events, whatever they may happen to be, that perform the generalized function of maintaining homeostasis. At all three levels, this generalized function is basic, with variations of how it is performed varying with the special capacities of natural bodies at the different levels.

While such generalized functionalism represents an interpretation of the panpsychist thesis, it clearly diverges from it in two important respects. The most obvious is that panpsychism characterizes mentality in terms of spontaneity, while functionalism by its very nature excludes this by postulating deterministic causal relations between environmental stimuli, mental representations, and behavioral responses. The fact that behavior is statistical is acknowledged to be only due to our ignorance and a spur to further investigations of underlying causal mechanisms. The second point of divergence with panpsychism is over the qualitative aspect of mentality. Because panpsychism attributes mentality on the basis of an analogical inference from our own experiences, the qualitative is regarded as essential to the mental, and is implied in the attribution of feelings to the most primitive of natural bodies. For functionalism, in contrast, the mental is defined by its functional role, and for this qualities seem incidental. They may be present at the level of toads and flies, but they can be absent at the level of atoms and molecules and still, provided homeostasis is maintained, mental attributions would be appropriate.

There is historical precedent for this separation of the mental from the qualitative. Recall from chapter 2 how Aristotle distinguishes the souls of plants from those of animals, and seems to deny any psychological aspects to the nutritive capacity. Also, Leibniz in his early pre-*Monadology* formulation of panpsychism (cf. chapter 2) defines souls in nonpsychological terms as substantial forms, and thus suggests for them a capacity that may lack a qualitative aspect. Both these formulations seem to be means of achieving a generalization of the mental that recognizes the difficulty of extending psychological capacities to natural bodies lacking sense receptors.

Some Criticisms of Functionalism

The generalized form of functionalism just outlined does seem to have the advantage of avoiding some implausible aspects of panpsychism's attempts to extend its account to inorganic natural bodies. But functionalism encounters more serious difficulties of its own when applied to linguistic mental representations, because knowledge about our use of language is derived in a way very different from our knowledge about the capacities of other species. In using language we follow a variety of kinds of rules, and the nature of these rules, as Chomsky observes, is known to us as participants in the practice of using language and not as observers of the behavior of others. A rule is a norm, a requirement acknowledged within a community that stipulates what *should* be done in a given situation. In contrast, descriptions of observed behavioral regularities inform us about what is *in fact* being done. Because of this difference between the normative and descriptive, the methods used in describing rules can be expected to be different from those describing behavioral regularities.

Indeed, invariable regularities such as the dispensing of drinks by coin vending machines, tropistic behavior of plants, and snapping responses of toads to flies seem on the surface of it very different from behavior that we associate with language and the concept of representation. If there is a reflex response to some stimulus object, this seems to insure that there is no representation with content. Someone shines a bright light in my eye and I blink. The internal state causing the blinking response performs the functional role of preventing damage to my retina, and will be evoked only if it detects the potentially damaging light source. But it is surely not by virtue of performing this function that the flash of light is a representation of the light source. If there is representation, it would seem there must be some response that is *not* reflex, one for which there are no innate structures explaining a law-like correlation between the representation and its external cause. On seeing an apple,

I may reach for it. But only if this reaching is *not* like the reflex blinking response to light, would we regard the internalized "apple" to be a mental representation.

Normative considerations seem to reinforce this contrast between a mechanical reflex response to a triggering stimulus and genuine mental representation because representation seems to be accompanied by the possibility of misrepresentation or error. As Fred Dretske has pointed out, where responses are reflex, there may be cases in which a triggering response evokes a response that frustrates the goals of the organism under conditions similar to those for goal-promoting responses. Dretske cites the earlier example of the toad responding with snapping to a dark moving image on its retina. Normally this image is caused by a fly and the response is goal-promoting. But a BB shot dangled in front of the toad would cause this same image, and would repeatedly evoke the snapping response, each time with harmful consequences.[8] An error can be recognized and corrected, but for the toad there seems to be no capacity for discriminating the BB shot from the fly and altering the response. In contrast, when we recognize that the object is not an apple but instead a pear, we correct our initial mistake and evaluate our original judgment as false.

Such considerations suggest the humanists' conclusion that there is an unbridgeable gap between our use of language and anything occurring in the behavior of lower animals. We apply such normative terms as "true" and "false" in evaluating our own judgments and what is said by others. Such evaluations are made from our standpoint as participants in the use of our language, not as observers of the behavior of others. We can say of the toad that its retinal image of a dark spot "misrepresents" its object in the sense that the response of snapping caused by the representation fails to promote the toad's goal of securing a source of nutrition. But this is simply our description of functional relationships between relevant stimuli and responses. It bears no relationship to the normative term "false" as used by ourselves in evaluating expressions within our language. Humanists must concede, of course, that learning takes place among lower animals: not all animal behavior is like the reflex snapping of the toad. But such learning can be accounted for in mechanical terms, they will argue, as shown by the "training" of machines to alter their outputs to a given range of inputs, and hence does not alter the contrast being drawn. The fact remains that evaluation is unique to us as participants in our language, and this separates us as a species off from all other forms of life.

The first of Chomsky's criticisms of Skinner's applications of instrumental learning models to language—the contrast between behavior as performance and rule-following as a competence—thus continues to reinforce the humanist belief in human uniqueness. There remains the undeniable fact that our evaluative terminology has application only to our rule-governed language. For humanism this introduces special features of language use that make it impossible to apply mechanistic models from animal behavior to ourselves. As occurring in lower animals, there are internal events that may be given functional definitions in terms of goal-promoting responses, definitions that assume some causal explanation of these responses. But it is a mistake to think that these events are "representations" in any important sense that applies also to linguistic representations. Through its use of language and its accompanying normative terminology, the human species is distinguished from all other species.

Panpsychism has no quarrel with this rejection by humanism of universal mechanism. It thus agrees with the following remark made by Wittgenstein about the incompatibility between applications of causal terminology and descriptions of language use: "But if it were shown how the words "Come to me" act on the person addressed, so that finally, given certain conditions, the muscles of his legs are innervated, and so on—should we feel that the sentence lost the character of a *sentence?*"[9] As Wittgenstein correctly recognizes, to characterize a sound as a sentence is to bring to bear normative standards for its formation and for its truth and falsity, standards applied by participants in language use. To describe the sound as an element in a causal sequence is to describe it in a fundamentally different way, a way incompatible with the application of norms.

But recognizing this does not at all commit us to the humanists' conclusion that all animal behavior can be causally explained in a way that distinguishes it from human behavior. We do not have to concede that mechanism applies to all but ourselves. Indeed, this is acknowledged by Wittgenstein; immediately before the passage just cited, he extends his conclusion to animal calls: "We say: 'The cock calls the hens by crowing'—but doesn't a comparison with our language lie at the bottom of this?—Isn't the aspect quite altered if we imagine the crowing to set the hens in motion by some kind of physical causation?" To describe the signal of the cock as a "call" is for Wittgenstein to implicitly compare it with a rule-governed sentence such as "Come to me," and this also precludes describing it simply as a term in a causal sequence. A sound wave may be a term in such a sequence, but neither a call nor a sentence can be.

The alternative of panpsychism being proposed in this work incorporates Wittgenstein's insight. It does this by analogically extending selected features of language use to lower forms by means of the concept of a sign. Intentionality is then ascribed to these natural forms as interpreters of signs, with the concept of a sign extended to include natural events in addition to the linguistic expressions and animal calls cited by Wittgenstein. The intentionality of sign interpretation is thus regarded as the defining characteristic of mentality. The normative concepts of truth and falsity are acknowledged to be unique to language and its conventional rules, but judgments of truth and falsity are also claimed to have analogs within primitive forms of sign interpretation. How these analogical extensions are made will be discussed when we turn to the topic of intentionality in the final part of this chapter.

For now, however, we consider the claim by humanism that a special human capacity grants to our species a special exemption from universal mechanism.

Self-Consciousness and Freedom

Recall that Aristotle and Leibniz, despite their willingness to extend mental attributions to other species, believed that we humans differ from other species in one important respect. Unlike other species, we have the ability to reflect on our own mental operations. The deer in the forest may smell the presence of a predator, expect its approach, and flee the scene. In expecting the predator, it has what is labeled a "first-order thought." We, in contrast, do not simply smell, expect, and act, but have "second-order thoughts" in which we are aware of having perceptions and beliefs, and of making decisions. A second-order thought, in the words of David Rosenthal, is a "roughly contemporaneous thought that one is in [a] mental state."[10] For Aristotle this special capacity qualified human souls for immortality; for Leibniz it provided us only with a special kind of knowledge, since immortality was ensured for all monads. Very few contemporary humanists share Aristotle and Leibniz's belief in personal immortality. But they do find the capacity for reflection on mental operations, or the capacity for what is called "self-consciousness," useful in drawing a metaphysical distinction between the human and infrahuman. It is our capacity for self-consciousness, they claim, that is the basis for our ability to make choices among alternatives. Lacking it, animals are pushed and pulled by McDowell's "biological imperatives."

How do humanists think that this capacity for self-awareness creates the distinction between the free and the determined? Their answer is that it releases us from mechanical pushes and pulls insofar as it enables control over desires. We have not only desires for objects, as occurs when a person has a craving for chocolate. We are also aware that we have this first-order desire, and may form a second-order desire not to have it. Thus, the person craving the chocolate may desire that he not have the craving, and this second-order desire provides him, humanists contend, with the means of controlling the craving and not acting in accordance with it. Similarly, a person may be ambitious for a promotion to a job with higher social status. Reflecting on this ambition, she may approve of it, that is, have a second-order desire to have the desire for promotion. In such a case, the second-order desire leads her to act in accordance with her ambition. Here she is not simply impelled by the first-order desire for promotion, but in some sense controls its effect on her by her approval of it. Such self-control, it is argued, is the source of our free agency. Lacking it, and capable only of having first-order wants for such goals as food, sex, preservation of young, and safety, lower animals cannot be said to freely choose what they do. Instead, their behavior must be explained solely in terms of determining antecedent causes, both environmental and physiological.[11]

As I indicated at the beginning of this chapter, philosophical humanism's attempt to create a metaphysical gulf between ourselves and the rest of nature should be greeted with some skepticism because it requires us to suppose a remarkable, unexplained development within a relatively recent stage of evolution. We can concede that self-consciousness is a unique capacity of humanity.[12] But once we understand the nature of this capacity, we see that it fails to provide the sought-for distinction between the free and the determined.

All thoughts are expressible in language, and second-order thoughts are no exception. When we say we believe something to be true, we use sentences of the form "I believe that p," where p is some proposition, as in "I believe that John will arrive soon." For desires, we use sentences of the form "I desire that p be the case," "I desire that I obtain o," where o is some object of desire, or more simply "I want o" ("I want some chocolates"). Such attitudes directed toward propositions are termed *propositional attitudes*. Self-ascriptions of these attitudes seem to be simple descriptions of the mental states of belief and desire, and it is understandable why writers have taken the second-order thoughts they express to be directed toward beliefs and desires as first-order thoughts.

But they actually function very differently from standard descriptions. First of all, their subject "I" does not function as a referring expression that indicates an object in the common environment of speaker and hearer. The speaker is instead using "I" as an address indicating himself as the source of the information, who it is that is conveying what is believed or desired.[13] And secondly, the predicates "believes that p" and "desires that p" are not used to ascribe properties. Sentences such as "I believe that p" and "I desire that p" are instead expressions of the attitudes of belief and desire, rather than being descriptions of them. If they were descriptions, then we could expect them to be based on some kind of evidence. But what could serve as this evidence? It might be psychological items such as characteristic feelings or sensations, but it is clear that no such items are regularly present when we make such ascriptions. My desire for chocolates may sometimes be accompanied by a characteristic sensation, say of hunger pangs, but this is accidental and occasional, and certainly does not qualify as evidence for the self-ascription of desire. The evidence could also be behavioral, but it seems clear that normally when I say "I want some chocolate" I have not observed myself behaving in a chocolate-seeking way. Rather, I am simply expressing to another what I want.

To these language-related reasons for rejecting the notion of a second-order thought, we can add psychological considerations of the kind raised by Ryle in his *Concept of Mind*.[14] I may presently hold a belief about the weather tomorrow. But as soon as I attempt to reflect on this belief, the reflection replaces the belief. A given thought occupies our attention in the present; to reflect on it replaces this thought with another that occupies another successor "now." To be sure, I can now recall having had a previous belief. But such recollection is not an exercise of a capacity to examine a belief while still having it—the belief is no longer being held at the time it is being recollected. Recall how Rosenthal describes a second-order thought as "nearly contemporaneous" with the thought to which it is directed. This phrase disguises a difficulty. Either the second-order thought is contemporaneous with the its first-order thought or it is not. The first case is impossible because of Ryle's replacement problem, and in the second alternative we no longer have a second-order thought but a recollection. As Ryle notes, the possibility of thoughts directed toward other thoughts such as beliefs or desires also poses the problem of an infinite regress. Suppose a person is capable of directing a second-order thought toward a first-order one. If this were indeed possible, there seems to be no reason for not being able to direct a third-order thought toward a second-order thought, to not only believe that one is having a certain belief, but believe that one is believing that one believes. If third-order thoughts are possible, why not also fourth-order, fifth-order, and so on without end? The most plausible way of terminating such an infinite regress of thoughts is to simply deny the possibility of the second-order thought that initiated it.

But what of the second-order desires cited in defense of the uniqueness of human freedom of choice? Surely, it will be said, such desires do exist and constitute a form of self-consciousness immune to the objections just raised against the possibility of second-order beliefs. In fact, we do seem to resist some cravings and approve of some motivations, and such self-control would seem to support the presence of this form of reflective consciousness. There is a simple explanation of this feature of our experience, however, that avoids granting this exception to the denial of second-order thoughts. All deliberation involves a conflict between motivations, and what are labeled as "second-order desires" are properly viewed as simply parts of this process. A person may crave chocolates, but act contrary to this craving by refusing to indulge it. But this simply means that there is some other desire, say that of good health, that competes with the craving, and becomes the basis for his action. Similarly, a person may be ambitious and approve of her ambition, but this approval is nothing more than her having an ideal of herself as independent or as one who follows her own path. This ideal is what she wants to realize, and becomes the guide of her actions. Again, there is no desire directed at another desire, but instead a desire to realize an ideal that reinforces her ambition.

Awareness of beliefs and desires thus does not qualify as a form of self-consciousness. There is another type of awareness, however, that does seem to qualify, an awareness sometimes referred to as "phenomenal consciousness," the awareness that we are having a certain sensation or feeling. This awareness seems best characterized as an exercise of our capacity to report our perceptions, sensations, and feelings in the form of avowals such as "I hear the sound of the radio," "I am having a visual image of what seems red and square," or "I feel a pain in my leg." To be aware is to either form representations for ourselves of these sentences or to use them to report what we sense or feel to others. This capacity to use avowals is clearly unique to ourselves as users of language. But the uniqueness of the capacity to use language is obvious, and has never been questioned by naturalists. What divide humanists from naturalists are the metaphysical implications that can be drawn from this unique capacity of our species, in particular, whether it can be used to distinguish a species with free choice from other natural forms whose behavior is determined. Phenomenal consciousness as manifested in the use of avowals has no bearing on this issue, and can be readily conceded.

Intentionality

Another reason given for our special exemption from universal mechanism is our capacity to make judgments. When we look at a colored object we can judge for ourselves and assert to others sentences such as "This is square" and "That is red." Tokens of these sentences functioning as mental representations within us are thought to be very different from the mental representations of toads snapping at flies. Mental representations in animals are causal intermediaries between the environment and behavior, functioning as both effects of environmental stimuli and causes of subsequent behavior. But the sentence tokens of our judgments are not causal effects of the objects to which they are correlated. Instead, our powers of conceptualization make it possible for us to withhold judgment and refrain from action. Using such considerations, some advocates of humanism have appealed to still another kind of consciousness called "intentional consciousness" to justify this distinction between representations as causal intermediaries and as vehicles of choice.

Intentionality may be defined as directedness toward that which may not exist. Beliefs, desires, and hopes are regarded as intentional states because of the possibility of the nonexistence of the objects or events toward which they are directed. Someone says to me, "It will rain tomorrow," and I believe him. Since the state of affairs toward which it is directed may not in fact exist tomorrow, my belief may be false. Similarly, I may desire or hope to become wealthy, but may not eventually realize my desire or hope, and I may intend to go for a walk within an hour and never take the walk. Desires, hopes, and intentions are thus to be counted along with beliefs as intentional states. Also classified as intentional are judgments and decisions as psychological acts. I judge now that it is raining on the basis of what I see, but there is the possibility that I am mistaken. Similarly, I decide now to go for a walk, but some contingency may arise that prevents me from actually carrying out my decision.

Can we attribute intentionality to lower animals? Some intentional states seem clearly to be specific to humans. Consider, for example, the intentional state of belief, which some writers are reluctant, and for good reasons, to attribute to lower animals. I may believe it will rain tomorrow based on what I have been told by another. If it fails to rain, then my belief can be said to be false in exactly the same sense as the statement made to me is false. This falsity is clearly relative to the conventional rules governing the sentence with which the statement was made. It is only because the sentence "It will rain" means what it does that we can appeal to observations in judging that it is false. The concept of falsity is thus language-relative, and when used to evaluate beliefs carries this relativity with it. For these reasons it seems nonsensical to say of a dog that it believes there is a bone buried in its backyard. Because the dog is incapable of using and understanding sentences, it makes no sense to evaluate such a belief as false, and such evaluation seems essential to the concept of belief.

But a wide variety of intentional states do seem attributable to lower animals. Consider, for example, the tribe of vervet monkeys studied by Cheney and Seyfarth.[15] Within this tribe, we are told, there are separate warning cries for eagles, pythons, and leopards, the principal predators of the area, with each cry evoking a characteristic response. On hearing the eagle cry, tribe members normally take cover under a tree or bush; for the python, there is typically climbing of trees; for the leopard call, there is typically fleeing into dense underbrush. Sometimes a call is a false alarm: there is no eagle observed to be up in the sky after hearing the eagle cry. This happens quite frequently when sounded by immature tribe members, only rarely when the call is made by an adult. Tribe members learn to disregard the immature calls, but at the same time continue to take cover when the alarm is sounded by an adult. Here we would quite naturally attribute expectations to those hearing an eagle alarm call, and expectation clearly fulfills the conditions for an intentional state. There may be no eagle up in the sky; the expectation may be disappointed, and there may be recognition that what is expected does not occur. We should not apply the evaluative term "false" to the expectation, because this is language-specific. But there is clearly an analog to belief in the truth of a proposition in the expectation of an eagle, and in the recognition of the nonoccurrence of what is expected there is an analog to a judgment of falsity. In this sense intentionality can be ascribed to the vervet monkeys.

Whether we can attribute an intentional term like "decide" standing for a psychological act to them is less obvious. The responses to the various calls are not reflex responses insofar as monkeys can learn to withhold them if what is expected does not occur. If an eagle is not seen when an immature member produces the eagle call, the next time this member produces the call others in the tribe will be less likely to flee for cover. Should we say that during this period of learning these others are deciding whether or not to respond to the call? Or does "decide" share with "believe" the feature of being language-specific? We used "expectation" in place of "belief" in describing the mental states of the monkeys, because "expectation" can take nouns as its object ("He expects his mother"), but "belief" typically takes propositional "that" clauses ("He believes that his mother will come"). But there seems to be no word in ordinary language that provides a similar general replacement for "decide." Admittedly, it sounds strange to attribute decisions to monkeys; decisions are usually made by weighing alternatives within contexts of practical inferences. If we do use "decide" in this situation, it is surely an extended sense in which many of its connotations are missing. The difficulties we face in choosing the appropriate specific ascription for a wide range of mental states and acts in lower animals should not obscure the fact, however, that we accept attributions of intentionality in some form or other as being entirely appropriate.

Warning cries such as those of the vervet monkeys represent a primitive level of communicated sign. At the still more primitive level of naturally occurring events, the same types of attributions would seem to apply. Consider, for example, the doe in the forest sensing a certain odor that for her is a sign of a nearby hunter. She then expects the hunter, and if she were to see him would recognize him as an instance of the type she expects. We can then say that what she expects is the significance of the sign, while what she sees is a significant occurrence recognized on a given occasion. As for warning cries as signals, this recognition is an analog of judgments of truth at the level of conventional language. But ordinarily the deer doesn't simply wait for this recognition, instead fleeing the potential danger. Besides having the *cognitive* significance of hunter, the sign has, for her, the *dynamic* significance of fleeing as the response necessary for self-preservation. If fleeing were a reflex response to the odor as stimulus, we would not, of course, refer to the odor as a sign. To describe it in this manner is to appeal to a comparison with language interpretation in which we exercise some self-control.

These considerations would seem to apply to Skinner's models of instrumental learning. In one of them, we may recall, there was a controlling stimulus such as a flash of red light that was paired with a rat's bar-pressing response and the reward of a food pellet. Like the odor for the deer, we can describe the red light as a sign with both cognitive and dynamic significance: the animal anticipates the pellet reward and interprets the light as a sign of bar pressing. If the pellet were not to follow, the rat would recognize a nonoccurrence of what was expected, and after such recognitions would cease to respond to the light by the pressing. We can describe the situation in the language of cause and effect, and inquire into the mechanisms that explain the changes in the animal's behavior. But to describe the light as a sign introduces a comparison to language of the same sort as the comparison invoked by Wittgenstein in discussing the parallel between a sentence and the crowing of a cock. With such a comparison, intentional descriptions in terms of expectation and recognition become appropriate.

More problematic again is the application of the word "decide" to the fleeing of the deer or the bar pressing of the rat. It seems even more out of place than for the responses of monkeys to warning calls, and yet we lack another term that can serve as an acceptable substitute. The best we seem to be able to do is to describe the behavior of the deer and the rat as "spontaneous," as not consisting of reflex responses to environmental stimuli, but instead of making responses that could be unlearned. With attributions of intentionality, therefore, we introduce the concept of spontaneity in which there is some degree of control on the part of organisms over their responses.

Philosophical humanism in the sense being understood here denies the possibility of such attributions. Norman Malcom introduces the term "intentional consciousness" to stand for intentional mental states, and applies it to persons being afraid of snakes, hoping for future profit, and believing that it will rain. He argues it can be sensibly attributed only to humans because it makes no sense to say that a fly takes flight because it is frightened or is aware of some danger. The fly can be said to have visual and tactile sensations, and in this sense has experiential consciousness, but it lacks our human-specific intentional consciousness. [16] In a similar vein, John Heil claims that "it is only when we introduce second-order representational capacities into a system that anything approximating the fine-grained character of intentionality is achieved."[17] Those organisms or "systems" without the capacity for reflective consciousness—and this seems to include for Heil all infrahuman species—lack intentionality. Keith Lehrer also argues that it is in virtue of possessing a unique kind of consciousness, that our interpretation of signs is distinguished from that of lower animals. Because of reflective consciousness, we are said to "understand signification," and through this understanding are able "to let a sign signify something." In contrast, a lower animal "cannot alter the signification of the signs it understands."[18]

If such remarks were intended only to emphasize the uniqueness of the human linguistic capacity, we could let them stand unchallenged. But they are designed for the larger purpose of drawing humanism's distinction between lower animals governed by mechanical causation and humans with freedom of choice. Of course, Malcom is correct in saying we don't attribute fear and hope to a fly, though it is not so obvious that such attributions are not appropriate for monkeys. But to the extent that a fly is capable of learning on the basis of past experience, intentionality seems present. We can also agree with Heil that language permits discriminations between objects that are impossible for any system of warning calls found among lower animals. If this is what is meant by saying that our intentionality is "fine-grained," there can be no objection. But there seems no relation between such discriminations and the suspect notion of reflective consciousness in the form of a capacity for "second-order representational systems." And finally, the conventionality of language permits the introduction of new terminology and letting "a sign signify something." But again, this is simply a restatement of our species' unique language abilities.

Indeed, we seem to have in our own experience some basis for conceiving the type of intentionality present within lower animals. I may be driving in my car listening to news on its radio. Suddenly I see a pothole, and swerve to avoid the anticipated jolt, while continuing to listen. The sight of the pothole is like the odor for the deer

and the red light for the rat: it combines both the cognitive significance of the expected jolt and the dynamic significance of swerving.
But as a sign being interpreted in this way, consciousness seems to
be minimal, and there is certainly nothing remotely related to the
exalted "reflective consciousness" that is thought to be peculiar to
ourselves. My focus of attention is on the news I am listening to,
with the sight of the pothole and swerving functioning at some level
peripheral to this attention. At this level learning seems to occur: if
I were to see the pothole on several future occasions, fail to swerve
in time, and feel no jolt, I would not swerve in the future. Cognitive
scientists postulate different modules of the brain that run in parallel. Some of these seem to be remnants of earlier stages in the evolution of our species, and their survival in our experience in such
forms as learning to swerve provides us some understanding of
forms of intentionality present in our evolutionary predecessors.

So far we have singled out two modes of sign interpretation for
attention: cognitive interpretation, in which there is expectation and
recognition of occurrences or nonoccurrences of the expected, and
dynamic interpretation, in which there is a decision or some mental
act analogous to a decision. In characterizing an event as a sign, as
contrasted with the cause of a reflex response, we assume the presence of both of these modes. Where there is learning there is, therefore, sign interpretation, and where there is interpretation there is
intentionality. But completeness requires us to add a third mode,
which we can refer to as *emotional interpretation*, what, at the
human level, we describe as aesthetic attraction and aversion. On
smelling the odor, the deer expects the hunter and prepares to flee,
but the odor as sign also arouses an *aversion* analogous to what we
experience as fear. Similarly, the rat on seeing the flash of red light
expects food and bar-presses, but the expectation is accompanied by
a positive motivation that we describe as an *appetition*. It is surely
anthropomorphizing the situation to describe this as hope, but the
emotional response of the animal can reasonably be said to share at
least some features of this emotion.

For organisms exhibiting learning, it seems plausible to attribute
intentionality in all three cognitive, dynamic, and emotional modes.
But panpsychism is a doctrine claiming that mental attributions can
be made of all organized, self-maintaining natural forms, and these
may include viruses, molecules, and atoms that do not exhibit learning behavior. What form of mental description is appropriate at these
most primitive of levels? Here the answer seems to be that at these

protoexperiential levels emotional interpretation predominates in the form that Hartshorne describes as feeling, with the cognitive and dynamic modes present only in incipient forms. The infinitesimal degrees of feeling that exist at these lowest levels of organization can be conceived as faint traces of satisfactions and dissatisfactions that get progressively intensified as organization becomes more complex and specialized and more advanced forms of sign interpretation are possible. The spontaneity of behavior present in organisms with the capacity for learning is reduced, but where feeling is present would not seem to be entirely eliminated.

But why accept such extensions of mental attributions? We do have available to us the negative argument that we have no justifiable grounds for denying mentality and spontaneity at primitive levels of organized natural forms. Once we reject humanism and concede spontaneity at any subhuman level, say at the level of primates such as apes and monkeys, we seem to lack a basis for denying it at a still more primitive level. Learning behavior as associated with intentionality may seem a reasonable point of demarcation, but we have no a priori grounds for excluding organized natural forms that fail to exhibit such behavior. Some may choose to attribute some degree of spontaneity to living organisms, while withholding it from the inorganic. But life is defined as the combined capacity for reproduction, either asexual or bisexual, and for metabolism. There seems no necessary relation between these capacities and the presence of spontaneity; it seems possible for there to be reproduction and metabolism within a natural body without mental spontaneity. And it seems just as reasonable to conclude that their absence does not require the absence of spontaneity. Below the organic level, comparisons to the human case are based only on persisting unity of organization and homeostasis, but nevertheless such comparisons constitute analogies, albeit ones with a restricted base, and an inference is still possible. We have, then, this negative argument for panpsychism in the general form advanced by Whitehead and Hartshorne: Because there are no grounds for demarcating any one level from those more primitive with respect to mental attributions, it is plausible to ascribe spontaneity to any organized body exhibiting homeostasis.

This negative argument conveys a degree of plausibility to the thesis of panpsychism to the extent it renders the humanist alternative implausible. As an independent argument, however, it commits the *fallacy of ignorance* (*ad ignoratium*), the fallacy of arguing from our ignorance of any level of demarcation of the mental from the nonmental to the conclusion that there is no demarcation. It may be successful in convincing us that the panpsychist thesis may possibly be true, but it falls short of convincing the skeptical that it warrants their acceptance. A stronger argument must wait until chapter 5, in which the topic is mechanist attempts to explain the emergence of mentality.

CHAPTER FOUR

Mental Ascriptions

So far I have been presenting panpsychism as a metaphysical doctrine and locating it relative to the alternatives of philosophical humanism and universal mechanism. The initial reasoned basis for the doctrine we have seen to lie in analogical inferences that compare human behavior and anatomical structures with those of other natural forms. In the absence of sense receptors and learning behavior, the only basis for this extension to nonliving forms is the observation of unified wholes maintaining themselves against environmental forces. At this stage we need to look more closely at mental ascriptions in general because features of them help to understand problems with their extension and the attractiveness of the humanist alternative. We begin with problems related to ascriptions of sensations and feelings, and then turn to ascriptions of propositional attitudes. Finally, we look more closely at ascriptions of mental states to infrahuman species and the relationships between human freedom and spontaneity of behavior within natural forms. These must be clarified if we are to give an adequate response to the humanists' division between the human and infrahuman.

Ascribing Sensations

Recall from chapter 1 Wittgenstein and Ryle's claim that ascriptions of sensations such as pain are direct and noninferential—for we seem to make them simply on the basis of observations of another's behavior. This behavior constitutes criteria for the application of a sensation word such as "pain" rather than being the basis of an analogical inference. It is obvious, however, that when we apply sensation words to ourselves these behavioral criteria become irrelevant. We use avowals such as "I feel a pain," "I see a red apple," and "I hear a loud sound" to report what we feel, see, and hear to others, and we regard these avowals as direct reports of what we experience. Sensation and feeling terms have both a first-person and third-person use, and retain the same meaning when used by a speaker to report what he or she experiences. The word "pain" does not change meaning in the sentence contexts "I am in pain" and "He is in pain," although in the third-person sentence behavioral criteria are applied that are absent for the first-person avowal.

It is not a simple matter to specify exactly how the two different uses of the same word are related. In his criticisms of the view that behavior constitutes criteria for mental ascriptions, Hilary Putnam argues it is possible for a person X to be constituted in such a way that he grimaces when experiencing pleasure and smiles when in pain, and contends that in such a case the words "pleasure" and "pain" would not have changed their meanings when applied to him, contrary to Wittgenstein's criterial view.[1] We could judge as false the assertion "He is in pain" when observing the grimacing, but may not regard this as a change in meaning. But how would we find out about the discrepancy between what is described on the basis of normal behavioral criteria and that person's experiences? If it is observed behavior of X that brings this about, then we would simply enlarge the criteria we apply, and would regard the case as one in which one item that is normally present within a cluster including others happens now to be absent. We would then modify our applications of "pleasure" and "pain" for that particular person. This would simply be an illustration of the fact that all criteria admit of exceptions and that there are statistically rare abnormal cases in which normal criteria break down, such as for the albino animal that provides an exception to the application of normal coloration criteria to a given species.

It is more likely, however, that first-person avowals rather than behavior would be the basis for judging the presence of some kind of error. Let us suppose we know the person to be honest and, as far as we have been able to observe, an invariably reliable informant, and that he describes himself as feeling pleasure when exhibiting sad behavior, and as being in pain when he is smiling. Given his history of veracity, it is likely that our trust in his verbal reports would override normal behavioral criteria, and that we would regard X as an exception in applications of these criteria. More generally, it is the coincidence between verbal reports and behavior that serves to fix behavioral criteria used in mental ascriptions. If across the general population discrepancies were to develop between behavioral criteria and first-person verbal reports, our trust in the veracity of others could override and lead to a change in behavioral criteria. The meaning of the mental terms as derived from the first-person reports would then remain constant in the face of changes in behavioral criteria, and force a change in these criteria. The meanings of the sensation words would eventually change as the criteria change, but the change would be induced by corrections on the basis of first-person reports.

This priority of first-person reports would seem to be maintained if we used recordings of brain processes as criteria for ascriptions of sensations in place of behavioral criteria. Whenever a brain pattern of type Z occurs in our subject X, we might judge him to be in pain. Again, if discrepancies were to arise between X's first-person avowals and our ascriptions based on such criteria, the avowals would normally take priority and force a revision of the criteria, at least as applied to X.

It is also possible, of course, that we judge our subject X to be untrustworthy, as would occur if he were to sometimes make mistakes about obvious observational matters, or substitute one word for another that should be used properly. Then if he were to say "I am in pain" when smiling and "I am experiencing pleasure" when grimacing, we would probably use behavioral criteria to either judge him as misleading us or guilty of a misuse of language. But from the fact that behavioral criteria may sometimes be accorded priority, it does not at all follow that they typically have this status. Normally we trust others, and it is only difficult determinations about the trustworthiness of informants that force us to decide whether first-person reports or behavioral criteria used in third-person ascriptions are to have priority.

Wittgenstein suggests that a verbal report such as "I am in pain" is a type of verbal behavior replacing groans and cries. If this were so, again we would have a situation in which we must decide which of the features in a behavioral cluster are to be weighted more heavily, and we might decide that the verbal behavior is to count more heavily than the nonverbal. But this solution can't be correct. Although a groan and a cry can be uttered with the intent to deceive, unlike the verbal report "I am in pain" it cannot be said to be true or false, nor does it have a corresponding third-person description of the form "X is in pain." It is precisely because the first-person verbal report is not simply another item of behavior that it can be used to correct third-person descriptions employing behavioral criteria.

In recent years an alternate way of justifying mental ascriptions has been developed that appeals to a basic method of explanation in the natural sciences. In the sciences the existence of a theoretical entity such as a certain quark or a force field is postulated on the basis of its providing the best available explanation of observed phenomena. Thus, the existence of a certain quark may be postulated on the basis of explaining observed interactions of particles, even though we have no observational means of directly observing the quark. The hypothesis that this type of quark exists must meet the standards of simplicity, coherence with other accepted scientific theories and background assumptions, and consistency with observed data. Similarly, magnetic and gravitational fields are postulated as providing the best explanation of the behavior of bodies that are influenced by them. Now we cannot directly observe the sensations or feelings of another person. But we can postulate the existence of these mental events—so it is argued—on the grounds that they provide the best explanation of the behavior that we do observe. Why is that man writhing on the floor holding his stomach? It could be because he (or it) is an unfeeling robot with implanted electrodes being controlled by some wireless device in the hands of a manipulating technician. But the best explanation, that is, the simplest and with the greatest overall coherence with what we accept, would be that he feels a pain in his stomach; hence we regard ourselves as being justified in ascribing the pain to him.[2]

This best-explanation justification is flawed in at least two ways. First, it seems obvious that the best explanation of the writhing has no relation to what we describe with "pain." The best explanation would cite electrical/chemical processes in the nervous system of the individual, for these, after all, are causing the observed behavior. The pain as felt from the perspective of the one having it would itself seem to be irrelevant to the explanation of behavior. Many philosophers accept the view that a particular pain is identical with a particular brain process, and through this identity the pain could be regarded as the cause of the behavior. This assumes that the concepts of identity and difference can be applied to relations between the physical and mental, and this assumption is controversial. But even if we do accept physical–mental identities, whatever causal powers the pain has in its qualitative, felt aspect, they would be derived from the neurophysiological process with which it is identified. The best scientific explanation would be formulated in the language of neurology in which there is no mention of felt pains.

The second problem with the best-explanation view is that it seems unable to account for the special relationship between third-person and first-person sensation ascriptions. Suppose we do infer that the best explanation of the writhing is that X is in pain, and X asserts "I'm not in pain." Again, if we have found X to be consistently trustworthy and there is no aberrant behavior, we could accept this as a falsification of our explanatory hypothesis. But there is obviously no parallel for this in the natural sciences, and thus the assimilation of sensation ascriptions to explanatory hypotheses in the sciences is suspect.

There is also a practical dimension to sensation ascriptions that is typically absent for theoretical explanatory hypotheses. Normally it is not simply curiosity that leads us to ask what pains a person is enduring, or what he or she is seeing or hearing. Asking and answering such questions take place in a context of cooperation and mutual care among members of our species. If a person is in pain, this typically evokes our sympathy and perhaps assistance. If another can't see an object, we often take measures to ensure that she does. As we shall see, this cooperative feature has implications for the panpsychist thesis.

We now turn to the ascription of propositional attitudes, in which cooperative and interactive features are much more prominent. Here we have the same problem of explaining how a single term can have first- and third-person uses. In addition, we have a dual use within third-person ascriptions, and a propositional component with no application to creatures incapable of language use.

Social Aspects of Attitude Ascriptions

Ascriptions of propositional attitudes are of the form "X φs that p," where φ represents a verb such as "believes," "desires," "fears," or "hopes," and p expresses the proposition toward which the attitudes of believing, desiring, etc. are directed. Thus, we might say of John "John believes that the boat will arrive tomorrow" or "John hopes that the boat will arrive soon." Belief ascriptions are commonly asserted on the basis of what a person says. Thus, on Monday John might say "The boat will be coming in on Tuesday." On the assumption that John was sincere in what he said, another might then assert "John believes that the *Seaside Princess* will be arriving tomorrow." Here John's original remark is paraphrased within the belief ascription, with "*Seaside Princess*" being substituted for "the boat" and "arriving tomorrow" for "coming in on Tuesday." The ascription functions as an interpretation of what John said, a paraphrase making it more easily understood by the intended audience. Other propositional attitudes such as desires and hopes are also commonly based on what others say and then interpret. Thus, John may say "I hope the boat comes in Tuesday," and the corresponding third-person ascription becomes "John hopes the boat arrives tomorrow." More generally, if X says "I ϕ that p," then, assuming sincerity, another might assert "X ϕs that q," where q is a paraphrase that interprets the original p.

Such ascriptions serve a two-fold purpose. First, they enable us to predict and explain actions. If we know that John wants to return to the mainland after a night's rest, then on the basis of his belief that there will be a return boat the next day, we can now predict he will stay overnight and take the next boat back, or explain after the fact why he stayed overnight rather than taking a flight back that afternoon. For such prediction and explanation, the question of whether John's belief is true or false is irrelevant: false beliefs are just as effective as true ones. Such prediction and explanation are based on our knowledge of regularities of human behavior, and are no different in kind, although often much more difficult to accomplish in practice, than predictions and explanations we apply to objects in nature such as pieces of metals, liquids, plants, and animals.

But there is also a second use of attitude ascriptions that requires social interactions that we have only with members of our own species. The point of paraphrasing and interpreting someone's remarks in the process of ascribing a propositional attitude is to make ourselves understood to an audience. Gaining this understanding makes it possible for both this audience and ourselves to then evaluate the proposition toward which the attitude is directed. If it is false or unjustified, then we may be able to inform the subject and prevent some sort of harm. Will the next boat in fact be arriving tomorrow? If not, John's belief is false and his hope unjustified. He should probably be leaving today, and in most circumstances we would inform him of his mistake.

We have, then, two uses of propositional attitude verbs such as "believe," one to predict or explain, the other to interpret or evaluate. Why do single words assume both functions? Why has language not evolved two words to perform two distinct roles? The answer seems to be that the combination is an essential aspect of the cooperation and social control characteristic of human life. If we recognize someone as holding a mistaken belief and predict that on the basis of this belief he or she will act in harmful ways, we usually feel obligated to point out the error and avert the harm. *X* may believe that the boat will come tomorrow; I know it will not. By correcting the error I aid him in avoiding a needless wait. This correction is made possible by the verb "to believe" being used both to predict *X*'s behavior and to correct the mistake of one with whom communication is possible.

The capacity to combine prediction of behavior and recognition of error, and to use both to control others seems to have developed quite late in primate evolution. Students of animal behavior have noted an important difference between chimpanzees and monkeys with respect to the ability to recognize another's error and take measures to correct it.[3] In one experiment, an adult female chimpanzee is placed in a glassed-in compartment outside a cage. In the presence of the female a snake is placed by an attendant underneath a box that can be easily picked up. The female's infant is then placed in the cage. The mother has the capacity to recognize the ignorance of her offspring, and reacts by screaming to the infant as a warning of the danger. If let in the cage, the mother will lead the infant to safety. No such behavior is observed among monkeys. They can signal danger, as shown in the studies by Cheney and Seyfarth of the vervets, but not in response to what they recognize as ignorance on the part of their audience.

Attitude ascriptions are sometimes not based on what others actually say. *A* observes John skating warily on the ice, staying at the edge and avoiding the center of the pond. *A* then uses the sentence "John believes that the ice is thin" to describe to *B* John's mental state and to possibly predict his future behavior. Here there is no relaying and interpretation of a remark actually made by John, but instead an ascription based on behavior. Even in such situations, however, there seem to be linguistic elements relevant to the ascription. *A* not only sees John's behavior, but observes the ice as the circumstance in which this behavior is occurring. He then formulates to himself a judgment about the ice's condition that could be verbally expressed to another. In describing John's belief, A would seem to use this information to answer a question about what John would say in these circumstances, with the answer being a judgment about what A thinks John would say if queried. In this respect it represents a relaying of this conjectured remark. There does not seem to be, therefore, a sharp distinction between a belief ascription based on what a person says and one based on how that person behaves. In the first case, there is an interpretation of what is actually said; in the case in which behavior is the basis, there is an interpretation of what the speaker thinks the person would say in the circumstances being observed.

What is true of beliefs also seems true of other propositional attitudes such as wants, hopes, and fears. Often we reach conclusions about them on the basis of what persons say, and produce interpretations of these sayings. As for beliefs, if the basis for the ascription is behavior, we interpret what we think the person would say he wants, hopes, or fears in the circumstances being observed.

Words such as "believes," "wants," and "hopes" occur in both first-person and third-person forms, not simply in English, but in all the world's languages. They must therefore have common meanings in these languages that justify this dual use; if they did not, we would find different words to express the different meanings of the two uses. For some first-person uses of attitude verbs such as "believes" and "wants" this shared meaning can be explained on the basis of common criteria for application. I may judge that another wants to eat a piece of cake on the table at a reception by his behavior: he circles it, eyes it longingly, wets his lips, and so forth. On the basis of this behavior I conclude "He wants to eat the piece of cake." I may also find myself circling the table, looking at the cake, and so on, and even though I may not feel the want, I may judge on the basis of my own behavior that in fact I too want the piece of cake. In such a case, the common meaning of "want" in the third-person "He wants the cake" and first-person "I want the cake" is readily explained on the basis of the common behavioral criteria. On some occasions the basis for a mental ascription is a verbal report or expression by another. X may say to me "I believe it will rain" and, trusting his sincerity, I say to another "X believes that it will rain." Since my ascription is simply a relaying of what X said to me, the common meaning of the verb "to believe" in X's expression and my ascription is readily explained. Similar considerations apply to the first-person "I am in pain" and "He is in pain" discussed earlier. If the latter is based on the former, if it represents a relaying of what someone has reported in the first-person, the common meaning of the sensation word "pain" is readily accounted for.

But other cases of third-person uses of the same mental word seem more puzzling, and these have occasioned much discussion by philosophers. Often we don't seem to apply verbs such as "believe" and "want" to ourselves on the basis of observing our own behavior. Instead, we express these attitudes directly in the manner described in chapter 3, and often use the verbs to express how their propositional attitudes are to be understood. I may say "I believe that it will rain" as a way of expressing my uncertainty about the weather; if I were certain or confident, I would use sentences of the form "I know that p" or "I'm certain that p." In such cases, "believe" is an indicator of what J. L. Austin called "illocutionary force," and is not itself descriptive of self-observed behavior. Instead, it conveys how p is to be understood by the audience, the degree of confidence in its assertion by the speaker. In such cases, it does not seem possible for another's judgment about my belief—based on observations of behavior—to conflict with my own expression of belief. Another person X sees me leaving without my umbrella on a clear day, and concludes "Clarke doesn't believe it will rain." Suppose I have just told another "I believe it will rain" as a way of expressing my hesitation about the future weather. Then X's ascription of nonbelief would not seem to contradict my expression of belief—I certainly would not retract my first remark on X's pointing out to me my behavior. Since I was not describing myself by my first-person expression, I cannot be contradicted by X's description. In this case the first- and third-person uses of "believe" occupy different logical spaces between which there can be no contradictions, and this seems to force us to conclude that the word has two different meanings.

This conclusion is most implausible, however. Natural languages tend to develop different words for different senses, unless words are used for very different purposes on unrelated topics. If the first-person sense of "believe" were entirely different from that in the third person, we would expect that within natural languages there would evolve two different words, and in fact this has not occurred. As noted, the first-person "I believe that p" is typically used to express uncertainty about the truth of p, while the third-person "He believes that p" is claimed by many philosophers to have as its sole use the assertion of a psychological state. We have seen, however, that this third-person ascription has two uses, one of which, the interpretive–evaluative, is certainly not asserting a matter of fact about a subject. There is then no difficulty in explaining the use of the same verb in the two persons. To say "I believe that *p*" and express hesitation is to invite correction and aid of the kind that is made possible, as we have seen, by the combination of uses found in third-person ascriptions. Of course, a first-person belief sentence can also be used to assert a psychological state on the basis of behavior. I might assert "I believe there are ghosts" on the basis of observing my own behavior in old, deserted houses. In this case, my assertion is not primarily an expression of hesitation, and what I assert could be corrected by saying "He doesn't believe there are ghosts" on the basis of my behavior as observed by others. But this simply shows that there is a predictive–explanatory use in the first-person in addition to the expressive one that invites evaluation, and further supports the view that "believe" has varying uses that occur in combination.

Without propositional components to be evaluated, attributions of perceptions, sensations, and feelings obviously differ from those of propositional attitudes. For sensations and feelings we have no basis for correction of any kind: it makes no sense to say that Smith feels a pain, although it is really a tickle. But as noted earlier, sensation and feeling ascriptions do share a cooperative aspect with ascriptions of propositional attitudes. To describe someone as being in pain to an audience is commonly to imply that the audience should come to that person's aid or that comfort and care is in order. If the cause of the distress is known, sometimes there is an implied warning to the audience to prevent this cause from inflicting the same effect on them. In all such situations, we don't use the relevant mental terms to simply describe as a means of satisfying our curiosity, but typically employ them in a wider context of cooperation. (Of course, this needs qualification, because for both propositional attitude and sensation ascriptions there are also malicious uses to deceive and inflict harm. Overall, cooperation dominates.)

So far we have considered only mental ascriptions as members of our own species. But this is of interest to us primarily for its lessons in extending mental ascriptions to infrahuman natural forms.

Mentality and Spontaneity in the Infrahuman

The features of mental ascriptions of sensations just described complicate the way we ascribe mental states to lower animals. Contrary to Fechner's view described in chapter 2, my brother and my dog must be regarded as very different for the purposes of mental ascriptions. The whimpering of a dog would seem, at least on some occasions, to be a form of communication, but it is very different from a first-person avowal of pain. In the absence of a shared language, for the dog we must rely on comparisons between behavioral and anatomical criteria of the kind described in previous discussions of analogical inferences. In using these inferences, however, we are employing a mental term that has a use in making avowals. Similarity of behavior may be the base of the inference when applied to infrahuman species, but our understanding of the projected term is determined in part by first-person forms used in communication with members of our own.

There are thus important differences between ascriptions we make of other humans and those we make of lower animals. For humans we apply behavioral criteria directly, but can use first-person reports as a basis for correcting a third-person ascription. This may eventually lead to a change in behavioral criteria and a change in meaning of the mental terms being applied. For lower animals, in contrast, there is no possibility of correction by a first-person report, and the tie between first- and third-person is broken.

This special feature of mental language as applied to the infrahuman is noted by Nagel, who remarks that "we ascribe experience to animals on the basis of their behavior, structure, and circumstances, but we are not just ascribing to them behavior, structure, and circumstances. . . . Here the special relation between the first- and third-person ascription is not available as an indication of the subjectivity of the mental."[4] This inability to use behavioral and anatomical criteria to indicate "the subjectivity of the mental" Nagel finds "definitely unsatisfactory," because we believe that other creatures "have their own reality and their own subjectivity." The situation described by Nagel stems from changes in the use of mental terms when extended to the infrahuman. In the absence of first-person avowals, they are applied only on the basis of behavioral and anatomical criteria. At the same time, they retain the implication of subjectivity at the infrahuman level in the form of having a perspective on an environment. This implication is the grounds for the belief in subjectivity Nagel appeals to. It seems derived from the standard combined first- and third-person uses of mental terms, although for creatures the first-person use is not operative as a corrective.

There is also at least some degree of social interaction that seems implied when we extend mental terms beyond their standard uses in both the first and third person. As noted, we use first-person forms such as "I believe that p" or "I am in pain" to solicit cooperation, whether in evaluation or aid in alleviating distress; corresponding third-person forms such as "He believes that *p*" and "He is in pain" are means for evaluating and aiding others. From this it would seem to follow that such mental terms will have no justifiable application to those for which such interactive relations fail to exist. We may extend them perhaps to prelinguistic infants, caged and domesticated animals, and for pets under our care. We do give food to the dog that is said to expect it and treat its foot if we judge it to be in pain. But no interactive relations typically exist for animals in the wild, not to mention for insects and protozoa, and for them, what seems to be an essential feature of mental attributions is lacking. This lack of social relations may explain the reluctance of philosophical humanism to attribute to other species full-fledged mentality.

How then do we justify attributing mentality to creatures with which we do not interact? The answer of panpsychism must, I think, take the form of extending the attitudes of care and concern that underlie social cooperation with our fellow humans to other natural forms. We justify mental attributions to the infrahuman because we believe we *should* adopt an attitude of care and concern toward other species, and, at least in an attenuated form, toward natural forms exhibiting unity of organization and homeostasis. Does this mean I should care about the mosquito I flatten with a swat or the plant cells in the piece of celery I chew on? Or the bacteria I destroy by taking medicines? Clearly in such cases of minimal complexity of organization concern is properly minimal, although even here panpsychism holds that our attitude should differ, if only in the slightest degree, from what we have toward a rock we crush with a hammer or a computer scheduled for recycling. But what of the atoms in the rock or in the plastic of the computer? Assuming these qualify for mental attributions by the panpsychist thesis, it is surely absurd to think these merit concern of any kind. At this inorganic level, panpsychism seems forced to appeal to attitudes of a different kind. These will be discussed when we turn to religious implications of the doctrine in the final chapter.

For now it is sufficient to note that mental language, when applied to members of our own species, is not used to simply report matters of fact, and this feature is carried over when this language is extended to natural bodies with evolutionary origins earlier than ours. Nagel seems correct in emphasizing that to assert that a natural body has a qualitative perspective is not simply to make a linguistic decision to extend mental terminology. There is, in addition, an implicit comparison to our own perspectives and use of the indexicals "I," "now," and "here." In this sense, the panpsychist thesis is a realist thesis, as maintained in chapter 1. But special features of this mental language also guarantee that its extended use is not to assert some special type of fact about natural bodies in addition to such properties as their mass, size, and shape.

Problems related to lack of social interaction also arise when we attempt to justify attributions of spontaneity to the infrahuman, and the solution to it seems to be similar. To say of someone that she acted freely, as Peter Strawson has noted,[5] is to adopt a certain attitude toward that person, an attitude entirely different from that we adopt toward infants and the criminally insane. Freely performed actions seem to have two essential features. They are, first, in some sense under the control of agents, what is done by them as unified individuals, not simply caused by their glands and muscles as their component parts. And second, they are actions that agents can be held accountable for, both for the action itself and for consequences that could have been reasonably foreseen. Accountability takes the form of being blamed for what is not regarded as fitting or appropriate or what brings about harm; praise is for what is fitting or has beneficial consequences. The one-year-old infant who tips over and breaks a glass is usually not scolded, unlike the twelve-year-old boy who is. The difference in treatment in both cases arises from our attributing freedom to the boy, who can be responsive to reasons, but not to the infant. As before for attributions of mentality, when we attribute freedom to someone we are not describing some fact about her—certainly not the presence of some mysterious mental act of will causing a given action—but instead implying the relevance of normative evaluations within prudential, legal, or moral contexts.

Understood in this way, it is obvious that freedom cannot be attributed to lower animals in the wild, because they stand outside the communicative network of accountability, praise, or blame used in applying the concept of a free action. (Again, pets and domesticated animals, to the extent their behavior can be controlled, can sometimes be included in this network, although we hesitate to apply "free" of them.) It makes no sense to say of a squirrel that it freely built its nest at the top of a particular oak tree or that a rabbit freely chose to burrow at a certain location because these animals are never blamed for mistakes or praised for successes. They are like infants and the insane in lacking accountability.

For these reasons, we don't find philosophers in the panpsychist tradition attributing freedom to lower animals. Instead, they choose the term "spontaneity" as an analog to "freedom," using it in place of the latter in their descriptions of infrahuman species. Spontaneity implies a form of self-control by individuals over their own movements, but this is the behavior of those outside the network of human interactions and for which there is no accountability. The thesis of panpsychism has then come to include, through the writings of Whitehead and Hartshorne, the claim that a degree of spontaneity of behavior exists in all those natural forms to which mentality can be attributed. In this way, mentality has been associated with spontaneity as a type of agent-determined behavior.

The danger in such accounts is that they can mislead us into regarding spontaneity itself as a kind of fact about natural forms that stands outside the investigations of the natural sciences. We have seen how attributing a free action to a person is not to be describing some special nonphysical cause of that person's behavior, but rather to imply accountability. If spontaneity is regarded as an analog to freedom—that is, as freedom in the sense of self-control minus accountability—then it clearly also would seem not to be a feature of natural forms that provides a special nonphysical, mental explanation of behavior. But then this leaves undecided exactly what role spontaneity is supposed to fulfill.

One answer can be provided by identifying spontaneity with indeterminacy of behavior. Reflex and stereotyped behavior, in which the same response is invariably made to the same external environmental causes in conjunction with internal structural conditions, is then by definition not spontaneous. If spontaneity is identified with indeterminacy in this manner, then to attribute it is clearly not to attribute any kind of positive cause to behavior in addition to what is external from the environment and internal to structural organization. It is, rather, simply to deny that all behavior is determined by antecedent causes, whether external or internal. Besides this negative characterization, spontaneity also implies some form of self-control that we attribute to natural bodies as organized wholes, but there is no requirement that we identify such self-control, whatever it may be, with some nonphysical cause.

To attribute spontaneity to nonhuman natural forms with self-maintaining unity of organization is to extend our species-specific concept of freedom to these natural forms. This attribution implies indeterminacy of behavior, but would seem not to be simply the attribution of indeterminacy. What then is spontaneity, if not indeterminacy of behavior? After abstracting from the species-specific features of freedom as defined by social relations of accountability, praise, and blame, what remains of the concept of spontaneity? Our answer is that the other essential condition of freedom, that of self-control, is present also where there is spontaneity. This self-control is one we associate with attributions of mentality. In fact, we do ascribe mentality to lower animals, attributing to them wants, expectations, sensations, and feelings, and it seems possible to generalize from such ascriptions to attributions of feelings to very primitive natural forms. In our human species-specific case, attributions of freedom imply the same sort of possibilities of influence and control that we have noted exist when we attribute mental states to others. This liability to influence and control associates mentality with freedom: where the one is present, so normally is the other. Because we do extend mentality to species over which we have no direct influence, we seem justified on the basis of this association to also extend the concept of freedom in the altered form of spontaneity. We do this even though one of the conditions for freedom, that of accountability, is absent. Just as mental ascriptions become dissociated from evaluation when applied to the infrahuman, so spontaneity becomes disassociated from accountability. Analogical projection of mental terms thus represents an abstraction from these two features of evaluation and accountability that are present when we apply them to members of our own species.

This association of mentality with spontaneity also provides a means to justify attributions of spontaneity through the concept of a sign as an object of interpretation. This is made possible by identifying mentality with sign interpretation in the manner indicated in chapter 2. Attributions of freedom are made only of those with a linguistic capacity that enables them to be influenced by praise and reproaches. Spontaneity as the analogical extension of freedom is then attributed on the basis of the similarities between the interpretation and use of language and that of signals and natural events as more primitive types of signs. If the fleeing of the deer is a reflex response to environmental stimuli, we cannot apply sign terminology, and our description is appropriately couched in the terminology of mechanical causation. On the other hand, if an odor is characterized as a sign interpreted by the deer, we are implicitly making a comparison with language, and spontaneity as the analog to freedom is applicable. The degree of spontaneity we attribute varies with the degree of similarity of the sign interpretation with the interpretation of language. It is minimal for sign interpretation restricted to that kind of emotional interpretation we label by "feeling," significantly greater for the interpretation and use among primates of signals sharing some of the features of human language.

The foregoing constitutes, I think, a plausible explanation of why we do attribute mentality and spontaneity to lower animals. It also helps to explain, though not justify, why humanists have created their distinction between humans blessed with freedom and self-consciousness and dumb brutes whose behavior is determined by antecedent causes—what Whitehead calls a "bifurcation of nature." This separation stems from species-specific evaluation and accountability that characterizes our use of propositional mental terms and the application of "free" to actions. In effect, philosophical humanism is an assertion of the obvious and indisputable fact that the capacity to use discursive language and establish with it developed interactive social relations is unique to the human species.

But although we may have an explanation of why we apply mental attributions to lower animals, we have at this stage a very weak argument in favor of panpsychism's attributions of mentality to all natural forms with self-maintaining unity of organization. Is qualitative mentality and spontaneity attributable to insects, plant cells, molecules, and even atoms? Possibly, we may answer, because there is nothing logically inconsistent in such attributions. But in their favor we have only the very weak analogy between our own structures and behavior and what we appeal to as "appropriate" forms of structure at primitive levels of complexity. We may have no reasonable basis for establishing a line of demarcation separating those forms endowed with mentality from those that lack it, but this in itself fails to establish that some line of demarcation, albeit with difficult borderline cases, does not exist.

At the end of these first four chapters outlining panpsychism and its contrast to alternatives, we are thus left with an inconclusive defense of the doctrine. In the next chapter I consider a way of improving on this. This improved defense in turn serves to introduce the theological alternative to panpsychism in chapter 6 and the relation between panpsychism's conception of eternal mentality and the religious attitude in the final chapter.

CHAPTER FIVE

Mentality and Evolution

That matter could be created out of nothing we regard as an irrational dogma of Christian theology inconsistent both with Einstein's equation $e=mc^2$ relating energy to matter and with the law of conservation of energy. If matter is in fact a form of energy, and energy can neither be created nor destroyed, then how could God have possibly created matter? Martin Heidegger's question "Why is there something rather than nothing?" thus admits of no answer. The existence of matter is simply a brute, inexplicable fact. But the question "Why is there mentality rather than simply insensate matter?" is regarded by many in a very different way. They think that during the evolution of our universe there suddenly appeared on our planet, and probably also on countless other planets or their moons within our universe, living forms with mentality, that is, forms with an individual perspective from which to encounter an environment. Before the appearance of these forms, there was lifeless matter devoid of such a perspective; after their appearance the stage was set on this planet for the eventual evolution of the human species with its special mental capacities.

Panpsychism regards belief in such a transition to be as irrational as belief in the Christian dogma of the instantaneous appearance of matter. The generation of mentality from matter never occurred, because mentality in some form or other has always existed. Its existence, like that of matter, is therefore a brute, inexplicable fact. Of central interest to us in this chapter is the argument—what I refer to as the "Origination Argument"—against the belief that there was at some point in time a transition requiring explanation from a state in which bodies existed with only physical attributes to one in which there were bodies with perspectives and the capacity for experiencing. I shall be contending that this argument offers us a plausible positive case in favor of panpsychism that helps compensate for the relatively weak analogical inference used to initially justify it.

Mechanism and the Origination Argument

Daniel Dennett's engaging and ambitious *Darwin's Dangerous Idea*[1] is perhaps the most thorough philosophical defense to date of universal mechanism as applied to evolution. The foil for Dennett's argument is John Locke's claim that mentality cannot originate out of bare matter. Matter by itself, Locke claimed, can be conceived as being in eternal motion, and through its changes as producing changes in the shape (figure) and size (bulk) of material bodies.

> Yet Matter, incogitative Matter and Motion, whatever changes it might produce of Figure and Bulk, could never produce Thought: Knowledge will still be as far beyond the power of Motion and Matter to produce, as Matter is beyond the power of nothing or nonentity to produce. And I appeal to everyone's own thoughts, whether he cannot as easily conceive Matter produced by nothing, as Thought produced by pure Matter, when before there was no such thing as Thought, or an intelligent Being existing.[2]

Although Locke couched the problem in terms of the specifically human capacities for thought and possession of knowledge, it can be reformulated as explaining how mentality, regardless of how primitive its form, can be generated from the motions and combinations of insensate material elements. Just as Leibniz had invoked God through the principle of sufficient reason (cf. chapter 2) to explain the existence of monads, so Locke contends that the only explanation for the presence of mentality is the existence of God as the Universal Mind coeternal with matter. Only such an eternal Mind-as-cause can explain how mentality as we are aware of it for ourselves could come into existence.

Locke's argument for God's existence and a recent reformulation by Richard Swinburne is indeed very weak, as I hope to show in the next chapter. But although his argument may be weak, Locke's problem of explaining the origination of mentality from bare matter remains very real. This much is conceded by John Mackie in his criticisms of Locke, who concedes that "having to postulate a fundamental natural law of emergence for awareness is something of a difficulty for the materialist."[3] Unlike Mackie, Dennett is unwilling to acknowledge any difficulty; he regards the origination of mentality as simply another stage in the progression from primitive to more complex forms of organization, with this progression to be explained by the combination of random genetic variation and forces of natural selection of Darwinian evolutionary theory. It is thus no more difficult to explain than the emergence of multicellular species with central nervous systems from an earlier evolutionary stage with only single-celled organisms.

The route to this conclusion is reached by applying universal mechanism to Darwin's theory of evolution. The first stages of evolution are to be explained by the laws of physics and chemistry. Shortly after the Big Bang, physicists tell us, subatomic particles formed the atoms that became the building blocks of the universe.[4] Atoms then combined to form molecular compounds, and then these compounds combined to form macromolecules with differentiated structure. At some stage, silicon-based, self-replicating crystals appeared that the chemist Graham Cairns-Smith speculates formed the basis for the development of self-replicating sequences of amino acids in the form of ribonucleic acid (RNA) and deoxyribonucleic acid (DNA).[5] These sequences were incorporated into self-replicating macromolecules, the earliest of which seemed to have been free-standing versions of our present-day viruses with self-replicating, single-strand RNA. The probabilities of this sequence of stages of increased organization occurring, given the laws of physics and chemistry and the tendency toward disorder described by the Second Law of Thermodynamics, is a matter of dispute. Suffice it to say that universal mechanism makes the debatable claim that if we had sufficiently detailed knowledge of initial conditions prevailing on a given planet, we could deduce from the laws of physics and chemistry the exact details of the stages of development just described; alternatively, given duplication of these conditions on another planet, exactly the same stages would occur in exactly the same temporal sequence.

The possibility of variability of replicas through random mutations within strands of RNA is introduced with self-replication. This then introduces the explanation of development in terms of natural selection by the environment that is central to Darwin's theory of evolution. Such a theory can explain the evolution of macromolecules with DNA, and then the succeeding stages of prokaryotes (photosensitive bacteria and algae) that began about 3.5 billion years ago, and then about one billion years later the appearance of eukaryotes, single-celled organisms with nuclei-containing genes consisting of DNA and with organelles as specialized internal bodies. In early stages, variability was produced by genetic mutations. This in turn led to bisexual reproduction as a means of increasing variability within a population by the laws of Mendelian genetics, to the evolution of multicellular organisms about 700 million years ago, and finally to the plants and animals from which those species surviving on our planet are descended.

How evolutionary theory explains these successive stages can be illustrated by the frequently cited example of changes in a species of moth during England's Industrial Revolution. At the beginning of the nineteenth century this moth had light gray wings that matched the bark of the trees on which they tended to rest. The effect of this matching was to hide them from their main predator, the birds of the area. With the Industrial Revolution came factories burning coal and producing soot that darkened the trees near the factory towns. The effect was to remove from the moths their camouflage, because now they were a light gray against the darkened background of the trees, making them easy prey for local birds, and leading to a drastic reduction in their numbers. Among the species of moths, however, there was variability of color, with some a darker gray than others. The probability of a moth with darker wings surviving the predators and reproducing was significantly higher than for the light gray moths. As a result, the genes of the darker colored moths were passed on to succeeding generations, while those of lighter color were not. Within fifty years or so after the onset of the darkening of the trees, it was observed that members of this species had darkened wings that now matched those of the region's trees, and that the population had been restored to its previous numbers. Genetic variation within the population plus natural selection in the form of predators had brought about a change in succeeding generations that enabled the survival of the species.

The processes of genetic variability and natural selection can explain changes over time within a given species, as in the example just given. But they can also be used to explain the origination of new species that exploit different resources of their environments and the extinction of species with insufficient variability to cope with environmental changes. In fact, the entire course of evolution from the stage of self-replicating macromolecules to the present is regarded as being explained by these factors of variation and selection. Universal mechanism claims that deterministic laws dictate the successive stages of this development. The laws of biochemistry explain how a particular combination of genes or genotype is transmitted from parents to offspring. The variability of this inheritance introduces the variability within a population of shape, color, and behavioral traits, that constitutes the phenotypes of individual members. Relative to the selective forces of a given environment, this variability will invariably produce observed evolutionary changes over time. Dennett follows Manfred Eigen in referring to "algorithms" for evolutionary change.[6] An algorithm is a computational rule, and apparently what underlies applying this term to evolution is the conviction that one with sufficiently detailed knowledge of the initial conditions prevailing on the planet Earth when self-replication first occurred, and of the environmental changes that were to follow, could have predicted all the details of later evolutionary changes. Alternatively, the combination of variation and natural selection is being described as a mechanism that, if supplied with a given input of initial conditions, would generate exactly the same result on successive reruns. A world in which both the chemistry of our planet and its physical, chemical, and biological laws were duplicated would have exactly the same evolutionary history.

The algorithmic view of evolution seems to be supported by computer simulations of simplified models of change over time. Perhaps the most widely discussed is John Conway's "Game of Life" in which possible sequences are generated from a cell in an initial state relative to the states of eight neighboring cells on a two-dimensional grid. From possible initial states are mapped simulated future states of equilibrium and alternative patterns of growth and extinction.[7] Models have also been devised by Norman Packard that demonstrate by simulation how evolution of a population of organisms achieves, through genetic variability, a balance between an organism's innovation in devising sensorimotor strategies to flourish in a changing environment and its conservation (or memory) within its gene pool of those functions that are successful.[8] Scientists cannot recreate the earlier stages of evolution, but through simplified models they can provide computer simulations of these stages, and then compare these simulations with what can be observed in present evolutionary changes. This suggests for mechanists that evolution is algorithmic, that is, a consequence of a series of causally determined sequences.

It is important to distinguish evolutionary theory as a theory of the natural sciences with extensive empirical confirmation from universal mechanism as a metaphysical theory. Evolutionary theory can provide us with explanations of past changes and can be successful in predicting future changes without requiring us to admit that all such changes are the effects of invariant causal mechanisms. Nor does the success of simplified computer simulations using algorithms for change require us to regard evolution as representing an algorithmic process. Universal mechanism rests on a certain view of the scientific enterprise that is not entailed by any highly confirmed theory, and its errors will be discussed later in this chapter. But similar doubts cannot be raised against evolutionary theory itself as one of the great triumphs of modern science.

Our present purpose is served by noting how universal mechanism applies evolutionary theory to explain the origination of mentality. The capacity to sense objects in its environment, either by touch or by distance receptors, has obvious adaptive value for an organism, both in avoiding predators and securing sources of nutrition. Indeed, the evolution of single-cell and then multicellular organisms seems necessarily to be accompanied by such a capacity as a means of maintaining themselves in their environments. Similarly, the capacity to learn from prior experience and on the basis of what is learned anticipate the future gives organisms a flexibility of response that at a certain level of complexity of organization is necessary for survival. Signaling enables cooperative behavior in the form of mating, maintaining group cohesiveness, and mutual avoidance of predators, and thus we assume this capacity also evolved through the same processes of variation and selection. And finally, discursive language conveyed an advantage to the human species, enabling it to flourish in a way impossible for those hominid species that preceded it and probably competed with it. The mentality we attribute to ourselves and other forms of life are thus accounted for by slow accretions in mental capacities at these successive stages through the mechanisms of evolution over hundreds of millions of years.

Fred Dretske provides an evolutionary explanation of the origination of mentality, which he describes as "consciousness." We don't "have to start with consciousness," he says, to understand how, through a process of natural selection, it comes into being. What natural selection starts with as raw material are organisms with assorted needs and variable resources for satisfying these needs. You don't have to be conscious to have needs. Even plants have needs. They need sunlight and water. . . . For creatures capable of behaving in need-satisfying ways, . . . the benefits of information are clear. Information about external (and internal) affairs is necessary in order to coordinate behavior with the circumstances in which it has need-fulfilling consequences. . . . What natural selection does with this raw material is to develop and harness information-carrying systems to the effector mechanisms capable of using information to satisfy needs by appropriate directed and timed behavior. Once an indicator system is selected to provide the needed information it has the function of providing it. . . . As a result, the organisms in which these states occur are aware of the objects and properties their internal representations represent. They see, hear, and smell things. Through a process of selection they have become perceptually conscious of what is going on around them.[9]

Such an account seems to render obsolete Locke's problem of mind originating out of matter. For universal mechanism, mentality is the causal effect of material processes that are described by physics, chemistry, and evolutionary biology. To know the laws of these sciences and the chemistry of our planet from about four billion years ago is to know exactly how mentality originated from material elements and their combinations in the law-governed progression from molecular compounds, to replication of these compounds, and then to those organisms that Dretske calls "indicator systems" that became aware of representing their environments as a means of fulfilling their needs.

But is this really a solution to Locke's problem? The capacity to differentially respond to objects in their environments certainly did convey an adaptive advantage to some organisms. A system capable of differential responses can be said to "process information." But there is no necessary relation between this capacity and having the qualitative perspective that is characteristic of mentality. Mechanical devices can be constructed, after all, that differentially respond to environmental changes, such as for servomechanisms like thermostats that respond to temperature changes by sending signals to furnaces or signaling devices that turn on lights outside when a guest is detected. Mental attributes have application to such devices only in metaphorical senses.

Why did not evolve robot-like combinations of molecules with the capacity for differential responses that also lacked mentality? One answer may be that mechanical devices are relatively inflexible, and this inflexibility would pose an adaptive disadvantage. But this answer is unconvincing because inflexibility is characteristic only of primitive devices, not of more sophisticated devices recently developed that can adapt to changes over time. Evolutionary theory should predict the emergence of organic zombie-like equivalents to these sophisticated devices as a means for coping with a more demanding environment. The conclusion we seem forced to draw is that the laws of physics, chemistry, and biology can perhaps explain the evolution of some form of complex organization enabling differential responses to environmental conditions. But in themselves they do not explain how anything similar to the sensations and feelings that we are aware of came into existence.

Dretske contends that organisms with needs existed before the advent of mentality (for him, consciousness) and that mentality arose as a way of satisfying these needs. If this were so, then these needs must have been satisfied prior to the introduction of mentality, for if not satisfied, these organisms would have been eliminated by the forces of natural selection. But then we can ask what advantage mentality itself could have conferred, if the needs were already being met. Further, any naturalistic, nondualistic account of the mental must deny causal efficacy to it. The explanation of why an animal responds to a given stimulus in a certain way is to be traced to the nature of this stimulus and the structures of the animal's sense receptors, central nervous system, and motor response mechanisms. That the animal has a certain experience, say pain, is thus causally irrelevant to a given response, such as withdrawal from a pain-inducing object. But if mentality per se is causally irrelevant, it is again difficult to see how its presence conveys any evolutionary advantage. When introduced it would simply be an adventitious addition without consequences for survival.

Under discussion so far have been primitive feelings and sensations as means of providing information about an environment. But similar considerations also apply to the evolution of learning and communication through signals and language, all of which convey an adaptive advantage. Learning behavior, both conditioned reflex and instrumental, can be simulated with computer and robotic technology to produce machines that change their responses as the environment changes. Yet we do not attribute either consciousness or mentality in general to these machines (although we can imagine them having mentality, as in Stanley Kubrick's film *2001*). That communication in the form of signals and even linguistic expressions can be simulated is shown by the construction of computers that, at least for restricted questions, pass the Turing test of providing answers to questions that can't be distinguished from those given by human subjects. Again, applying simply the laws of physics, chemistry, and biology may explain the evolution of organic zombie-like equivalents of these machines, but this again fails to provide us with an explanation of the origination of intentionality as a form of mentality. As for differential responses to the environment, to explain the evolution of communicative capacities conveying an adaptive advantage is to fall short of an explanation of the origination of mentality from matter, because mechanical simulation of these capacities demonstrates they can be present without the presence of mentality.

That genetic variation within a population and natural selection provide an implausible explanation of the origination of mentality becomes clearer when we attempt to conceive how the first form of mentality came into existence. Let's suppose that mentality originated with the emergence of eukaryotes as single-celled organisms capable of exploiting the energy resources of their environment. One such organism reproduced asexually a number of replicas of itself among which there was variation, and one of the variant replicas, let's suppose, was endowed with a faint trace of feeling and hence could be said to have its own perspective, or as some prefer to say, its unique "subjectivity." Let's label this variant Alpha. Would the feeling perspective of Alpha confer on it a competitive advantage? It is difficult to see why, because the primitive feeling would be sufficient unto itself and without instrumental value, in this respect like the sunset we enjoy for its own sake or the taste of a good wine we savor. And if this original primitive feeling were an isolated occurrence and self-sufficient, it would not confer an adaptive advantage on the organism experiencing it. It may have been the precursor to the experience of signs, which, when interpreted cognitively and dynamically, could be used to anticipate and to differentially respond to the environment. This successor experience and its attendant intentionality might be thought to have adaptive value, although I have just argued it is the behavioral capacity rather than the experience itself that is adaptive, and this capacity can be mechanically simulated. But the original experience itself would seem to have conferred absolutely no adaptive advantage, and thus its continuance and later elaboration remains unexplained.

Some may want to reply that this shows simply that Alpha's experience must have had intentional aspects, that simultaneous with that original feeling there were anticipation and differential responses conferring adaptive advantage. But it is most implausible that full-fledged intentionality would have suddenly appeared in Alpha as a mysterious novelty without precedent. Such sudden transitions certainly do not seem characteristic of other stages of evolution, and it seems arbitrary to postulate it for Alpha.[10]

It is, of course, a familiar problem for evolutionary theory to explain how traits evolved whose early antecedents have no adaptive value. Wings convey an adaptive advantage to birds, but the same cannot be said of the stumps we see on young chicks, which we can suppose are the wings' more primitive antecedents. Indeed, the stumps seem to be an impediment, and of negative value. Here evolutionists have a ready explanation in terms of what is called "exaptation;" they can claim that a feature with adaptive value at one stage can be co-opted and utilized later. Thus, fins on fish or balancing appendages on amphibians can be hypothesized as the materials from which wings gradually evolved. The situation is different, however, when we attempt to explain the origination of mentality. So unlike is this from what preceded that there is no question of utilizing what went before. We are confronted with a totally new aspect apparently without any biological explanation for its origination.

Critics of panpsychism have attempted to reply to various versions of the argument just outlined. They grant that the introduction of mentality represents a novelty. They insist, however, that this does not preclude a causal explanation of this introduction. With sufficient knowledge of the laws of nature and circumstances prevailing at the time of introduction, they claim, we could provide this explanation.[11] But they never specify the form this explanation could take. It is the great merit of Dennett's attempt at an explanation that it clearly identifies random variation and natural selection as providing the only possible explanation. Everyone concedes, including the most convinced mechanists, that a satisfactory explanation has not actually been produced. But the failure of Dennett's attempt goes further. It enables us to see that no such explanation is possible.

The arguments just given against universal mechanism's explanations of the origination of mentality are an essential first stage to the strongest positive argument available to panpsychism, the Origination Argument.[12] If the laws of physics, chemistry, and evolutionary biology cannot explain the origination of mentality, how can we account for its existence? One way, and the way chosen by Locke, is to claim that an explanation is provided by postulating a Universal Mind that somehow creates out of itself (an "outflashing" as described by Leibniz) the various forms of mentality that exist. If we reject this alternative, as in the next chapter I shall argue we should, the most plausible alternative open to us would be to endorse panpsychism's claim that mentality has always been present at levels predating those at which life arose, that is, at the molecular, atomic, and particle levels where there is the appropriate form of organization. No Alpha could ever have existed, because mentality was never generated from matter, just as matter itself was never generated from nothing. And without such generation, there is no need to continue the futile search for an explanation of mentality's origination.

As noted in the preface, versions of the Origination Argument for panpsychism had their early supporters in the nineteenth century. The cosmology of this period speculated that the stars and planets composing our universe formed from a vast gaseous nebula composed of atoms. To avoid the abrupt transition from matter to mind and to preserve continuity in evolution, it was argued that there was originally a "mind-dust" from which sentient creatures evolved. Recent cosmology based on the Big Bang hypothesis has complicated the case for such an account, however. We now pause to consider the problems it raises for panpsychism's claims.

Does the Panpsychist Thesis Extend to Fundamental Particles?

In chapter 1 I posed in a preliminary way the problem of determining the scope of the panpsychist thesis. Some of its advocates, notably Whitehead and Hartshorne, extend it to fundamental particles as those elements in nature that by definition cannot be decomposed into more simple elements. Subatomic particles were once believed to be these fundamental particles. Current physical theory now holds that many of these particles are wholes relative to the more elementary quarks and leptons. Quarks and leptons thus now enjoy the status of fundamental particles, although it is conceivable that physics in the future will discover still more basic elements as the unanalyzable building blocks of nature.

As noted in chapter 1, the difficulty with attributing mentality to fundamental particles, whatever physics determines them to be, is derived from the nature of the analogical inference initially used to justify panpsychism. In using this inference we progressively abstract from specific features of our own bodies and their behavior as we extend mentality to more primitive natural bodies. As we descend to inorganic forms in which sense receptors and learning behavior are absent, we have at least unity of organization persisting through time and maintenance of homeostasis with a surrounding environment as a basis for attributing an attenuated form of mentality. Fundamental particles by definition are not organized wholes with parts, and hence do not fulfill even this minimal condition for mental attribution. They are, to be sure, individuals persisting through time, but individuals so different in nature as to apparently exclude them from the scope of the panpsychist thesis. To admit them would seem to require such a weakening of the concept of mentality that it becomes vacuously general.

In reply, it can be pointed out that analogical reasoning always requires a decision about what counts as a relevant similarity for inclusion in the premiss base. A decision must be made whether there are sufficient similarities between organic and inorganic natural bodies to justify extension of mentality to the latter. Once having decided in favor of this extension, it seems arbitrary to select out unity of organization as a necessary condition and exclude fundamental particles from panpsychism's scope. There is some force in this reply, although it seems that restriction to organized wholes is not simply an arbitrary decision. Certainly the more similarities in the base, the more plausible the panpsychist thesis, and unless forced to, we should not resort to the expedient of accepting this additional weakening of the base.

The question arises, then, whether the Origination Argument in conjunction with current physical theory does indeed force us to extend the thesis to fundamental particles. Nineteeth century cosmology may have postulated the existence of atoms as organized wholes within the gaseous nebula as the original elements, but current cosmological theory is based on the existence of a Big Bang about 14 billion years ago from which our universe was generated. Steven Weinberg's description of the universe a few milliseconds after this event seems to indicate that no organized wholes could possibly have existed during this interval, because at this early stage "none of the components of ordinary matter, molecules, or atoms, or even the nuclei of atoms, could have held together."[13] This description implies a sequence in which fundamental particles combined to eventually form atoms as organized wholes and the basic constituents of more complex organized wholes in the form of molecules and eventually single-celled organisms. But if this account is accurate, there was at some early stage a transition from fundamental particles without internal organization to organized wholes. And if we refuse to ascribe mentality to fundamental particles, we are left with the same problem that the Origination Argument was intended to solve. The effect has been only to push back by several billion years the unexplained, mysterious transition from bare insensate matter to organized wholes with perspectives.

We should recognize this impasse as the result of a basic conflict between the analogical inference used initially to justify panpsychism and any solution to the physical–mental transition problem. The more similarities between the anatomy and behavior of human bodies, the more plausible the extension of mental attributes. If the most primitive natural bodies were bacteria and protozoa, then the analogical justification of panpsychism would be very strong indeed. But of course any living organism is a complex whole whose parts—whether molecules, atoms, or particles—exist in freestanding form. The Origination Argument is intended to be a means for compensating for the weakness of analogies when extended to these parts. But resorting to this argument forces the extension of mentality to progressively more dissimilar bodies. Current physical theory seems to force us to terminate this with fundamental particles as the natural bodies most dissimilar to our own.

Panpsychism has available to it three alternative strategies for dealing with this problem. The first is to simply admit fundamental particles to be within the scope of its thesis. The effect of this, as we have seen, is to virtually abandon its initial analogical basis, and rely solely on the Origination Argument. This strategy is consistent with considerations related to the religious attitude that will be raised in the final chapter. But since whatever meaning the term "mentality" has in the formulation of the panpsychist thesis is derived from the analogical inference, this alternative would seem to be chosen only as a last resort.

The second alternative is to exclude fundamental particles from the scope of the thesis, and as a consequence of descriptions provided by current cosmology, abandon altogether the Origination Argument. The sole basis for panpsychism would then be provided by the analogical inference described in chapter 1. One consequence of this strategy is to make the religious attitude irrelevant to the panpsychist thesis. Because of the weakness of the analogical inference used to initially establish panpsychism, this would seem to be a strategy to be avoided at all costs.

There is another alternative that would seem to be a plausible way of avoiding the disadvantages of the two just outlined. This is to appeal to the incomplete knowledge of contemporary physics regarding the earliest stages of our universe. The history of physics suggests that the particles Weinberg describes as existing immediately after the Big Bang will some day be discovered to be wholes with parts, and hence there was no time at which natural bodies with a degree of organization failed to exist. The Original Body existing prior to the Big Bang is conjectured by cosmologists to have had some type of unknown structure. We can conjecture that some features of this structure were retained within particles existing immediately after the universe-generating explosion. Until physics provides a definitive account that conflicts with this conjecture, this alternative retaining both the analogical basis and the Origination Argument seems to be the most attractive of the three alternatives.

Having acknowledged the difficulty posed for the Origination Argument in this digression, we can now return to the argument itself. It stands in stark contrast to philosophy's most widely accepted view of the origination of mentality. This standard view is that mentality is a property that somehow "emerged" within living organisms at a relatively early stage in the history of our planet. We now consider the conception of emergence being appealed to by this view.

Resultant and Emergent Properties

Despite the complications introduced by fundamental particles, the Origination Argument outlined previously is proposed by panpsychism as the most plausible solution to the problem of accounting for the origination of mentality from bare matter. It is important to distinguish panpsychism's use of this argument from the view that mentality is what is referred to as an "emergent" property defined in terms of relations between wholes and parts. If in fact mentality did somehow "emerge" as a property of certain wholes, say living single-celled organisms, then panpsychism must be rejected as false. The parts of these wholes would then be natural bodies fulfilling the panpsychist criteria for mentality and yet lacking this mentality.

Discussions of emergence tend to provide a common analysis of it that overlooks important differences of application. In fact, part–whole relations within natural forms occur at many levels and stages in evolution and take a variety of forms. The hierarchies of organized forms present obvious examples. They include atoms as organized combinations of particles, molecules with atoms as parts, which may then combine to form macromolecules, single-celled organisms whose parts are these macromolecules, and multicelled organisms composed of cells. Within these hierarchies there occur a variety of part–whole relations that we can rank according to their *strength*, that is, the degree of organization they exhibit. The weakest relation is that of *spatial juxtaposition*, as occurs for the grains of sand that constitute a heap. The next strongest is that which occurs when there are bonds and other relations between independently functioning elements, as for the array of atoms that constitute a crystal or the array of cells that constitute a fungus. We can refer to this relation as *simple aggregation*. Next in strength are those wholes that are *structured aggregates*, with structures that relate elements with specialized functions, such as for plants composed of cells related by fibrous transport mechanisms or starfish as organisms lacking a central nervous system. Human societies, with their transportation and communication infrastructures, are perhaps best included in this category. Finally, there are wholes as *organized unities* with specialized parts, as apparently represented by atoms and molecules, and certainly by single-celled organisms and multicelled organisms with central nervous systems. There are obviously borderline cases that will be difficult locate in any one of these categories, such as worms with central nervous systems so primitive that it perhaps disqualifies them as organized unities. But as a rough classification this is sufficient for our purposes.

Jaegwon Kim has distinguished two kinds of relations between properties of wholes and the properties of their parts.[14] A *resultant property* of a whole W is a property that can be derived by the laws of physics, chemistry, and biology from those of its parts P. Kim contrasts this to an *emergent property* of a W, a property that cannot be derived from its P. Examples of wholes with resultant properties seem to be present where there is juxtaposition and simple aggregation of parts. The volume and mass of a heap of sand, for example, is the sum of the volumes (plus interstices) and masses of the grains constituting it. Macroproperties of a gas in a container such as pressure and temperature can be derived by the laws of statistical mechanics from the microproperties of kinetic energy of constituent gas molecules. For many crystals as simple aggregates, chemical bonds and positive and negative charges of elements provide the basis for explaining properties of wholes in terms of properties of atomic parts. Many of these properties of wholes are novel in the sense of not being present in the parts. Popper notes that "crystals and other solids have the property of solidity, without solidity (or pre-solidity) being present in the liquid before crystallization."[15] Solidity is thus novel and yet resultant.

But for wholes in the form of structured aggregates and organized unities, the derivation is more complex. For a plant or an animal developing from a seed or fertilized egg, there is a relation between the microlevel of genes in the form of DNA and their phenotypic expressions in macroproperties such as size, shape, coloration, and (in the case of animals) behavioral traits. But this relation is contingent on development taking place in the appropriate environment, and thus we have no simple derivation from parts P to whole W. Instead, if W is to be derived from P, the derivation must be relative to some environment E in which the development of W from P took place. Where we have such a derivation relative to E, we can refer to a *broad resultant property* of W relative to E, as contrasted to the *narrow resultant properties* that might be claimed for wholes as juxtaposition of parts and some forms of simple aggregates. Even for simple aggregates there may be broad resultant properties that require a certain environment, such as for chemical bonds that are formed only within a fixed temperature range.

This concept of a broad resultant property can be applied to evolutionary development over a period of time in which a type of whole W evolves from a type of parts P relative to an environment E. Adherents of universal mechanism claim that evolved properties of wholes are broad resultant properties that could be derived by all-knowing investigators from properties of antecedent parts and environmental conditions by the laws of physics, chemistry, and biology. The fact that such derivations cannot be actually carried out is due to our ignorance. Opposed to this is the view that there is real indeterminacy in nature; that is, objective probabilities of events occur; that are not due solely to our ignorance of complexes of causal factors, and as a consequence at least some properties of wholes will be emergent properties. Understood in this way, the concept of an emergent property, like that of indeterminacy, is a negative concept used to indicate the absence of a derivation under conditions of omniscience. Emergent properties are properties that are neither broadly nor narrowly resultant.

Chaos theory describes patterns of large-scale order arising from a series of events that are themselves indeterminate and hence unpredictable. The key relation in defining a resultant property is that of derivation, and the theory provides a novel way of understanding this derivation. Recent developments of chaos theory present us with the prospect that large-scale macroproperties of wholes may be derivable from indeterminate events, and thus indeterminacy at the microlevel would be consistent with the evolution of wholes with broad resultant properties. The law of large numbers in probability theory provides a simple illustration of how this could occur. Let's say that we have an unbiased coin that for a given toss has a probability of $\frac{1}{2}$ of turning up heads. For a given toss it is indeterminate whether the coin will turn up heads or tails, and for limited sequences we could have any proportion of head outcomes relative to tail outcomes. But the sequence of tosses, if continued in the long run, will converge on an even number of head outcomes and tail outcomes. In a similar way, events in evolutionary history could themselves be indeterminate, yet yield over time determined collective outcomes. Thus, we may attribute genetic variation within members of a certain population of animals to chance, and environmental changes with selective effects also to chance, but at the same time recognize over long periods of time common patterns to evolutionary changes within the population. In such a case we would have types of broadly resultant properties derived from what is indeterminate.

We should note, however, that what we identify as a resultant property will depend on the degree of specificity with which we describe it. It follows from the law of large numbers that at some point in time the proportion of heads to total tosses of the unbiased coin will continue to be $\frac{1}{2}$. But we cannot predict from the law the number of tosses at which this result is reached. In similar fashion, it may be true that a population of moths placed in the circumstances described in the example given previously in nineteenth century England will invariably, after a period of time, change their coloration to match their changed environment. But there is no assurance that with the most detailed knowledge of circumstances we will ever be able to predict the exact temporal interval over which such change occurs. Further, gray is an indeterminate color for which there are many shades and matching allows of degrees. The coloration of moths may roughly match the background of trees after a given period of time, but it does not follow that there is a match that satisfies more demanding standards. For every resultant necessary property under a general description, there will invariably be many alternative contingent emergent properties under more specific descriptions. When applied to evolutionary development of phenotypic features, the resultant–emergent contrast is simply a contrast between more general or more specific descriptions.

The resultant–emergent contrast discussed so far applies to observable properties such as size, shape, coloration, and behavioral traits, and as restricted to such properties, admits of reasonably clear applications. Much confusion arises, however, when philosophers attempt to extend the contrast to the problem of explaining the origination of mentality. One difficulty should be obvious from the discussions of the previous chapter. We attribute mental states for different purposes than we attribute ordinary descriptive properties, and mental attributions have special features. To learn about a belief or a pain is not to acquire descriptive information about a person of the same kind as when learning of her height or weight. If this is so, then the fact that we have a clear (if perhaps unanswerable) question about whether a given descriptive property of a whole is resultant or emergent in evolution is no assurance that this question will make sense when applied to the mental.

Questions about the origination of mental capacities for learning and language use are, of course, asked within the natural sciences, and are answered in the same way as for any other behavioral trait. But philosophers have asked the question of origination about mentality as such, and for this question neither the resultant nor the emergent answer seems possible. The *only* way of arguing that mentality is resultant is provided by evolutionary theory in a form similar to that advanced by Dennett and Dretske and discussed previously. But we saw there how evolutionary theory fails to provide an explanation of mentality in terms of what existed prior to it. That mentality is not resultant has been argued on the basis of the possibility of mechanical simulation of mental capacities. Behavioral capacities such as differential responses to environmental objects, learning, and language use may be classified as resultant from variation and selection, provided we choose an appropriately general description of the behavioral capacity. But since each of these capacities is capable of computer simulation, the origins of mentality—the endowment those possessing it with a qualitative perspective and the appropriateness of attitudes of concern—remain unexplained.

But equally unsatisfactory is the answer of emergence, for we have seen that to classify a property as emergent is to concede there is no explanation for the origination of mentality and to leave us with a deeply unsatisfying mystery.[16] The widely accepted version dates the emergence of mentality in the form of sentience back no earlier than the first living organisms, although exactly at what stage in the evolution of these organisms—whether at the bacteria-like prokaryote stage, the amoeba-like eukaryote stage some two billion years later, or even at the stage of multicelled organisms—is left indefinite. Why was life in the form of self-reproduction and metabolism a necessary condition for mentality? Why did environmental conditions in conjunction with a certain level of organic complexity give rise to a qualitative perspective? Throughout the history of science there have been questions whose answers came only much later. There are also many questions posed within current science whose answer must await the future. Questions about the origination of mentality, however, seem to be of an entirely different order. These are questions that are *in principle* unanswerable. Unlike questions about the events immediately following the Big Bang, we can be confident that science will *never* provide answers to them. To say that mentality is an emergent property is simply to concede this permanent ignorance.

Through the influence of Russell and Quine, many have come to accept the nominalist prohibition against multiplying entities beyond what is necessary: *Entia non multiplicanda praeter necessitatum*. One reason for accepting this prohibition is that it prevents raising unanswerable questions. For example, if we refuse to countenance Platonic forms, then the question "What is the relation between Forms as universals and particulars?" is rejected on the grounds that it presupposes what is in fact mistaken. Parallel to the nominalist prohibition is a general prohibition against multiplying mysteries beyond what is necessary: *Res occulta non multiplicandum praeter necessitatum*. On the basis of this principle we reject the question "Why is there matter?" by appealing to the law of the conservation of energy, because it is inconsistent with the presupposition of the question.

Similarly, to reject the doctrine of emergence in favor of panpsychism is also to adopt this principle and reject the question "Why is there mentality?" Because mentality has always been present in the most primitive natural bodies, the question admits of no answer.[17] We can, of course, formulate questions about why and how mentality came into existence, that is, put together words that ask these questions. But these are no more answerable or meaningful than the corresponding questions about the existence of matter. At some stage the regress of questions about origins must come to an end. Panpsychism's solution is to bestow on mentality the same kind of priority in terminating this regress as is bestowed on matter. Mentality, like matter, simply is a fundamental feature of what is, and all questions about its origins must therefore be dismissed as meaningless.

So far I have made no mention of accounting for the introduction of spontaneity during the course of evolution. We consider now the question of whether spontaneity is a concept antithetical to the methodology of the sciences, and examine the role it may play in evolutionary development.

The Role of Spontaneity in Evolution

We have noted how spontaneity entails indeterminacy, but because of its association with mentality, spontaneity is itself not entailed by indeterminacy. There may be indeterminate events that simply occur without assignable causes, but we need not attribute spontaneity to them. Universal mechanism correctly recognizes that admission of indeterminacy is inconsistent with the principle of causality, but mistakenly regards this principle as a methodological principle of science. The causal principle states that every particular event e that occurs is the effect of some determining physical cause c and can be explained by a uniform generalization of the form "C is the cause of E" where C and E are types of events of which c and e are particular occurrences. There are many events for which we are not able to produce such uniform explanation of causal laws, but if we accept the principle of causality we must regard this as due to our human ignorance and as setting a task for further inquiry. To take a simple example, suppose that adding fertilizer to a lawn results in faster grass growth two-thirds of the times the fertilizer is applied. Then we can state the statistical generalization that the probability of growth (G) on the condition that fertilizer is added (F) is 2/3, or $p(G/F)=2/3$. The principle of causality implies that there are other causal factors such as sufficient water (W) and sunshine (S)

whose presence or absence explains why the increased growth did or did not occur. Discovering these factors allows us to convert the statistical generalization into the uniform or deterministic generalization $p(G/F\&W\&S)=1$ stating that given the presence of fertilizer, water, and sunshine, plant growth will invariably occur. With this additional information, we could explain grass growth on a given occasion as the effect of the causal factors.

Why is the principle of causality regarded as a central assumption of the natural sciences? The reason is that there is a widespread conviction that to abandon the principle is to introduce a block to scientific inquiry. To accept the statistical generalization $p(G/F)=2/3$ and the indeterminacy of grass growth as final, as in the nature of things and not due to temporary human ignorance, is to give up the search for those causal factors that provide a complete explanation. Alternatively, it is to leave it a mystery why growth does or does not occur on a given occasion. This seems to be the reason that Dennett, Eigen, and others wish to apply universal mechanism to evolution and for their referring to evolutionary processes as "algorithms." Once it is conceded that there may not be a deterministic causal explanation of a given evolutionary change such as the emergence of a new species, it is thought that we inhibit science's search for natural causes of the change. Science seems to require the principle of causality as a regulative ideal to ensure its continued search for causal explanations. It is then argued that for panpsychism to claim the presence of mentality and spontaneity during all stages of evolution is for it to introduce elements of mystery that are inconsistent with the continued advance of science. Worse still, it seems to imply that there are special mental causes of evolutionary development that are, in principle, outside the scope of the sciences.

No such commitment to the principle of causality is presupposed by scientific inquiry, however. There is no solution to the metaphysical problem of deciding between determinism and indeterminism: the problem is simply the practical one of deciding on the appropriate degree of specification of causes and effects. Statistical generalizations can be converted into uniform generalizations by more exact specifications of a cause, as we saw in converting $p(G/F)=2/3$ into $p(G/F\&W\&S)=1$ by replacing the single cause F with the complex cause $F\&W\&S$. But it is just as true that every uniform causal generalization can be converted into a statistical one by further specifying the effect. Let's grant that further inquiry has discovered $F\&W\&S$ as the cause of G, the increased growth of the plant.

But how much growth, and after what temporal interval? By specifying the effect, say as one centimeter of growth after one week's interval, we introduce the possibility of replacing the uniform generalization G_1 by a statistical one S_1: sometimes fertilizer, water, and sun produce the specified growth in this interval, sometimes not. Of course, this statistical generalization S_1 can be converted into a second uniform generalization G_2 by further specifications of the cause. But G_2 can in turn be converted back into its corresponding S_2 by further specifications of the effect. And so on indefinitely, with the limits imposed by the practical advantages of specifying the cause as balanced against the time and energy expended in the search for this specification. The principle of causality as a regulative ideal is the demand that for any given statistical S_k we admit the possibility of a uniform G_{k+1} with a more specific cause. When more precise means of measurement become available and our supporting knowledge improves, we then set out to formulate this uniform generalization. But this is clearly an unreasonable demand that can never be met if we continue specifying the effect through the same improvements in observation. If taken seriously, the demand would result in unreasonable and unsustainable costs to society, and cannot be one imposed by a scientific enterprise contributing to the benefit of humanity.

Universal mechanism does have domains of applicability in which there is contemporaneous variation, as contrasted with the relation of a cause and effect separated by a temporal interval. Physics as applied to such phenomena as gravitation and electromagnetic radiation yields theories from which uniform generalizations in the form of functional laws can be derived. For these laws of the form $y = f(x_1, x_2, \ldots, x_n)$, the specification of numerical values for the dependent variable y and the one or more independent variables $x_1, x_2, \ldots, x_n$ is limited only by the precision of our measuring instruments. We can be confident that in these domains determinism prevails, and that the relevant laws of physics provide constraints on all future evolutionary development. But as noted in chapter 1, panpsychism as understood in this work is a theory applying only to self-maintaining bodies with an appropriate degree of internal organization, and can thus readily concede determinism in those domains in which such organization is absent. If from the theories of physics of deterministic form we could deduce laws applying to organized self-maintaining bodies, universal mechanism would be established outside the restricted realm of fields and wave phenomena. But such reductions have been singularly unsuccessful, and the project attempting them has been very sensibly abandoned as its difficulties become apparent.

If universal mechanism's principle of causality has no reasonable application to events as elementary as grass growth, it is far more unreasonable to apply it to evolutionary change. Those like Dennett and Eigen who apply the principle in the form of a claim that evolution is an "algorithmic process" are surely hand waving at possible explanations of events under the grossest of descriptions. We could, of course, make these descriptions more specific. But what would be the point of generating answers to these questions about progressively more specific effects? Explanations of past evolutionary change and predictions of what will occur are of enormous importance to the survival of the human race on this planet and the exploration for other life forms on other planets. But to continue the search for these explanations and predictions implies no mindless commitment to the existence of an "algorithm" by which any conceivably detailed specification of change could be deduced.

Similar considerations apply to computer simulations of evolutionary changes such as those of Conway and Packward discussed in the beginning of this chapter. These simulations will provide models of evolutionary change whose empirical confirmation will depend on how the outputs of the models are specified. That models with certain general descriptions of these outputs can be confirmed does not require us to assume that there are confirmed models, even in science's distant future, with indefinitely higher degrees of specificity of description. All can agree that the broad outlines of evolution are determined by the laws of physics prevailing at the origination of the universe. But the devil is in the details, as the saying goes, and it is in such details that spontaneity has its place.

Adherents of universal mechanism constantly have before them traditional theology's invocation of an all-powerful supernatural Creator and Designer of the universe. Belief in this Creator was the foil against which Darwinian evolutionary biology struggled, and the struggle continues into the present with attempts by creationists to discredit or explain away its discoveries. Such a theology did represent a block to scientific inquiry, and to combat it remains essential to progress in formulating causal explanations of evolutionary change. Also before mechanists is the discredited vitalism of nineteenth century biology with its invocation of vital causal forces to explain embryological development. If mentality and spontaneity are present in the earliest stages of evolution, then it is thought we must explain evolutionary development by two different kinds of causes: the physical causes described by the natural causes and mysterious mental (or vital) causes whose existence is the basis for attributions of spontaneity. It is thought that this introduction of mental causes should be rejected as antithetical to the progress of the sciences.

The reply to this is the same as given in the previous chapter. When we attribute mentality and spontaneity to infrahuman natural forms, we are simply extending to them attributions analogous in progressively attenuated respects to those we apply to our fellow humans. Mentality is projected on these natural forms on the basis of an analogical inference whose base is shared behavioral and anatomical features. But characteristic of mentality as a generalized attribute is the combined first- and third-person uses of specific mental terms, and this is sufficient to project both a qualitative aspect to the perspectives of infrahuman forms and spontaneity. In such projection we abstract from features specific to our communicative relations with other persons. Spontaneous behavior is that which is done from the point of view of the organism, and in this respect is not simply the effect of a natural body's internal structure in conjunction with environmental causes. To attribute it does not preclude an explanation of this behavior in terms of a set of uniform causal generalizations in which the effect as behavior is described at some level of generality. But the attribution of spontaneity is inconsistent with the dogma of universal mechanism that for any degree of specificity of effect there must invariably be a determining cause. In all these respects, the introduction of spontaneity is consistent with progress of the natural sciences, if not with certain misconceptions about scientific methodology.

Again, it must be emphasized that to attribute mental spontaneity is not to describe some matter of fact in addition to the facts investigated by the sciences. As emphasized in chapter 4, the language used to make species-specific mental attributions has socially interactive features of evaluation and accountability not present for standard descriptions. When we extend this language to infrahuman levels, we progressively abstract from features of our communicative relations with others. For the most primitive natural bodies we are left only with the recognition of qualitative perspective with a minimal degree of spontaneity. This extension shares with the mental language from which it is derived the feature of not describing some additional matter of fact.

If spontaneity is not an additional supplementing cause, what is its role in evolution? This question is perhaps best answered by considering an example. All of us have probably at one time or other observed the courtship behavior of pigeons in a park—the approach of males with puffed out neck feathers, the repeated rebuffs by females of their many suitors, the occasional selection by a female of an appropriate male, followed by mating. Clearly, the selection of a mate by a female has some influence, however slight, on the future evolution of the pigeon species, because this determines the mixture of genes inherited by offspring and hence the variability within the next generation of pigeons. How does this selection take place? Chance would seem to have a role, as there are many coincidental encounters between pigeons who happen to fly to the same park and be in each other's vicinity. There is also a causal story to be told in terms of the effect on a female pigeon of such stimuli as the different male displays and emitted chemical pheromones and the effect of hormones on her receptiveness. But to the extent (which for this species is undoubtedly quite limited) that we attribute the selection of a given male for mating to spontaneity we are assigning the selection to the pigeon rather than to external stimuli in conjunction with her internal physiological states. It was *her* selection from *her* perspective on her surroundings with *her* motivations and preferences, and this agent-centered way of describing what happened distinguishes her from an unfeeling, mechanical mate-selection device. In this respect we regard mate selection by the pigeon as similar in some respects to mate selection among members of our own species, a selection that we regard as *their* decision for which they can be held accountable.

Nature presents us with countless examples in addition to mating behavior. Ethologists have noted how animals such as gazelles develop strategies of survival when foraging in view of predators such as lions. One strategy would be to flee immediately on seeing a predator, but this requires giving up sustaining nourishment. To continue to forage after seeing the predator approach runs the risk of capture and death. General strategies seem to have evolved as innate behavioral capacities. But there can be variation in how they are applied by a particular individual in a given situation, how long it lingers foraging in view of the predator, and this will have consequences for the survival of both the animal and its genes into the next generation. We hesitate to say that a given animal "decides" on a given occasion to either flee or stay, since this would imply discursive reasoning by means of a practical inference. But what is analogous to a decision seems to be present, and is the basis for our attributing spontaneity with evolutionary consequences.

The capacities for mate selection by the female pigeon and for delaying fleeing while foraging are innate capacities shared with others of the same species. The exercise of these capacities contributes to the reproduction of the species. In attributing spontaneity in both cases, we are claiming that these capacities are those whose exercises on given occasions do not have unique outcomes in given perceptual situations. In this respect they are very different from the capacity for imprinting that is unique to newborn ducklings. As Ruth Millikan notes, imprinting has the direct function of ensuring following behavior necessary for the safety of ducklings and what she terms the "derived function" for a particular duckling of ensuring its following that individual, normally its mother, that it first perceives after birth.[18] As experiments have shown, substituting some other individual for the duckling's mother as the first object seen will invariably produce imprinting on this substituted individual. Underlying this behavioral trait, we suppose, there are causal mechanisms that determine this unique outcome on the appropriate occasion. But assuming the applicability of spontaneity, the capacities for mate selection and fleeing are entirely different from that for imprinting. We can describe in general their direct functions in terms of the selection of mates producing viable offspring and survival for reproduction, but from this no function to perform a particular response on a given occasion can be derived. In a given situation, the capacities can be exercised in alternative ways, as contrasted with a unique way that is the causal effect of antecedent conditions.

The example of mate selection and fleeing have as many variations as there are forms of courtship prepatory for bisexual reproduction and responses to predators. It seems that spontaneity in the sense just applied to these examples has *some* relevance to evolutionary change, however slight this may be in comparison to those produced as causal effects or by chance. The Lamarckian theory that behavioral traits acquired through learning can have genetic effects that are transmitted to future generations has been discredited as a biological theory, however satisfying it may be as an endorsement of the role of spontaneity. But panpsychism is not required to assign spontaneity a Lamarckian role. Any activity, regardless of whether it directly alters an individual's genotype, if effective in securing a mate and prolonging life sufficiently to produce and nurture offspring, will have future effects. In human affairs we assign a role to individual decisions in determining the course of history. It seems only a humanistic dogma that refuses to extend this role in a reduced degree to spontaneity in infrahuman species, and such an extension is consistent with the causal factors described in Darwin's theory.

Some may be willing to concede that spontaneity is present in animal courtship and fleeing behavior, but will balk at panpsychism's extension of this spontaneity to all natural forms. Again, the reply must be that, having made the concession at the aviary and mammal levels, it is arbitrary to assign within nature a demarcation between what occurs by either chance or causal determination and what occurs when mental spontaneity is present. Just as for mentality, we lack a biological explanation for the origination of spontaneity at any stage in evolution. This is because spontaneity in itself seems to have no adaptive value. Flexibility of response certainly has adaptive value: stereotyped behavior within a changing environment can lead to species extinction. But flexibility can be simulated by mechanical devices of increasing complexity, and we lack an explanation of why such complexity rather than spontaneity evolved. Just as for mentality, genetic variation and natural selection cannot explain the appearance of spontaneity rather than simply the appearance of traits capable of mechanical simulation. The conclusion drawn by panpsychism is that there was never a time when spontaneity was entirely absent.

The Origination Argument of this chapter presents panpsychism as a solution to the problem arising from the impossibility of ever providing an explanation of how mentality arose from bare matter. Lurking ominously in the background, however, is an alternative solution to this problem provided by Christian theology, and this deserves our consideration.

CHAPTER SIX

The Theistic Alternative

At the core of theism, as I shall understand it here, is the view that mentality can be attributed to the universe as the whole of which all individual natural bodies are a part. Just as we attribute mentality to certain natural bodies, so we must attribute it to this whole. Within theism there are many differences over how best to characterize this universe-wide mentality and its relation to the various natural forms. Under the sway of traditional substance dualism, medieval theology posited the existence of a Universal Mind. This Universal Mind was regarded as identical with that Cosmic Person named and prayed to as the "God" or "Allah" of the Judeo–Christian and Islamic religious traditions. In accordance with the models of agency found in their scriptures, this Universal Mind was endowed with the powers of creating the universe and individual minds, showing love and concern toward supplicants, legislating moral laws, and rewarding or punishing those who followed these laws or transgressed against them.

In reaction against this theology and its philosophic assumptions, we find thinkers in the nineteenth and twentieth centuries endorsing what is called "pantheism." This characterized universe-wide mentality in more indefinite and impersonal terms as "Being Itself" or as an animating force—what Henri Bergson termed an *Elan Vital*—somehow influencing the upward course of evolutionary development and counteracting natural tendencies toward dissolution. In this chapter I shall be considering, first, the general problem of extending our attribution of mentality from natural forms to the universe as a whole. I

129

then turn to two formulations of an argument for God's existence whose starting point is the same as the Origination Argument of the previous chapter. Of chief interest to us here is the alternative to panpsychism posed by this argument.

Universe-Wide Mentality

We can understand the term "universe" to be a singular term referring to that whole aggregate of matter whose parts are causally related to one another and to our planet. There are galaxies receding from us at such great distances that light from them will never reach us and which may exert negligible gravitational influence on our planet. Yet they do stand in causal relations to other galaxies that we can detect, and these other galaxies may directly have some minimal influence on our galaxy and the stars and planets within it. In this sense all parts of the universe stand in causal relations with every part, although certain of these relations may only be exerted through intermediaries. David Lewis describes possible worlds as concrete, material worlds that are causally isolated from our universe.[1] If indeed such possible worlds happen to exist (the hypothesis is, in principle, untestable), then our universe would not include all material bodies, but only those that stand in causal relations to ourselves.

Are there rational grounds for attributing unitary mentality to our actual universe? Philosophers in the past have referred to a "World Soul" that stands in relation to the universe as our actual world in a way analogous to that in which it was once believed our soul or mind stands in relation to our bodies. Such a conception assumed what is labeled "substance dualism," the view that the mind or soul is a type of persisting object standing in relation to a body, and one that has few adherents today. Some contemporary theologians endorse the view of Hartshorne that universe-wide mentality is to be conceived as a sequence of mental events related by psychic causation to the mentality of natural bodies. But however this universe-wide mentality is conceived, it would seem that belief in it would be at least initially based on reasoning related to that used to justify panpsychism. As we have seen, to attribute mentality to certain objects in our environment is to attribute to them a point of view or perspective on the basis of an analogical inference that compares certain structural or behavioral features of these objects with those used as criteria in attributing mentality to other humans. The closer the similarity between these features and the criterial features in the human case, the stronger the analogical inference. Our question then is: Can such attributions be extended to the universe as a whole?

It takes only a moment's reflection to realize that the answer is obviously no. As Hume noted in his *Dialogues Concerning Natural Religion*,[2] the universe exhibits none of the features, not even that of unity of organization and homeostasis, that we appeal to in justifying attributing mentality to natural forms. Far from exhibiting organization, current astronomy describes it as a chaotic aggregate of galaxies grouped into clusters in which there is continual creation and destruction of both member galaxies and the stars belonging to them. Moreover, the organization of the universe, rather than increasing, seems to be dissipating as galaxies recede from each other. Clearly homeostasis has no relevance; the universe is a whole including everything else as parts, and hence there is no external environment to which it is related and against which it maintains itself. Just as obviously, there is no specialization of parts that could be the basis for attributing some unified perspective, no central nervous system, no sense receptors, nor anything remotely analogous to these features that provide our initial basis for mental attributions. And so there seems to be no rational basis for universe-wide mental attributions, at least if this attribution is at all like that for natural forms. But if it is totally different from the attributions we make in everyday life, we have not the slightest idea of what it could be like. We have traded in any hope for justification in exchange for the acceptance of a mystery.

What then is the basis for the religious belief that the whole of which we are a part has a mental aspect? A psychological answer can be given by noting the human needs for security, hope, and consensus within communities on moral guidelines. Of these, hope is perhaps the most basic attitude to which religion gives expression. Religion exists, it can be argued, because of the human need for hope for a better future, and this hope is expressed within communities in the form of shared prayer. Now prayer must be addressed to some addressee or addressees with the capacity to listen and perhaps provide some help in realizing the hope that has been expressed. The history of religion is a history of progressive extensions in the scope and reduction in number of these addressees. For early animistic religions, the addressees were spirits inhabiting local landmarks of a restricted area. For polytheism, they became the plurality of gods of an entire nation, and finally with monotheism, the concept of a single god developed whose power and influence extended everywhere. Attributing the capacity to listen and help to the single deity of monotheism led to assigning the addressee of prayer a name—whether Allah, Jehovah, God, or whatever—and the personal name of this Listener and Helper requires the attribution of mentality. The possibility of praying and obtaining help anywhere and at any time then becomes generalized into the conception of an omnipresent addressee, and this in turn to have generated the belief that mentality exists everywhere within the universe.

Along with providing an omnipresent addressee of prayers, the concept of a unitary universe-wide mental perspective provides a means for common expression of the ideals and moral values of a community. People pray not only for direct aid for themselves and those close to them, but for the realization of shared ideals such as the ideal of peace among nations. They also express values they hold in common, values that in some religions become expressed in the form of moral commands thought to be invested with the authority of divine origins. It is thus possible to explain religious belief in the existence of universe-wide mentality in terms of psychological needs on the part of individuals within communities for an addressee of their prayers and the sharing of ideals and values.

I shall be returning in the next chapter to this relation between the addresses of prayer and theology when our topic is linguistic fideism. For now we can simply note that while this account of religion's psychological origins may provide an *explanation* of the religious belief in unitary universe-wide mentality, it certainly does not *justify* this belief. Indeed, the usual intent of those offering this explanation is to undermine this justification. And because we have seen that any attempt at justification through an analogical inference must be unsuccessful—at least if this inference is anything at all like that used by panpsychism to establish its thesis—at this stage we are without a justification.

The traditional theistic arguments, both ontological and cosmological, sought to justify belief in God's existence, but these arguments do not directly claim there is universe-wide mentality. Instead, they purport to establish that God under some aspect exists, and this aspect was thought to imply mentality. Thus, Anselm's ontological argument attempts to prove God's existence as a perfect being, but perfection itself is an ideal, and does not entail mental activity. The medievals assumed that God possessed such perfections as perfect love and knowledge, but these are not derived from the ontological argument itself. Thomas Aquinas' cosmological arguments attempt to prove God's existence as first cause, first mover, as a necessary being, and intelligent designer. Of these characteristics, only that of intelligent designer of the universe implies mental activity. The Argument from Design, purporting to establish the existence of this designer, has been convincingly critiqued by a succession of philosophers starting with Hume, with perhaps the most successful and thorough critique in recent times being provided by John Mackie.[3] I shall assume readers have no interest in replowing a field so neatly furrowed by others.

Of much more relevance to our topic is instead an argument for God's existence used by Locke in the seventeenth century to solve the problem he poses about the origination of mentality discussed in the previous chapter. Having rejected any mechanistic explanation of the origination of mentality from insensate matter, Locke thought the only remaining alternative was to postulate the existence of an eternal God as the cause of the mentality we are aware of in ourselves. On the way to reaching this conclusion he considered and rejected a version of panpsychism as an alternative explanation. Difficulties in his reasoning help to provide support for this rejected alternative.

Locke's Argument for God's Existence

Locke restates his argument several times in Book IV, Chapter X of his *Essay*, and any summary of it must be reconstructed from its different versions. It begins with the certainty we have of our own existence as thinking beings. "I think it is beyond question," he says, "that man has a clear idea of his own being; he knows certainly he exists, and that he is something."[4] He knows, moreover, that he has perception, thought, and knowledge, and therefore "we are certain now, that there is not only some being, but some knowing intelligent being in the world."[5] The question then arises of how to explain the existence of beings with the capacity for perception, thought, and knowledge. As we saw in the beginning of chapter 5, Locke argues that it would be impossible for such beings to exist unless there eternally exists some being with perception and knowledge, because matter itself cannot generate perception, thought, or knowledge. From the fact that thought exists in us and that thought cannot be generated from matter and motion follows the conclusion that God exists as the agent generating thought.

> Thus from the consideration of ourselves, and what we infallibly find in our own constitutions, our reason leads us to the knowledge of this certain and evident truth, that there is an eternal, most powerful, and most knowing being; which whether any one will please to call God, it matters not.[6]

The argument can be reconstructed as composed of two premisses leading to an intermediate conclusion, and finally to the conclusion that God exists. The first of the premisses, as we have seen, is that thought, intelligence, knowledge, and perception exist, as is self-evident from our own thinking and its capacities. Locke could have derived the self-evidence of this from Descartes' argument for the certainty of "I think," and, like Descartes, he could have assumed as self-evident that this thought includes intelligence, perception, and the other capacities listed. The second premiss is what he regards as the self-evidence of the fact that unthinking matter itself cannot be the originating cause of thought, or as he puts it, "bare incogitative Matter . . . could never produce Thought." The intermediate conclusion is that, if bare matter cannot generate thought, the only remaining alternative explanation of thought's existence is that some eternal thinking being generated it. God's existence as an eternal thinking being is then inferred as providing the only possible explanation of how our thought originates.

The argument can be summarized as follows:

> Our thought (intelligence, perception, etc.) exists.
> This thought cannot be generated from bare unthinking matter.
> Our thought could not therefore exist, if it were not generated by some Eternal Thought.
> Therefore, God as this Eternal Thought exists.

From the fact that thought exists, and the intermediate conclusion that this would not be possible unless it were somehow generated by Eternal Thought, we can deductively derive the conclusion.

Because it is regarded as self-evident, the second premiss is never seriously questioned by Locke. Panpsychism as understood in this work is also in agreement with it, although in its formulation "mentality" is substituted for "thought" and is extended to subhuman forms. As we have seen, this agreement is not based on the self-evidence of this premiss, as it was for Locke, but because of the implausibility of explanations of how mentality could have arisen from bare matter.

But although he accepts without extensive defense the second premiss, Locke does take great pains to establish the intermediate conclusion that causation by Eternal Thought is a necessary condition for the presence in us of thinking. To establish this conclusion, he argues for the elimination of other possible explanations of how thinking could originate, and all of these are relevant to the thesis of panpsychism.

Indeed, one of the alternatives he considers is a certain version of panpsychism, although not that developed here. This alternative is, as he phrases it, that the "eternal first cogitative being" is material, or that thought is a "property eternally inseparable from matter and every particle of it," and this matter is eternal. By adopting this alternative, we avoid violating the principle that thought (or mentality) cannot be generated from matter; it is now regarded as eternally associated with matter in the way that we associate our own thought with our body. Locke rejects this possibility on the grounds that matter is no more than the sum total of material particles as elements that are not themselves wholes with parts, nature's indivisible atoms, or what are regarded as the fundamental particles of contemporary physics. There are an infinite number of such elements, Locke thought, and the sum total of them could never produce the order and harmony that we observe in nature.

> And therefore if matter were the eternal first cogitative being, there would not be one eternal infinite cogitative being [God], but an infinite number of eternal finite cogitative beings, independent one of another, of limited force and distinct thoughts, which could never produce that order, harmony, and beauty which are to be found in nature.[7]

He also considers the possibility of one special atom or particle of matter being endowed with thought, but rejects this on the grounds that such particles are themselves indistinguishable in nature, and hence there is no basis for singling out one from the others. Every particle of matter, he says, "is capable of all the same figures and motions of another; and I challenge any one, in his thoughts, to add any thing else to one above another."[8]

Whether one or an infinite number of particles are endowed with thought, it is clear that Locke is presenting us with the problem posed by the Origination Argument of chapter 5. One way of avoiding the creation of thought (or mentality) is to postulate the existence of fundamental particles from the beginning of time that are endowed with mentality. As we have seen, this alternative conflicts with the analogical inference used as the initial rational basis for panpsychism. The appeal in the inference is to similarities between the structured bodies and behavior of our fellow humans and infrahuman natural bodies to which mental attributes are extended. Any significant analogy would seem to require natural bodies as structured wholes composed of parts, and both Locke's infinite collection of particles and his single particle fail to satisfy this condition.

Nevertheless, the Origination Argument may demand unstructured eternal natural bodies, despite the difficulty of applying an analogical inference to them. Writing before Darwin, it is understandable that Locke could not conceive how from such beginnings there could develop "the order, harmony, and beauty which are to be found in nature." For us, however, order arising from independent natural bodies follows as a consequence of evolutionary theory, and thus what was rejected by Locke is a viable option.

Locke considers another alternative that attributes eternal mentality to an organized body composed of parts. This alternative is that "some certain system of nature duly put together" is the eternal thinking being, a notion "which men are aptest to have of God, which would have him a material being, as most readily suggested to them, by the ordinary conceit they have of themselves, and other men, which they take to be material thinking beings." This he rejects on the grounds that such a system would consist of parts that lack thought.

> But this imagination, however more natural, is no less absurd than the other [that one atom is the eternal thinking being]; for to suppose the eternal thinking being to be nothing else but a composition of particles of matter, each whereof is incogitative, is to ascribe all the wisdom and knowledge of that eternal being only to the juxta-position of parts; than which nothing can be more absurd. For unthinking particles of matter, however put together, can have nothing thereby added to them, but a new relation of position, which it is impossible should give thought and knowledge to them.[9]

In the second premiss of his argument for God's existence, Locke had claimed that thought could not be generated from unthinking matter. He now extends this to the claim that combinations of unthinking particles into organized systems cannot possibly be endowed with thought. What is lacking in the parts cannot be present in the whole from which these parts are formed.

It is difficult to see how Locke can make this extended claim. He may have thought it follows from the argument's second premiss, since one form of generation of thought from matter might be regarded as the combination by juxtaposition of material particles. But if organized systems of material parts have existed from eternity, there will be no problem of generation, and we must therefore regard this extended claim as an independent one. Judged independently, it seems obviously false by Locke's own principles. We have just seen how he denies mentality (or thought and knowledge in his formulation) to indivisible particles of matter. Also, he takes as self-evident that we are thinking beings, and would agree that our thoughts are associated in some fashion with our bodies. Our bodies are organized wholes composed of parts that lack thought and knowledge, and thus provide a clear counterexample to his extended claim that combinations of unthinking matter cannot produce thought. Locke could perhaps argue (though in fact he does not) that our bodies are composed of parts with mentality, and might even agree with panpsychism that these parts are wholes relative to other parts with mentality. But assuming we withhold mentality from fundamental particles, eventually this regress must terminate in organized wholes composed of material, nonmental parts.

We must conclude, therefore, that Locke did not establish his intermediate conclusion that eternal disembodied thinking is a necessary condition for thoughts as self-evident to us, and without this intermediate conclusion, his argument for the theistic conclusion that God exists fails. If we grant his second premiss, the premiss that excludes the explanation provided by universal mechanism, there still remains the possibility of the existence of bodies endowed with mentality from eternity, whether these have or lack organization. For those with organization, Locke considers only the possibility of one such body, but there is nothing that seems to exclude the possibility of a plurality of them, each of finite duration, transmitting mental capacities to successors. Because this possibility is the thesis of panpsychism, if we grant him his second premiss, Locke only succeeds in presenting us with the alternatives of theism and panpsychism.

That Locke offers us this alternative is also shown by an equivocation in his conclusion that something that has mentality must have existed from eternity as inferred from the impossibility of bare matter generating mentality. As Mackie notes, this conclusion can be interpreted as saying either that (1) at every time there has been something mental, or (2) at every time there has been some one thing that has mentality.[10] (1) is consistent with panpsychism and the existence of a plurality of mental beings, while (2), the interpretation Locke assumes, entails the existence of God as the unique eternal mental being. Without justification, Locke imposes interpretation (2).

Panpsychism would seem to represent a far more plausible interpretation, however, because it is grounded in a method of analogical extension from familiar mental attributions. This contrasts to the utter mysteriousness of Locke's eternal thinking being or Universal Mind that is somehow supposed to cause the presence of thoughts in us. Such a being and the nature of its causative powers are by definition totally unlike anything of which we are aware in our own experience and practices. Indeed, Locke is vague about the way in which God as the eternal thinking being brings about thought in us. "All other knowing beings that have a beginning," he says, "must depend on him, and have no other ways of knowledge, or extent of power, than what he gives to them."[11] But he fails to tell us the nature of this dependence. Like Leibniz, he may have understood it in terms of mental capacities being implanted in us at birth as emanations from the divine, although this dependence can also take the form of participation in the activity of the Universal Mind, as for later idealist philosophers like Berkeley. It should also be noted that Locke makes no mention of the mental capacities of lower animals. True to the method of Descartes, only the existence of ourselves with our intellectual capacities is accepted as a self-evident premiss of the argument. This helps to establish his second premiss that such advanced capacities cannot be generated by combinations of matter, because the possibility of these capacities evolving from more primitive ones over long periods of time is not even considered, and the instantaneous generation of knowledge and intelligence from material elements is indeed inconceivable. The effect of this restriction to human mentality also avoids the need of explaining how the mentality of creatures is dependent on universe-wide mentality. Are the souls of all the billions of insects of this planet also implanted in them upon birth? If so, God will be very busy. Do all creatures or only a very restricted subset of them participate in the Universal Mind? To his great credit, Locke considers panpsychism as providing an alternative form of eternal mentality. But because of the pre-Darwinian framework within which he operated, he could never adequately pursue its implications.

Swinburne's Argument from Consciousness

I turn now to a recent reformulation of Locke's argument for the theist alternative offered by one who writes from the vantage point of evolutionary theory. Richard Swinburne's version differs from Locke's in three important respects, the first two of which serve to move it closer to the Origination Argument of chapter 5. First, his argument is directed toward the origination of animal consciousness, not human-specific "thought and knowledge." Second, he doesn't base it on the inconceivability of mentality arising from matter, but instead on the impossibility of the natural sciences providing an explanation of the transition. And finally, unlike Locke, he fails to consider the panpsychist alternative. Issues raised by Swinburne help to clarify the contrast between the atheistic panpsychism formulated here in earlier chapters and the theistic alternative.

Swinburne attempts to demonstrate in his *The Existence of God* that God's intentional intervention provides the only plausible explanation of the existence of consciousness. This demonstration is called the "argument from consciousness" for God's existence, and is one in a series of arguments, including the more widely discussed medieval ontological and cosmological arguments. Consciousness is extended by Swinburne to animals in a way that suggests it is understood as wakefulness, not self-awareness. It is denied of plant cells and all organized natural bodies that predate animal life. The problem for him is thus to explain how consciousness came into existence during the period in which animals evolved from their more primitive antecedent forms. Whether there is a separate explanation required for the origination of language-based consciousness in the human species is not made clear by Swinburne, although he implies that only the origination of consciousness at the animal level must be explained. However this requirement is understood, we should recognize his restatement of the problem, with its implicit acknowledgment of an analogical inference to animal consciousness, as marking an advance over Locke's exclusive attention to the perception, thought, and knowledge of which we are directly aware in our own experience. The possibility of a type of preconscious mentality whose origination also requires explanation is not considered by Swinburne. If he had, his problem would be identical with that with which the Origination Argument of chapter 5 begins.

Also marking an advance is Swinburne's view that the origination of consciousness requires an explanation. For Locke it was self-evident a priori that consciousness (or thought and knowledge in his version) could not be generated from bare matter, or that the generation was inconceivable. Now inconceivability would seem to have two different interpretations. It could mean logical inconceivability, that is, that mind and matter generation was somehow logically self-contradictory. For Locke this could have meant examining the idea of "matter" finding features that excluded "cause of consciousness," and indeed Locke suggests this in comparing the impossibility of matter generating thought to the impossibility of a triangle with more than three sides. But in fact, he doesn't carry through such an inquiry, and there seems to be no reason for thinking that he would have been successful if he had attempted it. Inconceivability can also be understood as incompatibility with the known laws of physics, chemistry, and biology. But again, Locke never attempted to demonstrate such incompatibility, and any attempt at such a demonstration would also seem futile.[12]

Swinburne's more sensible approach rests on the assumption that if consciousness were generated from matter, then the natural sciences should be able to provide an explanation of how this generation took place. There is no requirement that they produce such an explanation in the present; many phenomena await future explanation. But there must be at least the prospect that at some future stage in the development of the sciences that such an explanation be forthcoming. And it is this prospect that Swinburne correctly denies.

He bases this denial, however, on what I think we must recognize as faulty reasoning, for he regards it necessary that he demonstrate the falsity of materialist theories that identify the mental with the physical and demonstrate the truth of dualism with this. If materialism were true, he thinks, then science could explain the emergence of consciousness, while if consciousness is in fact distinct from material processes, and dualism true, he thinks that there could be no possible explanation of how it is generated by matter. From dualism it seems to follow that we can only establish correlations between the physical and mental and never any underlying explanation. From this theory it also follows that the fact of consciousness itself must necessarily remain unexplained by the sciences. But in arguing for dualism, Swinburne is relying on a highly controversial metaphysical position that has undergone sustained criticism for much of the twentieth century. It provides a most tenuous basis for concluding that the sciences cannot explain the origination of consciousness.

Moreover, it is not needed for this conclusion. We should grant, I think, the materialists their contention that consciousness does not constitute a process distinct from a physical process. There still remains, however, the contrast between material systems with a qualitative, conscious perspective on things and those material systems that lack these characteristics. We then face the problem of the sciences providing an explanation of how those natural bodies lacking a perspective generated those bodies that came to possess it. Evolutionary theory would seem to provide the only plausible means for solving this problem. But assuming the soundness of the Origination Argument of chapter 5, any attempt at an explanation through this theory must be judged a failure, not because of any temporary short comings in our experimental data or lack of ingenuity in crafting an explanation, but because no matter how complete the evidence, natural selection combined with variation between individuals cannot provide a plausible explanation of how some configurations of matter became endowed with consciousness. The emergence of behavioral capacities can be explained, but such capacities admit of mechanical simulation, and we still lack an explanation of why conscious systems emerged rather than their zombie-like mechanical counterparts.

We can thus agree with Swinburne's conclusion that science cannot explain the emergence of consciousness, although not with the reasoning he uses to base his ultimate conclusion that because science cannot provide the sought-for explanation, God's intervention must fill the gap. Only the intentional action of some conscious agent can explain the presence of consciousness in both ourselves and lower animals, Swinburne argues, and this conscious agent is for him God as the Universal Mind of monotheistic theology. But Swinburne offers us no help in understanding how such a Universal Mind brings about consciousness in certain natural bodies, and we are thus left with a mystery just as deep as the original mystery about the origination of consciousness.[13] Theology has rightly insisted that it is not under any obligation to explain why God exists, or why there is a Universal Mind. There is no more obligation on it than there is on science to explain the existence of matter. What exists from eternity is simply a brute fact. But change to a novel state demands explanation, and for this theology is under an obligation to provide us with a plausible explanation of some kind or other that goes beyond simply the pronouncement that God created creature mentality. On this score it fails miserably.

There are, in fact, just three different ways to deal with Locke's problem of the origination of mentality. One is to claim, as does Dennett, that there is some causal explanation that the sciences will someday provide. The second is Locke and Swinburne's way of appealing to an eternal Universal Mind from which mentality is generated. And finally, there is the panpsychist alternative that claims that the mentality of natural bodies is eternal, that mentality in this form is of the nature of things on an equal footing with matter, and hence no explanation of its existence is required. There are, I think, no decisive proofs for any of these alternatives. But we can weigh them against each other by the standard of relative plausibility, and here the balance seems to side with panpsychism. The Origination Argument and the difficulties with the theist alternative of Locke and Swinburne serve to tip the balance.

At this stage the attentive reader may be likely to jump in with an objection. Panpsychism ascribes to primitive organized natural bodies a type of mentality that is distinguished from perceptions and wants that are characteristic of animals. To this animal stage Swinburne extends the term "consciousness," apparently understood here in the sense of waking experience. Mentality as consciousness in this sense can in turn be distinguished from human mentality that at least intermittently takes the form of awareness of experiencing, or what we refer to as "self-consciousness." The contrast between consciousness in the extended sense and human self-consciousness corresponds roughly with Leibniz's distinction between perception and apperception (cf. chapter 2). Now the second and third stages (and there are other intermediate stages that could be distinguished) represent novel developments from their predecessor stages. It would seem to be incumbent on us to provide some explanation of why the later evolved from the earlier. But such an explanation would seem to be no different from that attempted by those who would explain the origination of mentality, whether in terms of evolution or divine action. To ask for an explanation here, however, is to ask panpsychism to forego the advantage that it claims over its competing alternatives. And if none is forthcoming, panpsychism cannot claim any exemption from the mysteries that beset these alternatives.

It can be further pointed out that embryonic and child development pose the same requirements for explanation. Let's grant with panpsychism that we can ascribe mentality to human sperm and eggs as single-celled organisms. (We overlook the synthesis from molecules of these organisms in the male testes and female ovary.) Nevertheless, this primitive form of mentality makes the transition at some stage to the sensations and feelings that it seems we can attribute to the developing fetus and eventually to the self-consciousness of the four-year-old child. Again, some explanation of these transitions seems called for. Under the influence of Leibniz's panpsychism, early nineteenth century biology postulated a tiny homunculus that remained constant through the different stages of embryonic development. But this has been decisively repudiated by modern biology, and with its rejection panpsychism would seem to face the same problem encountered by any who attempt to explain how mentality emerged from bare matter, whether in terms of causal mechanisms or divine intervention.

This objection ignores, however, the force of the Origination Argument. Its contention is only that evolutionary theory cannot explain the *introduction* of mentality, because in its most primitive form having a qualitative perspective fails to confer any evolutionary advantage. Pure feeling would seem sufficient unto itself, and without any instrumental value. Granted that it may have arisen as the result of some chance mutation, its transmission into future generations remains unexplained. But all must concede that progressively more advanced stages of mentality in the form of learning and the capacity for signaling and use of discursive language do confer evolutionary advantage, and for these capacities there is thus a ready explanation. Moreover, as the argument in chapter 5 showed, once established, the spontaneity inherent in mentality can play a role in its continuance and development, a miniscule role, to be sure, in primitive forms, but a progressively more important role in more complex and highly organized social organisms. Once its foot is in the door, there is no difficulty in providing an evolutionary explanation of the transition to higher stages. The problem for all but panpsychism is explaining how this foot was initially inserted.

The same considerations apply to embryonic development. Once DNA sequences have been established in the course of evolution and mechanisms developed for transmitting them from parents to offspring, we have biological explanations available, however incomplete they may presently be, of the transitions from one mental capacity to another more advanced. There is no more a problem explaining how a child develops self-awareness than there is in explaining how he or she begins to walk. The solution lies in understanding the complex interaction between internal biological mechanisms and triggering environmental conditions. The developed capacities of the human child are the evolutionary sequel to actual primitive feelings in the distant past. The real problem is explaining how these initial actual feelings came into existence. Again, panpsychism's solution of denying the need for an explanation on the grounds that mentality is in the nature of things seems more reasonable than attempts at explanation that hand-wave in the direction of science or are based on the conclusions of theology.

This chapter has been a discussion of theism's alternative solution to Locke's origination problem. It has examined only one form of argument for God's existence, and certainly from the weaknesses in this form we cannot conclude that no such argument can be formulated. Theism as based on a different form of argument remains a possibility, although well known criticisms of traditional arguments serve to undermine its credibility. But weaknesses in the argument from consciousness of Locke and Swinburne do serve to reinforce the view that panpsychism as a metaphysical doctrine is independent of theism, despite the historical connection of the two in the writings of Leibniz, Whitehead, and Hartshorne.[14] The version of panpsychism maintaining this independence can be titled *atheistic panpsychism*, and contrasted with the theistic versions of the tradition. This contrast establishes the separation of atheistic panpsychism from natural theology. But it certainly does not separate panpsychism from religion as a social practice and from religion's special attitude toward the ordering of our lives. The nature of the relation between panpsychism and religion is our final topic.

CHAPTER SEVEN

The Religious Attitude

To understand the relationship between panpsychism and religion we must first abstract a common religious attitude from the various forms in which it is expressed with the world's religions. This attitude is characterized here as one that regards mentality as eternal and places a priority on a sense of the eternal in the way we conduct ourselves. Understood in this way, the religious attitude is consistent with atheistic panpsychism and its denial of the existence of theology's Universal Mind. The religious attitude can be regarded as having a cognitive component with a propositional core expressing what is believed and an evaluative component requiring a certain direction to our lives from us. The chapter begins by outlining the differing senses of the eternal used in the propositional core, reviews traditional conceptions of theistic panpsychism, and specifies a form of panpsychism distinct from these earlier formulations. Next, it discusses a humanist view called "linguistic fideism" that diagnoses theology's error in making existential claims and providing explanations of natural phenomena. The next topic is the justification of the evaluative components of the religious attitude, and the final section provides a summary of the differences between panpsychism and the alternatives of humanism, universal mechanism, and theism as providing alternative solutions to the origination problem.

The Religious Attitude and Theology

As it was in the beginning, is, and always shall be.
World without end. Amen, Amen.

This Gloria Patri added at the end of the singing of Psalms is thought to date from the fifth century. It expresses the religious belief that there is something that has always been and will be—the eternal. This belief is a component of what we can refer to as the *religious attitude*, which includes also the evaluation that whatever this eternal something is, it is of greater importance than our transitory lives, and that we should somehow be influenced by our recognition of it. As William James expressed it in his essay "The Will to Believe," for those holding the religious attitude the eternal is believed to "throw the last stone." All religions affirm the importance of the eternal in their celebration of births, their ritualistic endorsement of marriages as promoting the propagation of the species, and in the mourning of deaths. Some religions have sought to do much more, of course, claiming themselves to be the sources of political power and guides of proper moral conduct. But all—from those of primitive societies to those of the most advanced—at least have as a common denominator a recognition of the centrality of what persists beyond individual transitory lives through their rites for birth, species propagation, and death.

What is the eternal aspect of things that is recognized in the religious attitude? In some ill-defined way it is regarded as being like ourselves. Animism has prevailed in some cultures, with the eternal being identified with immortal spirits inhabiting natural objects such as streams, prominent rocks, and trees. These spirits are conceived as having human-like emotions such as anger and as exhibiting preferences. For others, there has been a plurality of gods that compete for the attention of human supplicants. The dominant view of the eternal, at least in the West, has identified it with a single god as both the creator of the natural world and the source of moral standards. In some Far Eastern cultures, a qualified sense of the eternal in the form of temporal continuity is preserved in the very different form of ancestor veneration and the belief that for each family there is an unbroken succession of ancestors stretching back indefinitely into the past and influencing the present and future. Environmental and social circumstances seem to have influenced which of these answers was given. The Judeo–Christian and Islamic religions are those with roots in the lives of nomadic peoples living much of their lives with feelings of isolation and separation and needing the security of some omnipresent protector. Just as shepherds looked after their flocks, so there was felt a need for an Eternal Shepherd looking after the shepherds. But religions in the Far East tend to be those of peoples living in densely populated, close-knit agricultural communities whose members often assert imposing demands on one another. Here security is provided by one's neighbors, and religion is not needed to overcome a sense of isolation. Instead, priority is given to cultivation of distance through meditation from what are often oppressive social pressures and to the attainment of "tranquillity" or peace of mind. Mahayana Buddhism as originating in India and spreading to China and Japan is often described as atheistic by those in the West. Indeed, its sense of the eternal as shaped by the circumstances of its believers is very different from religions with roots in Judaism. But this only demonstrates the great variety of ways the religious attitude can be exemplified.

Despite this variety, there is at least one negative characterization that seems to be given by all religions. In none of them is the eternal identified with the material world of particles, atoms, and molecules, and their great variety of combinations. We have noted how the First Law of Thermodynamics affirms the eternality of matter as without beginning or end. But the world described in the Gloria Patri—"as it was in the beginning, is now, and ever shall be"—is certainly not regarded by the religious to be the physicists' world of material elements. Indeed, those holding the religious attitude at a certain level of sophistication would seem to agree that if the only eternal aspect of things were the physicists' world, then their attitude would be totally unjustified. Instead, they believe that the eternal aspect must be in some sense analogous to the experiencing that all of us are engaged in during our waking lives. Or in other words, the eternal must in some sense be characterized as being what we describe as "mental." The religious attitude can thus be understood as including the belief that mentality is eternal. I shall refer to this as the *propositional core* of the attitude. This belief is combined with the evaluation that this eternal aspect should be of central importance to us and that recognition of it should have an influence on the way we conduct our lives.

To understand the proposition that mentality is eternal requires understanding the adjective "eternal." It is used in a variety of senses, and it is important to identify those used by panpsychism and contrast them with those of traditional theism. The monotheism of early Christian theology described the eternity of God as timelessness in the sense of excluding change. It regarded any change in God as inconsistent with His perfection, for change implies the possibility of a transition from better to worse, and perfection admits of no degree of deficiency. To admit any imperfection in God would have the effect of reducing God's authority in the area of morality, since only the moral commands of a perfect being would seem to require total obedience. Traditional theology seemed to have regarded it as important that God be regarded as unchanging to preserve this supremacy of authority over all potential rivals. To not be subject to change in the natural world is to be outside time, because time as the measure of motion (which is change in the location of a body) by definition requires change. This sense of the eternal obviously has no application to natural bodies, which are subject to change during their careers and to generation and destruction.

Recent theology influenced by Hartshorne has challenged this interpretation of the eternal, arguing that it is inconsistent with God's involvement with natural events.[1] In place of this conception of the eternal as timeless, eternity is interpreted as everlastingness, as extending indefinitely backward into the past and forward into the future, and as subject to change. But what changes? Obviously, the physical universe, consisting of the totality of natural bodies, is constantly changing, and the matter of which it is composed is eternal. It is thus everlasting. Causal relations also exist between the material elements of which the universe is composed. It is difficult to see how the God of Hartshorne, if indeed everlasting, causally related to natural events, and, subject to change can be regarded as distinguishable from the physical universe. And yet for reformist theology, God as the unitary mentality of the universe is conceived as being not simply the sum total of material elements.

There is, however, another sense of the eternal that may be introduced in an attempt to make reformist theology's conception of God intelligible. The eternal can be interpreted as the perpetual "now" characteristic of mentality for which a continuing present defines a past and future. What is now present in our experiencing shifts to the past relative to the perspective of a new present, and each moment of our waking lives repeats this shift. When we say that mentality is having a perspective, we imply the temporal perspective of this continually changing present. Augustine's characterization of God as He for whom all time is the "eternal now" combines this constancy of a present with eternity as timelessness—the conception of traditional theism. But reformist theology can appeal to the fact that our experiencing seems to represent a combination of a perpetual "now" with change, as we live within a shifting present and are constantly changing. The God of the reformists seems to be simply a generalization of this combination to a universe-wide mentality that combines an eternal "now" with change that extends indefinitely backward and forward in time. The constancy of this "now" ensures that God is not identified with the sum total of material elements, and is still able to both causally interact with natural bodies and be subject to change.

Is the conception of an everlasting God subject to change and with the perspective of an eternal "now" an intelligible one? It is certainly not intelligible as a generalization from our own experience, because it ignores an essential aspect. For us, having the perspective of a "now" is accompanied by a sense of spatial location relative to other bodies that defines a "here." This "here" is constantly changing as we move among the objects of our environment. But the God of theism as the omnipresent has by definition no "here," and thus cannot combine the two aspects essential to what we understand as having a perspective. The reformist theology of Hartshorne and Swinburne seems to appeal to the perspectival "now" to distinguish God from the everlastingness of the physical universe, but in the absence of the perspectival "here" it renders the conception unintelligible.

No such difficulties face atheistic panpsychism's interpretation of the religious attitude's propositional core. For panpsychism, the eternality of mentality is understood as its everlastingness. Our bodies change, and as they change so do our experiences. These natural bodies themselves are subject to generation and destruction, birth and death. Prior generations of humans and of organisms from which humans evolved have been subject to generation and destruction and have undergone the combination of bodily and experiential change. Panpsychism is simply the belief that this succession of natural bodies with a qualitative perspective extends indefinitely backward and forward in time. It seems possible to also apply the constancy of the "now" to such change. If in fact there have always been natural bodies with perspectives on their environments, then there has always been a "now" defining past and future for those enjoying these perspectives accompanied by a "here" defining location within an environment. There has not, of course, always been concepts of time and place. These are late evolutionary arrivals accompanying the introduction of language with its indexicals "now" and "here," the use of periodic motions to measure durations of changes, and the introduction of conventional measures of distance. But if the central thesis of atheistic panpsychism is true, there has always been and will be an inarticulated "here" and "now" of a present perspective for natural bodies subject to change. No single body is everlasting, but some natural body or other with a perspective has always existed and will exist. The propositional core of the religious attitude that mentality is eternal is thus preserved, and without the implausibilities of reformist theology.

Through the writings of advocates such as Aristotle, Leibniz, Whitehead, and Hartshorne, panpsychism is associated with theism. But the tradition gives conflicting accounts of the relationship between God and the mentality of finite creatures. For some in the theistic panpsychist tradition, one role of a Universal Mind or God is making immortality possible. For Aristotle this is a restricted role, because as noted in chapter 2, it is imitation of the activity of the Prime Mover through contemplation that qualifies humans for immortality to the exclusion of all other levels of souls. How elitist we are to understand this conception to be is unclear. It is the human capacity for apprehension of necessary truths such as those of mathematics and for reflections on one's thinking that provides the qualification for immortality. But what of all those persons ignorant of mathematics and all those unreflective persons who simply judge, decide, and act, never reflecting on what they are doing? Do they also qualify? Aristotle seems to suggest a restrictive conception of immortality that extends it to members of his own profession, philosophers who engage in contemplation. But he may also be interpreted as saying that all humans have the capacity for discursive thought and reflection, and by virtue of this capacity, even if only occasionally exercised, they have gained the prize.

However this issue is decided, it is clear that for Aristotle all souls have a beginning in time that is independent of any influence of the Prime Mover. Once in existence, the Prime Mover functions as the object of striving for all souls, the object of their appetitions or desires. But the Prime Mover does not bring souls into existence. A soul at any level simply comes into being when there is a body with a potential for life that is capable of the activity appropriate to its level. Rational souls with immortality are thus at best sempiternal, having a beginning in time but no temporal end, while all others are of finite duration. Moreover, this immortality follows from their own characteristic activity, and not through any activity attributable to the Prime Mover.

Under the influence of Christian doctrine, Leibniz assigned to God the more substantial role of being the creator of all souls or monads, the same role assigned by Locke and discussed in chapter 6. The principle of sufficient reason is stated by Leibniz as the principle "that no fact can be real or existing and no statement true unless it has a sufficient reason why it should be thus and not otherwise."[2] The existence of each finite being with a beginning and end constitutes a fact falling under this principle, that is, requiring an explanation of why it happens to exist rather than not exist. The only basis for such explanation, Leibniz contends, is God as the unique necessary, eternal being, and thus God's sustaining of the existence of contingent beings provides the required explanation of their existence. He describes this creation as an "outflashing" of the divinity.

> God alone is the ultimate unity or the original simple substance, of which all created or derivative monads are the products, and arise, so to speak, though the continual outflashings [*Fulgurations continuelles*] of the divinity from moment to moment, limited by the receptivity of the creature to whom limitation is an essential.[3]

For Aristotle, a particular configuration of matter acquires at some stage the capacity for either nutrition, sensation, and rational thought, or perhaps two or more these activities in combination. This is simply a brute matter of fact. For Leibniz this fact requires an explanation that can only be provided by God's creative act.

Although for Leibniz in the *Monadology*, God initially brings souls into existence, He does not actively ensure their survival upon the death of the body, because they may continue in existence in different bodily forms apart from his intervention. "Not only is there no generation [of animals]," he says, "but also there is no entire destruction or absolute death."[4] Instead, each animal soul on the destruction of its body "is merely made ready for a great transformation, so as to become an animal of another sort," as when grubs become flies and caterpillars are transformed into butterflies.[5] A kind of immortality is thus ensured for every soul, no matter what its level, and God seems to have no direct role in this persistence of souls through bodily changes, although He did have a role in the soul's initial creation. As a sop to Aristotle and Christianity's belief in human immortality, Leibniz grants humans a special kind of immortality accompanied by memories of a former existence. God preserves, he says, "not only our substance [as he does for all souls], but also our personality, that is to say the recollection and knowledge of what we are."[6] Although immortality is ensured for lower natural forms, ours is at least a more desirable kind that preserves personality. Also, human rational souls are accorded the status of "spirits," and as such can "enter into a sort of social relationship with God."[7]

Whitehead and Hartshorne offer different accounts of God's role. For Whitehead, God provides an explanation for the striving of all creatures through what he terms His "primordial nature" as the repository of eternal objects as "lures for feeling." "God's immanence in the world in respect to his primordial nature," he says, "is an urge towards the future based upon an appetite in the present."[8] This explanatory role is similar to Aristotle's Prime Mover. Besides performing this explanatory role, God also provides for Whitehead a justification of the religious hope that our lives have not been in vain and that in some form we shall continue forever. This justification is provided by what Whitehead calls God's "consequent nature," which guarantees a form of immortality for mentality at all levels. The mentality of a given natural form is conceived by him, as we saw in chapter 2, as a sequence of psychic events called "actual entities" in which later events in the sequence selectively inherit or appropriate a portion of the content of events earlier in the sequence. That portion not appropriated would be lost forever were it not for its effect on God. Much as finite actual entities appropriate only a portion of earlier occasions in their sequences and selectively exclude some features of their environments, the sequence of actual entities constituting God appropriates the good achieved in the past of every finite actual entity within His consequent nature.[9] There is thus preservation from moment to moment for all actual entities, and hence preservation of particular psychic sequences after the death of the natural forms with which they are associated. An egalitarian form of immortality is thus ensured for all creatures, indifferent of ranking. This is accompanied by a denial of the personal immortality accompanied by "knowledge and recollection" so valued by Christianity and Leibniz. What alone is eternal as Augustine's "Eternal Now" is God as an actual entity always existing in a continually changing present and incorporating past experiences.

Hartshorne rejects the conception of an eternal object, and with this comes a rejection of the conception of God's primordial nature. For him appetition and desire are accepted as brute facts that require no explanation. God's only role in Hartshorne's system is to provide the justification of religious hope through what Whitehead terms His "consequent nature."

For both Whitehead and Hartshorne, God does not perform the role of bringing actual entities into existence. The sequence of actual entities we associate with a natural form throughout its finite duration has a beginning in time, and both accept this as a natural fact, not one requiring to be explained by divine intervention. It is instead the hope for continuance that must be justified by means of God's consequent nature. Sequences of actual entities are thus sempiternal, having beginnings in time, but without ends by virtue of God's preservation. God alone is eternal, and performs no role in creating these sequences.

We thus have widely divergent views among our representatives of theistic panpsychism regarding God's role. For Aristotle, the Prime Mover does not create souls, nor does it assume responsibility for their continuance after the death of the body. Because the soul is the form of a natural body, the dissolution of the body is accompanied by the disappearance of the soul. As we have seen, our hope for immortality leads Aristotle to create an inconsistent exception: humans (at least some of them) achieve immortality by virtue of the similarity between their characteristic activities and that of the divinity. But this occurs because of the nature of the human soul and its activities, not because of any intervention of the Prime Mover, who functions as only the object of appetition and desire. For Leibniz, on the other hand, by virtue of the Principle of Sufficient Reason, God is assigned the creative role of explaining how monads or souls come initially into existence. He does not explain, however, why their existence is continued: this is accepted as a consequence of the nature of monads as indivisible units and of human rational souls as spirits with special capacities. Finally, for Whitehead and Hartshorne, God is denied any role in initiating sequences of actual entities, but is introduced to justify a belief in a type of continuance after death for all natural forms. Unlike Aristotle and Leibniz, humanity is granted no special status.

We must accept as a historical fact an association between panpsychism and belief in some form of deity, as illustrated by the philosophers just surveyed. But we should not infer from this historical fact that there is an essential connection between the two, and indeed the divergence of roles assigned to God among advocates of panpsychism only serves to weaken the connection. These advocates all accept some aspects of mentality as inexplicable fact, whether its initiation (as for Aristotle, Whitehead, and Hartshorne) or its continuance or cessation (as Aristotle for the death of subhuman creatures and Leibniz for the continuance of monads). Certain combinations of these views would exclude God from playing any role in creature mentality. We could, for example, accept as inexplicable the initiation of mentality and accept the fact of its cessation, or perhaps combine the inexplicability of initiation with the brute fact of some form of continuance. For all such combinations, the conceptual link between panpsychism and theism is broken, and this frees us to interpret the eternality of the religious attitude in a way very different from both traditional and reformist theology.

Finally, it should be noted in passing that there is a religious tradition that separates panpsychism from the concept of unitary mentality. This tradition is Buddhism, in which we find claims of both restricted and unrestricted panpsychism. Restricted panpsychism of the Aristotelian variety is implied by the Gautama Buddha's instruction to care for both animals and plants.[10] Unrestricted panpsychism seems to be implied by the enigmatic saying of later Buddhist commentators that the Buddha nature is in all things. Whether restricted or unrestricted, the Buddhist form of panpsychism is not formulated in conjunction with a belief in some unitary consciousness within the universe. As has been frequently noted, judged by the standards of Western philosophy Buddhism is atheistic, with no mention of the existence of that Supreme Being central to the systems of the Western panpsychists that have been surveyed here. Yet its central beliefs are surely consistent with the propositional core of the religious attitude.

Linguistic Fideism

The God of the Judeo–Christian and Islamic traditions combines many roles. He is at once the eternal aspect of things, the means of providing an explanation for many features of the natural world, the unitary addressee of prayers, and as this addressee the source of hope for a better future, and finally, the provider of moral standards. There have been many arguments for the existence of this God, and of these we have considered here only one of them, the argument from consciousness of Locke and Swinburne. There have been in turn many refutations of these arguments, and I think it is fair to say that these refutations have been generally accepted as convincing by the philosophical community, despite repeated attempts at reformulation of the original arguments that are claimed to escape them. Yet religion remains a powerful force in contemporary society, not simply among the uneducated and superstitious, but among those who have understood and agree with the refutations of the theistic arguments.

One way of reconciling the weakness of theological arguments with the strength of religious faith is to adopt the position of *linguistic fideism*.[11] This view makes a careful distinction between descriptive forms of language used within the natural sciences and those used for religious purposes. Explanations of natural phenomena are the domain of the natural sciences. Here the existence of unobserved theoretical entities may be postulated, but only if they perform a role within an empirically testable theory. The descriptive language used here has standards for its correct employment that have been adopted within science as an institutionalized specialization. Success of the methods used within this specialization has vindicated its claims to provide explanations that trump any of those provided by alternative methodologies, including those of natural theology. This success leads us to conclude that as far as religious claims are couched in the descriptive language of traditional theology, they should be either rejected or reinterpreted in some other form of language. This blanket judgment is extended to those theological arguments that assume explanations for natural phenomena competing with explanations provided by the sciences.

For linguistic fideism, the fundamental mistake of theism is to regard the sentence "God exists" as being used to make a descriptive existential claim of the same general form as "Duckbill platypuses exist." "God" is a term within religious language, and as such does not name an object about which cognitive claims of any kind can be made. To assert the sentence "God exists" as the conclusion of an argument with descriptive premises describing features of the natural world is to fail to recognize the special features of this language. But if this is so, it is just as mistaken to assert with the atheists the sentence "God does not exist." This sentence is of a form entirely different from "Dodos do not exist" for exactly the same reason as the theists' affirmative existential claim. Nor are the agnostics correct in claiming that we should suspend judgment and neither assert nor deny "God exists." This also assimilates the religious existential sentence into a cognitive claim for which sufficient evidence is lacking for either confirmation or falsification.

Fideism distinguishes religious faith from cognitive belief that a proposition is true. Religious faith is claimed to be of the "believe in" variety that is allied to trust, for we say that a person can believe in God's existence and also believe in the almanac for weather reports or in the veracity of a person. To have faith in God or to believe in a person or source can be the result of a voluntary decision, or, as defenders of fideism like to phrase it, a "personal commitment," or a Kierkegaardian "leap of faith." In contrast, cognitive belief is of a "believe that" variety that seems to be independent of voluntary control. I don't choose to believe that the earth orbits the sun or that it will rain tomorrow, and once formed, no amount of effort on my part can rid me of the belief. Linguistic fideism explains this contrast between "believe in" faith and cognitive propositional belief in terms of the different uses of language in which the two types of belief are expressed. [12]

The characteristic use of religious language occurs in prayer addressed to a deity or deities by supplicants. Prayer is often the expression of hope for an ideal condition that is beyond the power of the supplicants to realize and of a trust that it will somehow be realized by the addressee of the prayer. "Our Father who art in Heaven, hallowed be Thy name," begins the Lord's Prayer of Christianity as a form of respectful address to the deity. Then follows the expression of hope that "Thy will be done, on Earth as it is in Heaven," the hope that the ideal divine order will someday be realized for us, and the expression of a trust that the addressee of prayer can be counted on to somehow bring this about. Sentences used to express this hope and trust are no more descriptive than are those in the imperative mood such as "Go to the store" and exclamations such as "Oh, what a beautiful day." Rather than being indicative fact-stating sentences, those used in prayer seem to be allied to those in the optative mood. To pray for peace on earth is to use the optative "Would that (or let) there be peace on earth" or some variant. Because the functions of prayer discourse are very different from those of descriptive discourse, the latter's criteria for success do not apply. We should not believe, then, that terms occurring within prayer such as "Lord" or "God" refer to that which is causally related to us, or that its sentences are to be evaluated as true or false on the basis of either empirical evidence or argumentation.

Linguistic fideism must face some obvious difficulties. All standard addressing forms of language would seem to presuppose the existence of an addressee or addressees. For me to say "John, close the door" presupposes the existence of the agent John in the sense that the command cannot be obeyed without this existence. Without such possibility of obedience, the act of commanding would not have been successfully performed. The command to close the door may not be true or false, but at least its address "John" must indicate what is assumed to exist. Similarly, to say "Lord, grant me good health" is to express the hope for good health, but it also assumes the existence of the addressee of "Lord." To learn that no such addressee exists would seem to deprive prayer of its point. This then raises the question of whether the existential assumption is true, and with this we enter the domain of natural theology.

Linguistic fideism can answer this objection, I think, but the answer somewhat complicates its position. The answer must concede that in earlier times all supplicants assumed the existence of an addressee of their prayers with power to grant or refuse them, and it is also true that today most supplicants make this same assumption. But the assumption is simply false because it fails to acknowledge the special functions of a language used to express shared hopes. Contemporary supplicants aware of these functions need not concede that prayer requires this assumption of existence, and they may insist that for them the addresses in prayer perform a role very different from the standard one in commands. They may continue to use such forms as "Lord" or "God" only as means of expressing continuity between the prayers of those in past generations with those in the present. One means of indicating that hopes for the realization of an ideal order expressed in the past are the same hopes as those expressed in the present is to continue the same forms of address. To change these forms or to forego them altogether would be to introduce a break in social continuity. By maintaining them, prayer performs its function of not only providing expression of common hopes and ideals shared by present members of the community, but also linking them to the hopes and ideals of the past. In this way, the present generation can regard its strivings as helping to fulfill previous generations' hopes for a better future.

The importance to us of maintaining forms of address used in the past is indicated by our resistance to changes in them. The possessive pronoun "thy" was in common use in the seventeenth century, and was adopted with capitalization in the phrases "hallowed be Thy name" and "Thy will be done" of the Lord's Prayer. It has been replaced by "your" in current English, and this change would seem to demand replacing "Thy" by "Your" in the prayer. But most worshippers would bitterly resist such a change, no matter how strong its linguistic justification might be. Their resistance seems to be rooted in a need to preserve the addressing forms of the past as a means of preserving social continuity. It is more obvious that they would resist any dropping of addressing forms altogether. Our shared hopes could be expressed by sentences of the form "We pray that . . ." or "We hope that . . . ," with addresses such as "Lord" or "Our Father" eliminated. But this would introduce an even more radical break with the past, and many of us therefore retain the forms of address, while rejecting the existential assumptions of past users of them.

To some this may seem to be simply a restatement of atheism dressed in the linguistic garb of discussions of "God talk." But it is rather a correction of past errors about the assimilation of religious language to language performing very different functions. Those of past ages and some in the present may think their form of address in prayer functions like "John" in "John, close the door," but in fact it functions very differently. Having assumed the addresses of prayer are directed to a type of supernatural person somehow analogous to human addressees, it was an easy step to assign causal powers to the addressee or addressees and use these to explain natural phenomena such as floods, earthquakes, rain, or droughts. But the advances of science have convinced us of the need to replace this form of explanation with one very different. It would also seem that such replacement would lead to reassessing the assumption about addresses that had led originally to introducing supernatural personal explanations of natural phenomena. To reject supernatural personal explanations thus leads us to reject the assumption that there is a supernatural personal addressee of prayers. And just as we replaced supernatural explanations of natural phenomena with natural ones within the sciences, so we realize that we must replace the existential assumption of addresses within prayers with a very different view. To adopt linguistic fideism is not to rob prayer and its use of traditional forms of address of significance, contrary to the views of such critics of linguistic fideism as John Hick and Roger Trigg.[13] Common expression of hopes and ideals and preservation of social continuity through traditional addresses perform important social functions—functions that rival in importance those performed by science in its pursuit of informational descriptions and explanations—and institutional religions are the primary means by which they are performed.

The version of linguistic fideism I have just outlined has the merit both of being consistent with our previous doubts about theism and of correctly acknowledging differences between describing states of affairs and expressing hope for the future. It also serves to explain the resistance of religious believers, including those fully aware of the advances of the sciences, to the arguments of agnostics and atheists. It is not necessary for such resistance to be irrational. Instead, it can result rather from an entirely sensible interpretation—admittedly one that is all too often not made explicit—of "God doesn't exist" and "Don't believe in God" as in effect commanding "Give up hope" or "Don't acknowledge the continuity between the hopes and ideals of past generations with yours of today." It is quite reasonable for believers to conclude that it is not in their interest to obey these commands.

Linguistic fideism thus presents us with an entirely plausible account of the religious language of prayer and the anthropomorphic, personal conceptions of a deity or deities as addressees that have provided the origins of theism. It also correctly identifies, I think, the basic error of theism as not due to weaknesses in the specific forms of arguments used to establish God's existence, although these weaknesses certainly exist. The basic error is instead that of regarding religious language as a descriptive form to which cognitive standards of evidence and argumentation apply.

Can linguistic fideism also be applied to the propositional core of the religious attitude? Is belief that mentality is eternal a disguised expression of hope for the eternality of mentality? Can panpsychism be interpreted as an expression of the hope that all nature shares with ourselves a perspective and a qualitative, spontaneous aspect? Critics of panpsychism have charged that it provides only an emotionally satisfying outlook, citing the weakness of the arguments used to establish the doctrine. That panpsychism provides an expression of hope not subject to cognitive standards might explain its continuing attractiveness in the face of the intellectual difficulties it faces.

But this application of linguistic fideism to panpsychism seems mistaken. The propositional core of the religious attitude is not susceptible to empirical test, because there seem to be no observations that would confirm or falsify the proposition that mentality is an eternal feature of natural bodies (chapter 1). But we must also recognize that linguistic fideism does not apply to this core proposition, which does seem to be either true or false. That argumentation, if not experimentation, is applicable to it is shown by panpsychism's Origination Argument that there has always been and will be natural bodies to which mentality can be ascribed. In this respect it is similar to some of the more speculative propositions of cosmology. The human species may never be able to determine whether the eventual fate of our universe is continuing expansion, equilibrium, or collapse to some condensed state. But we can be confident that propositions describing these three alternatives are either true or false. In similar fashion, we may never the able to demonstrate the truth or falsity of the proposition that mentality of natural bodies is eternal, but it nevertheless is either true or false, and in this respect very different from expressions of hope, which are evaluated differently as realistic or unrealistic.

There are, to be sure, implausible aspects of the panpsychist thesis, in particular the apparent inconsistency between the analogical inference used to initially justify it, and the Origination Argument. We have seen how the latter seems to require attributing mentality to fundamental particles without organizational structure, although the analogical inference seems forced to appeal to similarities between the persisting organization of organisms and more primitive natural bodies. But this simply emphasizes that for metaphysical theses we can at best apply the standards of relative plausibility, comparing one thesis with its competing alternatives, as we have compared panpsychism with humanism, universal mechanism, and theism. That we are able to make assessments of relative plausibility that weigh in favor of panpsychism is an indication that it is not simply an expression of hope to which cognitive standards fail to apply.

Some may object to distinguishing in this way the sentence "The mentality of natural bodies is eternal" expressing the propositional core from the sentence "God exists" as interpreted by linguistic fideism. The latter is the conclusion of arguments within natural theology, and the fact that these arguments that can be agreed with or contested demonstrates—so the objection may go—that this conclusion has descriptive propositional status. For this reason linguistic fideism is no more applicable to it than to the core proposition of the religious attitude.

But this objection fails to acknowledge that within the sentence "God exists" occurs the name "God" functioning as the address of prayers. It is this occurrence in both natural theology and prayer of a common name, together with the irrelevance of refutations of the theistic arguments by believers, that is the basis for the claims of linguistic fideism. Theism as a philosophical position has attempted to replace the addressee of prayers with a transcendental explanatory principle, and as a result we find the substitution of terms such as "Prime Mover," "First Cause," "Guiding Intelligence," and "Force Counteracting Entropy" for the personal address "God." Nevertheless, while the premises of theistic arguments may contain such terms or their equivalents, the conclusion of all arguments is finally "God exists," with the name "God" substituted for the definite description specifying the explanatory principle. It is this final substitution that makes relevant the charge by linguistic fideism that religious language is being misunderstood by theism as descriptive and propositional. No such substitutions are relevant, of course, to panpsychism's claim that natural bodies with mentality always have and will exist, nor is there any suggestion that such mentality is a potential addressee of prayer. If we accept the panpsychist thesis as true, this may arouse in us reverence and awe, but these emotional responses can be distinguished from the thesis itself. In contrast, the name "God" is necessarily associated with attitudes appropriate for one who asks for help of a divine provider capable of granting or rejecting requests. These features are sufficient to distinguish the panpsychist thesis from theism's claims for God's eternal existence.

So far we have avoided any discussion of the evaluative components of the religious attitude and relations between these components and the propositional core. What importance does the eternality of the mental have for us? How is it possible for acceptance of the propositional core to influence our conduct? Traditional theism stated a very simple relationship between belief in God's existence and conduct, namely that it is our duty to obey commands issued by God as somehow conveyed to us, and that somehow we would be better off if we obeyed these commands. The relationship for panpsychism between the propositional core of the religious attitude and associated evaluative components is more complex. To explain it requires examining the relationship between forms of practical inferences and the reasons for moral obligations overriding the prudential.

Practical Inferences and Moral Overrides

A well established tradition in modern philosophy insists on a sharp demarcation between practical prudential conclusions based on self-interest and moral requirements. The former are based on desires, or "inclinations" in the Kantian terminology, while the latter have a basis that is entirely grounded in "reason." To be moral is regarded as listening to the voice of reason in overcoming the temptations of inclination. That this separation of morality from desires is mistaken can be seen by briefly examining the similarities and differences between prudential and moral inferences.[14] Such an examination shows how moral conclusions share with the prudential variety the feature of being based on desires, differing only in the nature of these desires and the supplementing premises from which moral conclusions are derived. This enables us to see how prayer has relevance to morality and offers some limited justification for the evaluative components of the religious attitude.

A practical inference is a form of inference in which the conclusion states what should or ought to be done. This conclusion is based on premises that both express a desire for some state of affairs and assert what action is a means to obtain this state of affairs relative to a circumstance that obtains. For prudential practical inferences there is a first-person expression of a want or desire on the part of the agent deliberating about what he or she should do. Thus, someone might want to keep warm the coming winter and judge that buying a coat is necessary to accomplish this if the winter proves to be cold. Assuming it will be cold, she concludes that she should buy a coat. Her inference is thus of the form,

> I want to keep warm this winter.
> If it is a cold winter, to keep warm I must buy a coat.
> The winter will be cold.
> _____
> Therefore, I should (or ought to) buy a coat.

In this inference the action of buying a coat is a necessary means to the end of keeping warm. A second of type of inference has premisses presenting a number of optional means to an end, with an expression of preferences between these options. Thus, someone may reason as follows:

> I want to keep warm this winter.
> If it is a cold winter, I can keep warm by buying either a parka or
>   an overcoat.
> It will be cold, and I prefer the costs and alternative consequences
>   of the parka to an overcoat.
> _____
> I should buy a parka.

This weighing of alternative costs and consequences of means to ends is what we commonly understand by *deliberation* as a preliminary to a *decision*. Having accepted the conclusion "I should buy a parka," there is typically a decision on the part of the agent to so act.

It is important to notice how the premises of such inferences combine both expressive and descriptive functions. To say "I desire (or want) some end E" and "I prefer the costs and consequences of means M_1 over those for its alternative M_2," is to express a desire and a preference, and not to report some fact about myself. In contrast, to say "If circumstance C obtains, then doing M is necessary to attain E" and to assert that the circumstance C will in fact obtain, is to assert a relation between an action M and consequence E and assert C as a matter of fact. This assertive use of language is very different from the use of language to express desires and preferences. Finally, a conclusion of the form "I should (or ought to) do M" represents a third use of language to commit oneself to a course of action, and is related to the prescriptive use of language to issue commands to another. The language used to state this "should" conclusion is certainly not descriptive, though it is related to such language as a conclusion derived from premises stating circumstances and means–end relations.

There is general agreement on the basic features of the prudential inferences just described. Certainly no one has suggested that the ends or goals that individuals set for themselves are stated in descriptive, propositional form, or that they are accepted as true in the way we accept propositions about circumstances and causal relations. Beliefs may be relevant to desires, but the desires are clearly expressed in a form of language very different from that in which we express beliefs. It is thus generally conceded that what Kant termed "inclinations" guide our prudential deliberations.

The situation is very different, however, for moral inferences used in deliberating about what is morally obligatory; here there is much controversy. At the center of it is the question of whether we can sharply distinguish moral from prudential inferences with respect to their first premises. The rationalist tradition derived from Locke and Kant insists that moral first premises are propositional in form and known by "rational intuition," a special form of "rational self-evidence" distinct from the observational evidence of the empirical sciences. There are clearly important differences between the two forms of inference. But an examination of how moral deliberation is actually conducted within communities reveals that there is no need to create the rationalists' artificial separation of the moral from the prudential.

Instead, the two types of inferences are both practical in form, and distinguished only by the types of agents named in premisses and conclusion. Prudential inferences are *agent-homogeneous* inferences in which the first-person pronoun is used to both express the want in the first premiss and to state the obligation in the conclusion. Moral inferences, in contrast, are *agent-heterogeneous* inferences in which typically the first premiss expresses a want or desire shared within the community and the conclusion imposes a requirement on a single member. A distinctive feature of such inferences is also a Kantian universalization premiss that functions to relate the plural to the singular. It states that if most ought to perform an action that is a means to an end shared within the community, then any particular member of that community ought to perform that action also. Adding this premiss is necessary to infer from the obligation for most persons to act in a way to realize a shared goal to the conclusion that any given individual must act in that way. This prevents individuals from claiming themselves to be special exceptions to general rules of conduct applying to others.

To illustrate these agent-heterogeneous inferences, let's suppose that within the community there is a shared desire for quiet at night and that to achieve this just about everyone must close their windows when playing music. We say "just about everyone" because a very limited, controlled number of exceptions might not be overly disturbing. Then on the basis of the shared desire for quiet and information about means we could infer a moral requirement on any given member to close his or her window. In effect, we are concluding that what is necessary to be done by just about everybody should be done by each member. The inference used to conclude a moral requirement of a given member X is roughly of this form:

> We want quiet at night.
> Only if nearly everybody shuts their windows when playing music will there be quiet.
> If nearly everybody should shut their windows, then each member should also.
>
> _____
>
> X ought to shut his window when playing music.

The third premiss has the effect of denying the right of individual members to claim themselves exempt from a requirement to perform a kind of action necessary to achieve a common goal. The conclusion of the example just given is stated in the third person, but it could also take the first-person form "I ought to shut my window when playing music." It is through such moral inferences that we seem to impose requirements such as truth-telling and promise-keeping both on ourselves and others as based on shared desires for reliance and trust within the community. We regard the immoral person as one who denies the universalization principle by making a special exemption for himself from a course of action necessary to achieve a state of affairs that both he and others within the community desire to be brought about.

For every such moral inference there is at least potentially a prudential inference with an incompatible conclusion. For example, the individual X may want to have both fresh air in his house and to play music on his stereo system. With the circumstance left implicit, he might then use the following prudential practical inference:

> I want fresh air and to play music on my stereo.
> To attain both I must open the windows while playing music.
>
> ---
>
> I ought to open my windows while playing music.

In this way we generate the familiar Kantian conflict between duty and inclination. The duty to close windows is derived from a moral inference with a universalization premiss and shared desire, while the prudential obligation to open them is derived from an individual, or what we label a "selfish," desire. Normally we place priority on the moral over the prudential.

This priority should not be understood as the invariable subordination of the individual to social demands. A community may value individual autonomy and may regard it as morally obligatory that we respect the rights of others to pursue their goals provided this does not interfere with the rights of others to do the same. Also, the shared hopes and desires of a community change over time, and strong individuals are often instrumental in bringing about changes in social ideals by aggressively advancing *their* ideals and pursuing actions necessary to realize them. It is only later that these ideals become those shared by most in their societies. Before this change, we might be tempted to say that the prudential conclusions of the reformers should override moral conclusions derived from an established consensus that is destined to change. But it is more accurate to see such change as occurring within moral deliberation itself, with the reformers claiming themselves to be representatives of the community and expressing "we" premisses that differ from those of others. The conflict is between different claimants over the right to represent the community in expressing these "we" premisses. Until it is resolved, moral conclusions based on what is expressed by the de facto representative would seem to override the prudential.

Conflicting moral and prudential obligations are independently justified by separate moral and prudential inferences. Is there some way of justifying the priority we normally place on the moral conclusion over the prudential? As we saw, it is not necessary to bring about shared goals that everyone perform the types of actions necessary to realize them. A few liars and cheats will not prevent that general sense of trust of others so essential to community life. Why, then, shouldn't individuals seek to make themselves exceptions to moral rules? How do we answer the question "Why be moral?" It seems clear that there is no other form of practical inference that will provide the answer. Such inferences must be either agent-heterogeneous or agent-homogeneous in form, and must have premisses expressing either individual or shared desires. There seems to be no third form of inference in which the shared desires are compared with the personal, nor is it possible to establish priority of one over the other. As many writers have emphasized, this is what makes the resolution of conflicts between moral and individual demands often so very difficult. This difficulty would not exist if there were some form of inference we could appeal to in justifying the priority of the moral.[15]

It is here that the religious attitude, which may or may not be expressed through prayer, becomes relevant. Private prayer is often used to express individual hopes and desires for the future, and in this form may be relevant to prudential inferences if accompanied by consideration of actions as means of realizing what is hoped for and desired. But publicly expressed prayer is one of the chief means by which communities express their shared desires for future state of affairs, as when representatives of communities pray for peace and prosperity. In this plural "we" form, such expression may qualify for the first premiss of a moral inference. We have seen how prayer preserves, through use of established forms of address, continuity with past generations and their expressions of hopes and ideals, and is thus conservative in nature. It also expresses hopes whose realization may have to wait for future generations. As expressing shared desires, preserving forms of address, and projecting into the future, prayer places priority on what is social and continuous with past and future generations over what is individual and transitory. This is the same kind of priority we usually give to moral over prudential conclusions as based respectively on plural "we" and singular "I" premises.

Traditional theism within the Judeo–Christian and Islamic traditions interprets prayer as committing supplicants to belief in the existence of an eternal supernatural being. The importance of the eternal is in turn interpreted as the supremacy of this being and the authority of its commands as revealed in sacred scriptures. Guidance of conduct is understood in terms of a requirement obeying these commands. Fear of divine punishment and hope for rewards is intended to provide a prudential motivation to subordinate individual wants to moral requirements. Indeed, theists argue that without the belief that God exists, and acceptance of the authority of His commands, there would be no foundation for morality. The question "Why be moral?" would have no answer, or to use the literary expression of this position, if God is dead, "anything goes."

But there is a way of avoiding this choice between theism and "anything goes" in conduct, because the interpretation of prayer by the linguistic fideism previously mentioned has the effect of also endorsing the evaluative components of the religious attitude. As we have seen, public prayer is regarded as one of the central means by which communities express the shared desires used as first premises of moral inferences. Its forms of address derived from past generations affirm continuity between the hopes and desires of these generations and those of the present. The expression of desires for what is unlikely to be fulfilled within the lifetime of the present generation provides a link to an indefinitely extended future. Prayer thus seems to acknowledge the importance of the community as extending indefinitely back in time and forward into the future. This continuity is contrasted with the transitory nature of individual lives and the impermanence of changing individual desires. To the extent that the hopes expressed by prayer become incorporated into moral inferences in which specific types of action are prescribed, this can be regarded as representing an acknowledgment of the priority of the moral over the prudential in cases of conflict.

Prayer as interpreted by linguistic fideism and related to moral inferences thus provides an endorsement of the evaluative components of the religious attitude as affirming the overriding importance of belief in eternal mentality and committing believers to use this belief to guide conduct. But its endorsement must be regarded as limited in scope because the concept of eternity central to this attitude is abandoned in favor of continuity with past and future generations. It is conceivable that someday all religious supplicants on the entire planet will be able to agree on a single form of address that is claimed to preserve links to those of all past generations. Even so, these past generations would be members of the human species whose duration has been relatively brief and whose continuance into the indefinite future is by no means certain. Although it does function to emphasize the priority of the moral over the prudential, the social practice of prayer therefore provides an incomplete version of that sense of the eternal central to the religious attitude.

The fact that different forms of address occur in the prayers used within different communities further limits the scope of continuity. Perhaps the extreme form of exclusiveness is in the prayers of animistic religions addressed to spirits believed to be restricted to the locale of a particular village. It also exists, however, in the prayers used within the major monotheistic religions. To use "God" as a form of address links supplicants to the members of communities worshipping the god of Abraham, David, and Jesus in the past. But it does not link them to those within Islamic communities in which "Allah" has been the form of address. Even more obviously, it fails to link them to Mayahana Buddhists and all other peoples of the world whose prayers have no comparable form of address. The forms of address used in prayer evolved as means of promoting a sense of identity and uniqueness within communities, and to this extent they exclude both those of past generations with different histories and those of future generations not in the line of direct lineal descent from present members of the community. For this reason prayer as practiced within the various world religions has tended to reinforce social divisions.

Panpsychism's understanding of the evaluative priority of the eternal and its guidance of action suffers from no such limitations of scope because the continuity with past and future implied by prayer is extended indefinitely backward and forward in time. As a result, the moral overriding the prudential becomes interpreted as the priority of desires continuous with the appetitions of evolutionarily prior natural bodies over present transitory desires of human individuals. This can then guide conduct by justifying the priority we give to moral over prudential conclusions in cases of conflict. There is also the type of guidance of conduct discussed in chapter 4 in which the topic was interactive implications of mental terms. By placing priority on the eternal, we accept the responsibility for maintaining and enhancing natural forms other than those of our own species. We do this not because it is simply in our human self-interest, but because it is morally required of us to act in this way toward creatures with their own perspective evolving from an indefinitely remote past. In this way, the thesis of panpsychism does not simply make an assertion about the eternal existence of mentality justified on purely intellectual grounds. Through the evaluative components of the religious attitude, it also imposes a responsibility for actions preserving the diversity of life, and its justification is in part derived from the values promoted by these actions.

Before turning to a concluding summary, it is important to note a basic feature of the practical inferences just surveyed. Descriptive premises occur within all of them that must be accepted as true before a commitment is made to the actions required in their conclusions. Typically this acceptance must be based on evidence that is less than conclusive. Will this winter be cold? It may not be, but recent history makes a cold winter more likely, and on this basis I may decide to buy a coat. Metaphysical propositions such as the panpsychist thesis are, in some respects, similar to these descriptive premisses within the contexts of practical inferences. Although they are unlike descriptive premises in not being justified on the basis of empirical evidence, we have seen how the justification of the panpsychist thesis falls short of being conclusive, given the weakness of its analogical base. Given its consequences for action, however, we cannot suspend judgment in the face of this lack of proof any more than we can suspend judgment about the coldness of the coming winter when faced with the question of whether to buy a coat. Instead, we must decide to accept the thesis or reject it, and the wisdom of the choice is in part determined by the advantages gained by acting on the basis of it.

The Positive Drift for Panpsychism

This final chapter has been primarily devoted to demarcating the conception of the eternal held by atheistic panpsychism from that of theism. What alone is eternal for panpsychism is the existence of natural bodies with individually finite careers with a qualitative perspective accompanied by a "now" defining the past and present and a "here" defining a location within an environment. That mentality in this form is eternal is regarded as the propositional core of the religious attitude. By way of summary, it is helpful to contrast this secularist version of panpsychism with its principal alternatives. As in all practical reasoning, in the field of metaphysics we seldom find conclusive arguments demonstrating the truth of a favored viewpoint and decisively refuting a rejected alternative. Instead, we attempt to delimit a range of incompatible alternatives and then develop arguments purporting to show that one alternative warrants our acceptance on the grounds of having more plausibility than its competitors. Because of practical implications for conduct, a choice among inconclusive alternatives must be made, and it is incumbent on us to make the best of our situation. The following is a brief review of some arguments in previous chapters for favoring panpsychism over its alternatives.

Humanism

Characteristic of philosophical humanism is its insistence on the "great divide" separating human mentality from that of other natural forms. Members of infrahuman species may enjoy sensations and feelings and have a perspective on their environments, but such mentality constitutes "epiphenomena" in relation to underlying causal mechanisms, and these lower forms are to be regarded as automata whose movements are the effects of antecedent determining causes. We humans alone have freedom to choose between alternative courses of action, and this freedom is derived, humanists claim, from our capacity for self-consciousness, which is in turn an outcome of our unique ability to use discursive language. On the basis of quite obvious unique linguistic capacities that all agree exist, humanism thus claims a metaphysical distinction between the free and the determined.

Chapter 3 was an answer to the arguments of philosophical humanism. Self-consciousness in the strong sense required to make the distinction is an illusion, while in a weaker sense as the capacity for reporting sensations, its basis is simply a special use of language. Our concept of freedom is similarly derived from our ascriptions of responsibility and our regard of others as meriting praise and rewards and being liable to criticism and punishments. It is true that such ascriptions are applied by us only to fellow humans other than infants and only occasionally to pets or other animals under our care with which we socially interact. But the fact that we don't scold or praise a mouse is a fact about our relationship to the mouse, not a fact about the mouse as a mechanical system that contrasts it with ourselves.

Humanism obviously represents a denial of the propositional core of the religious attitude as defined in this chapter because it restricts mentality accompanied by spontaneity to a species of relatively recent duration. If we associate humanism with linguistic fideism, then the sense of permanence derived from religious practice extends only back to those past generations using the same addressee(s) of prayer.

Universal Mechanism

As we saw in chapter 3, the alternative to humanism is naturalism. Naturalism denies any metaphysical distinctions between the human and the infrahuman. What holds metaphysically for one natural form with a perspective holds for all, no matter what differences may exist between mental capacities. Naturalism has two varieties. Panpsychism is the variety that agrees with humanism in its insistence on human freedom of choice, and analogically extends this freedom in the form of spontaneity to natural forms exhibiting unity of organization and homeostasis. Universal mechanism is the variety of naturalism that agrees with humanism's claim that all movements of lower animals are the determined effects of antecedent causes, but more consistently extends this determinism to human behavior.

Mechanism does avoid the implausibility of humanism's "great divide," and we can only applaud its avoidance of this human conceit. But it encounters difficulties of its own. One arises from its attempts to explain away our intuition that we can indeed choose between alternative courses of action. A book is lying on the table before me. I am convinced that I could let it continue to lie there or pick it up. Either course of action is now an open possibility for me. And once having decided to pick up the book, I am also convinced that a few moments ago I could have let it lie on the table. Such convictions have been explained away by subtle reasoning offered by determinists. But the convictions we have about our choices seem to be more secure than the reasoning used in denying these convictions. In addition, there is, for mechanism, the difficulty posed by our practice of criticizing and praising the actions of ourselves and others, a practice that seems to have no point if what was done was the determined effect of antecedent causes. We can regard the criticisms and praise as part of a system of causes that determine future behavior. It is more plausible, however, to regard the evaluations as appropriate because the actions to which they are directed were outcomes of choices.

Why does mechanistic materialism deny these convictions? The denial seems to be based on naturalism's continuity principle and an assumption about the scientific method as applied to natural bodies. Panpsychism accepts metaphysical continuity between the human and other natural forms, and thus on this point there is agreement with universal mechanism. But it denies that the scientific method must assume that every natural event, including the behavior of natural bodies, is the effect of determining causes. Scientific inquiry does proceed by seeking increasingly precise specifications of causes. Often such specifications produce laws as uniform generalizations from which events as determined effects can be logically deduced. But more typically the generalizations are statistical generalizations from which only the probability of a given event can be inferred. These statistical generalizations could be converted to deterministic, uniform generalizations by specification of the cause, but, in turn, every uniform generalization can be converted back to a statistical generalization by further specification of the effect. The scientific method does not require that further specification of cause take priority over specification of effect. Whether the cause or the effect is further specified is determined by practical demands and available information, not by the inherent logic of scientific inquiry. Determinism in the form of a principle of causality is thus not a requirement of the scientific method, and the nature of this method cannot be used as a basis for universal mechanism.

It is, however, inconsistent with the scientific method to postulate nonphysical, and thus in principle unobservable, causes of natural events. Panpsychism has been historically associated with dualist metaphysical systems that have postulated special mental causes of the behavior of natural bodies, but there is no essential relation of the doctrine to dualism. To claim, as does panpsychism, that all natural bodies meeting certain conditions have perspectives with qualitative and spontaneous aspects is not to claim that there are two distinct causes of these bodies' behavior, one physical, the other specific to its qualitative and spontaneous aspects. The basis for attributing mentality to primitive natural forms is only an analogical inference from obvious features of our own experience to natural forms exhibiting anatomical and behavioral similarities to ourselves. The importation of causal terminology is but a spurious addition to such attribution.

Finally, universal mechanism, like humanism, must be recognized as inconsistent with the propositional core of the religious attitude, the belief that mentality with its attendant spontaneity has always existed and will always exist into the future. This theory insists on providing a mechanical explanation of mentality as a resultant property of mindless matter. As noted in chapter 5, such attempts so far have amounted to no more than a hand-waving extension of Darwinian principles of random variation and natural selection. Such principles may be cited in explanation of increases in complexity of organization and changes of behavioral repertoires, but they fail to explain how qualitative perspectives conferring no adaptive advantage evolved. Assuming its claim that mentality in natural bodies is eternal is justified, unrestricted panpsychism (unlike the restricted variety) faces no corresponding difficulties of explaining the origination of mentality.

Theism

Theism offers its own explanation of the origination of mentality in natural bodies. The Universal Mind as the addressee of prayer is postulated as being eternal, and this in itself is sufficient to satisfy the requirement of the religious attitude's propositional core. Unitary mentality of a form very different from the mentality of natural bodies is claimed to be eternal, with the mentality of natural bodies somehow appearing during the course of evolution as the result of a "superadding" activity on the part of the eternal Universal Mind. Does this provide a plausible solution to the problem of explaining how mentality originated? Only if we can understand the process by which the eternal Universal Mind somehow causes the introduction of that presence of perspective with qualitative and spontaneous aspect that is characteristic of the mentality of natural bodies. Given the totally mysterious nature of this special type of causation, however, this understanding is surely impossible. Theism may provide a propositional core for the religious attitude, but it offers no satisfactory solution to the origination problem. As we have seen, panpsychism faces no such problem because it claims mentality of natural bodies to be eternal. Because there was no moment in time when natural body mentality came into being, mentality being co-eternal with matter, there is no need for the contrived explanations of either universal mechanism or theism about how it originated.

Although it rejects the unitary mentality of theism in favor of an eternity of plurality of perspectives, atheistic panpsychism of the kind developed in this work has no quarrel with religion as a social practice. Prayer as the expression of shared hopes and ideals has played a role in moral reasoning by often providing its shared "we" premises. The use in prayer of addresses such as "God" or "Allah" serves to link present expressions of hopes and ideals to those expressed by past generations of communities, and in this way preserves a sense of cultural identity. The error of theism is correctly diagnosed by linguistic fideism as the confusion between the language of prayer and language describing states of affairs. Lacking a developed science to explain natural events, it was understandable that in earlier ages addresses of prayer were assigned referring functions, their referents were believed to exist, and their referents were employed as explanatory causes. No such confusion can be excused after the development of the empirically testable explanations characteristic of modern science.

I have just offered a brief outline of some advantages offered by panpsychism over its principal competitors. Are these sufficient to justify our acceptance of the doctrine? We advocates of panpsychism must acknowledge some implausible aspects. As noted, these arise primarily from the conflict between the use of an analogical inference to initially justify panpsychism and the Origination Argument used in defense of it. The Origination Argument requires us to ascribe mentality to subatomic particles because current cosmological theory describes an early universe in which only these existed. We must acknowledge the possibility of our being required to ascribe mentality to fundamental particles without internal organization, if indeed these are determined to be the only elements existing shortly after the Big Bang. Such ascriptions of mentality seem inconsistent, however, with the use of an analogical inference as the means of initially justifying the panpsychist thesis. As noted in chapter 2, such an inference becomes progressively weaker as we reduce the structural and behavioral similarities between ourselves and more primitive natural bodies. If mentality must be ascribed to fundamental particles without structure to preserve the Origination Argument, then it is difficult to see what basis remains for any analogical inference. In extending the term "mentality" to these primitive bodies, we seem to have stripped it of any content derived from its application to our own experiences.

The religious attitude requires eternity for the mental, and the Origination Argument claims this for the past. When we consider eternity into the future, we also face difficulties, this time in the face of projections by cosmologists of either an end to life due to the universe's continuing expansion or a contraction leading to a violent explosion paralleling that of the Big Bang. Either fate would seem to be inconsistent with panpsychism's claim for the eternality of mentality.

While daunting, these difficulties serve only to reinforce the recognition that there is no conclusive demonstration of panpsychism, and that it does have its implausible aspects. But so do its competitors, and on balance panpsychism must be judged to be on stronger grounds. The remote past and future of our universe continue to be matters of speculation, and there is certainly no inconsistency between all current guesses about the universe's origins and eventual fate and the panpsychist thesis. As for the analogical inference to the most primitive of natural bodies, we must emphasize again that the inference is only to the conclusion that there is *some* form of perspective with *some* qualitative aspect, however intermittent, and *some* spontaneity, although perhaps only infinitesimal. So removed from our own forms of experience is this primitive form of mentality that it is impossible to imagine what it would be like to have such a perspective. But although it is beyond our powers to imagine, we can conceive its presence, and reason to this presence from premisses on which there is agreement. The objection that "mentality" as used in the analogical inference becomes too indefinite to be useful only represents an undue reliance on what is imaginable.

Despite difficulties, then, there remain solid theoretical reasons for accepting the thesis of panpsychism. There are practical reasons as well, and these should perhaps be weighed more heavily. As emphasized in chapter 4, attributions of mentality imply attitudes of concern and responsibilities for care that are inappropriate for mechanical systems. Preservation of the world's great variety of species becomes for panpsychism a responsibility toward natural forms that share basic similarities with ourselves. Guided by the evaluative component of the religious attitude, panpsychism places importance on the permanent and shared over the transitory and individual, and this makes sense of our intuition that moral conclusions should be given priority over prudential ones in cases of conflict. It does this by extending the link to past generations provided by prayer to natural forms predating the arrival of the human species. In this respect, it preserves what is valuable in theism while avoiding theism's irrational aspects.

Such considerations establish, I think, panpsychism as more plausible than the broad perspectives that have dominated philosophic discussions. The doctrine with a long and honorable history must be restated, to be sure, in a way that removes some of the more implausible aspects with which it has been historically associated. But once restated, what James termed the "drift of reasons positive and negative" tilts us toward its acceptance.

Notes

Frontispiece

The Chuang Tzu, from *A Source Book in Chinese Philospphy*, ed. and comp. Wing-Tsit Chan (1963), 209, 210.

Preface

1. See Paul Edwards, "Panpsychism," *The Encyclopedia of Philosophy*, 22–31; and Karl Popper, "Some Remarks on Panpsychism and Epiphenom-enalism," *Dialectica*, 177–186.

2. William James, *The Principles of Psychology*, 1: 149, 150.

3. Ibid., 181.

Chapter 1. Introduction

1. Nicholas Humphrey, *A History of the Mind*, 120 ff. In this account, consciousness is restricted to organisms with a "high-fidelity" feedback loop within a cerebral cortex. This is said to exclude organisms such as amoebas, worms, and fleas.

2. For speculation about the possible internal structure of the top quark, see Tony Liss and Paul Tipton, "The Discovery of the Top Quark," 54–59. The authors conclude, however, that present evidence supports this

quark's status as fundamental: "For now we must conclude that the top quark, though massive, is indeed fundamental; it has no parts."

3. D. S. Clarke, *Philosophy's Second Revolution*, 72–80.

4. That we cannot apply "a conceptual grid that is alien to their intrinsic nature" to conscious events is argued in Colin McGinn's "Consciousness and Space." McGinn singles out the inapplicability of spatial categories as the reason for the ineffability of the mental, but also inapplicable would seem to be our referential, quantitative, and causal categories.

5. Such confusion occurs in Gilbert Ryle's criticisms of John Stuart Mill's analogical arguments on the grounds that they are based on the single case of the experiences of the individual making the inference. See Ryle, *The Concept of Mind*, 53, 54.

6. For this definition see his *The Logical Basis of Metaphysics*, ch. 1.

Chapter 2. Versions of Panpsychism

1. For a more complete survey of recent versions of panpsychism see David Griffin's very useful *Unsnarling the World-Knot*, 77–116.

2. That Socrates' conception of the soul is borrowed from Pythagoras is indicated by participation in the dialogue of Simmias and Cebes, both followers of Pythagoras.

3. Aristotle, *De Anima*, 412a 18–27.

4. A similar kind of restricted panpsychism is implied by the moral instructions of the Gautama Buddha, in which we find criticisms of those monks "who live on the food provided by the faithful, [and] continue addicted to injuring plants or vegetables; . . . He [the true follower] refrains from injuring such plants or animals" (*The Tevigga Sutta* in *Buddhist-Sutras*, ch. III, sec. 1). Nowhere in the Old and New Testaments or Koran can similar sentiments to be found.

5. *De Anima*, 429b 2–4; 430a 20–25.

6. Gottfried Leibniz, *Monadology*, 66, 67. In *Discourse on Metaphysics, Correspondence with Arnauld, and Monadology*.

7. *Monadology*, 71.

8. *Monadology*, 1, 3.

9. Leibniz, draft of the letter of November 28, 1686 to Arnauld. Translated by G. Montgomery in *Discourse on Metaphysics*.

10. Letter of November 28, 1686 to Arnauld.

11. This leads Arnauld in his letter of March 4, 1687 to Leibniz to correctly conclude that the dispute between himself and Leibniz over substantial form is "only a dispute regarding a word." Arnauld chooses Aristotle's wider definition of substantial form of the *Metaphysics*, according to which, substantial form is the definition or formula of a thing. By this definition a statue can be said to have a form. Leibniz chooses a definition of substantial form derived from *De Anima*. Here form is the soul as actuality of a body.

12. Edwards, "Panpsychism," 22–31. Edwards' criticisms are directed also toward Friedrich Paulsen, who also extends panpsychism to trees and plants in his *Introduction to Philosophy*.

13. *Monadology*, 28, 30.

14. At any rate, this is the view formulated in the *Monadology*. In the earlier *Discourse*, he draws a sharp distinction between the souls of lower animals and "intelligent souls which alone know their actions, and not only do not perish through natural means, but indeed always retain the knowledge of what they are" (*Discourse*, XII).

15. *Monadology*, 14.

16. *Monadology*, 19.

17. *Monadology*, 23.

18. Draft of letter of November 28, 1686 to Arnauld.

19. As set forth in Bertrand Russell, *A Critical Exposition of the Philosophy of Leibniz*.

20. Cf. Alfred North Whitehead, *Process and Reality*, 108.

21. Ibid., Part V, Sec. III.

22. Ralph Waldo Emerson, "The Sphinx," in *Ralph Waldo Emerson: Selected Essays, Lectures, and Poems*.

23. In his *The Civilization of Experience: A Whiteheadian Theory of Culture*, David Hall contends that Whitehead employs a method of "analogical generalization" that serves "as a means of coordinating various elements of experience in terms of the extension of a key notion derived from a single element of experience" (11–21). This may be so, but the nature of this extension remains unspecified by Whitehead.

24. Whitehead, *Science and the Modern World*, 129.

25. Ibid., 78.

26. Ibid., 99.

27. Ibid., 108.

28. Ibid., 85.

29. Ibid., 53.

30. For criticisms of it, see my "Two Aspects of Hartshorne's Metaphysics."

31. For Hartshorne's criticisms of Whitehead's postulation of independent "eternal objects" see his *Whitehead's Philosophy*, 59.

32. See "Why Psychicalism? Comments on Keeling's and Shepherd's Criticisms," 67–72 for a brief account by Hartshorne of his method of analogy. Behavioral criteria derived from human application, he says, are "generalized beyond common sense" in stating the panpsychist thesis, and this generalization must be through an argument from analogy: "The argument from analogy, whatever its defects, is all we have."

33. See Kitaro Nishida, *A Study of Good*.

34. See, for example, Charles Hartshorne, *Creative Synthesis and Philosophic Method*, 6; and Hartshorne, *Beyond Humanism*.

35. Hartshorne, *Creative Synthesis*, 6.

36. Ibid., 35.

37. Thomas Nagel, "Panpsychism" in *Mortal Questions*, 181–195.

38. The concession of token-token identities is one that I don't think should be made, because expressions such as "my pain now" are not referring expressions, and only such expressions can function as terms of identity statements. The issue is controversial, and the concession is made here only to advance the argument. I also pass over Saul Kripke's contention that mental/physical identities must be necessary, a contention which, if true, would establish the necessity Nagel is seeking.

39. See Hartshorne's "Physics and Psychics: The Place of Mind in Nature" in *Mind in Nature*, 93; and *The Logic of Perfection*, 229. In the former work Hartshorne describes psychic causation as two-way: "We in our human way share in the subhuman emotional life of cells; they in their subhuman way share in our emotional life." Hartshorne regards this two-way interaction between whole and parts as "the key to the influence of body upon mind." Griffin claims that promise for solving the traditional mind–body problem is the principal reason for adopting panpsychism (or what he calls "panexperientialism"): "The most important reason for trying a panexperientalist position, of course, is that it provides hope of actually solving the mind–body problem." See his *Unsnarling the World-Knot*, 92. Like Hartshorne, the solution arises, Griffin thinks, from the experiencing

of brain cells: "brain cells are themselves regarded as centers of experience (so that there is no problem of *dualistic* interactionism)" (235). A similar view can be found in Timothy Sprigge's *The Vindication of Absolute Idealism*, 104. That the "noumenal filling" of brain processes is psychical, argues Sprigge, "allows a far more promising account of how they interact with the consciousness of the organism as a whole."

40. A similar criticism is made by James Van Cleve in "Mind: Dust or Magic? Panpsychism Versus Emergence," 215–245. Van Cleve states the difficulty in terms of the emergence of the mental from the physical rather than in terms of explanations of mental/physical correlations. If the regress terminates in fundamental particles, Van Cleve notes, "we must admit a kind of emergence after all—of the higher mental functions from the lower mental functions." The problem of emergence is discussed in chapter 5.

41. Arthur Schopenhauer, *The World as Will and Representation*, 1: 99–105.

42. Gustav Fechner, *Elements of Psychophysics*, 1: 3.

43. Fechner, "Concerning Souls" in *Religion of a Scientist*, 135.

44. Ibid., 136.

45. Fechner, "The Soul Life of Plants" in *Religion of a Scientist*, 166, 167.

46. Ibid.,169, 170.

47. David Chalmers, "Facing Up to the Problem of Consciousness" in *Explaining Consciousness*. See also Chalmers's *The Conscious Mind*, (244), in which Chalmers poses this possibility on the grounds that "consciousness arises from functional organization" and the fact that information-processing systems have functional organization. See Searle's criticisms of Chalmers' view in David Chalmers and John Searle, "Consciousness and the Philosophers: An Exchange," 61, 62.

48. Chalmers's application of information theory to the particle level is endorsed by William Seager in his "Consciousness, Information and Panpsychism" in *Explaining Consciousness*, 269–286.

49. Whether there is a sense of "information" in this organizational sense can be applied to both thermodynamics and biological organisms has been hotly debated. Ernst Mayr argues that information realized in organisms is distinct in *The Growth of Biological Thought*. In contrast, E. O. Wiley applies a generic sense of information to both physics and biology in his "Entropy and Evolution" in *Entropy, Information, and Evolution*.

50. That this confusion is common within recent comparisons of human with artificial intelligence is pointed out by Raymond Tallis in *On the Edge of Certainty*, 90–103.

Chapter 3. Humanist and Mechanist Alternatives

1. John McDowell, *Mind and World*, 115. McDowell goes on to qualify his distinction between the human and the nonhuman, saying that while animals lack "Kantian freedom," they do have "self-movingness" (182). The qualification still seems to let the original distinction stand.

2. For the definition of an emergent property, see Jaegwon Kim, "Emergent Properties" in *Emergence or Reduction? Essays on the Prospects of Nonreductive Physicalism*.

3. In some accounts, these representations are said to correspond to expressions within specific languages; in others, notably that of Jerry Fodor in *The Language of Thought*, representations are encoded in a form that is invariant across different languages, with decoding taking place during speech production. I ignore these differences between the different accounts in this summary exposition.

4. For these definitions of the meaning and reference of mental representations, see Jerry Fodor's *Psychosemantics*.

5. For these examples, see Ruth Millikan, "Biosemantics," 281–297; and Mohan Matthen "Intentionality and Perception: A Reply to Rosenberg," 727–733.

6. Millikan, "Biosemantics."

7. Orientation to light is an example used by Fred Dretske to illustrate what he calls "type III" representational systems. See his *Explaining Behavior*, 62ff. and his earlier *Knowledge and the Flow of Information*.

8. Fred Dretske, "Misprepresentation" in *Belief: Form, Content, and Function*, 17–36. The problem of misrepresentation is also discussed by Fodor with his examples of cows on dark nights causing "horse" tokens in *Psychosemantics*, 99ff.

9. Ludwig Wittgenstein, *Philosophical Investigations*, I, sec. 493.

10. David Rosenthal, "Two Concepts of Consciousness," 329–359. Rosenthal's second-order thoughts correspond to John Locke's "ideas of reflection," ideas that it is possible for us to have of "the mind's operations."

11. For this view that second-order desires are the source of human freedom see Harry Frankfurt, "Freedom of the Will and the Concept of a Person," 5–20.

12. Some panpsychists, however, have implausibly denied this. C. H. Waddington in *The Nature of Life*, for example, claims that "even in the simplest inanimate things there is something which belongs to the same realm of being as self-awareness" (121).

13. The pronoun "I" thus functions as an address, not a referring subject. For arguments for this see my "The Addressing Function of 'I'," 91–93.

14. See Gilbert Ryle's *Concept of Mind*, 163–167.

15. Dorothy Cheney and Robert Seyfarth, *How Monkeys See the World*.

16. See Norman Malcom and D. M. Armstrong, *Consciousness and Causality: A Debate on the Nature of Mind*, 31.

17. John Heil, *The Nature of True Minds*, 202.

18. Keith Lehrer, *Metamind*, 288–290.

Chapter 4. Mental Ascriptions

1. Hilary Putnam, "Other Minds" in *Mind, Language and Reality*, 342–361.

2. For this view, see Paul Ziff, "The Simplicity of Other Minds," 575–584. Ziff proposes this as a solution to the problem of other minds, but makes it clear that to say of another he has a mind is to say that he is in some mental state such as having a pain. Ziff's account is endorsed with qualifications by Putnam in "Other Minds." For a version of this theory see also William Lycan, *Judgment and Justification*, 116–126.

3. Cheney and Seyfarth, *How Monkeys See the World*, 218–235.

4. Nagel, "Panpsychism" in *Mortal Questions*, 181–195.

5. See Peter Strawson, *Freedom and Resentment and Other Essays*.

Chapter 5. Mentality and Evolution

1. Daniel Dennett, *Darwin's Dangerous Idea*.

2. John Locke, *Essay Concerning Human Understanding*, Bk. IV, Ch. X, 10.

3. John Mackie, *The Miracle of Theism*, 13.

4. The processes of formation are described in Steven Weinberg's *The First Three Minutes*.

5. Graham Cairns-Smith, *Genetic Takeover*, 45ff. See also Richard Dawkins, *The Blind Watchmaker*, 148–158; and Dennett, *Darwin's Dangerous Idea*, 156–158.

6. Dennett, 48–60; and Manfred Eigen, *Steps Towards Life*, 12.

7. For descriptions of the simulations by Conway and his colleagues, see Martin Gardiner, *Wheels, Life and Other Mathematical Amusements*; Mark Bedau, "Weak Emergence" in *Philosophical Perspectives: Mind, Causation, and World*; and Dennett in *Darwin's Dangerous Idea*, 163–173.

8. See, for example, Mark Bedau and Norman Packard, "Measurement of Evolutionary Activity, Teleology, and Life" in *Artificial Life II*, 431–462.

9. Dretske, *Naturalizing the Mind*, 164.

10. Cf. Paulsen's question in *Introduction to Philosophy*, 99: "Is the first feeling in the protoplasmic particle something absolutely new?" To this he answers that if it is, then there is "creation out of nothing."

11. This objection is stated in Edwards' "Panpsychism," 22–31, and by Van Cleve in "Mind: Dust or Magic? Panpsychism Versus Emergence."

12. A version of this argument can be found in Nagel's "Panpsychism." For a good discussion of it see William Seager's "Consciousness, Information and Panpsychism."

13. Weinberg, *The First Three Minutes*, 5. See also the description of the universe by Graham Collins' "Fireballs of Free Quarks," *Scientific American*, 16–17. Ten microseconds after the Big Bang it was in an exotic state where "ordinary protons and neutrons melt together and form a fiery soup of free-roaming quarks and gluons," a state which can now be reproduced in some particle physics laboratories.

14. Jaegwon Kim, "'Downward Causation' in Emergentism and Nonreductive Physicalism" in *Emergence or Reduction? Essays on the Prospects of Nonreductive Physicalism*.

15. Karl Popper, "Some Remarks on Panpsychism." This is used as an argument against panpsychism, indicating that Popper regards mentality, like solidity, as being a resultant property, a naturally necessitated effect.

16. That the emergence of the mental from the physical is mysterious is acknowledged by one of its early advocates. Samuel Alexander in his *Space, Time, and Deity* concedes that the emergence of a property of a whole must "be accepted with the 'natural piety' of the investigator. *It admits of no explanation*" (46).

17. Humphrey dismisses panpsychism in *A History of the Mind* with the comment that it "is one of those superficially attractive ideas that crumble to nothing as soon as they are asked to do any sort of explanatory work" (203). This represents a complete misunderstanding of the doctrine: it is designed to put an end to the flood of bogus explanations of the origins of mentality that masquerade as "scientific." The advantage of panpsychism is precisely that it avoids the need for futile "explanatory work."

18. Ruth Millikan, *White Queen Psychology and Other Essays for Alice*, 14ff.

Chapter 6. *The Theistic Alternative*

1. David Lewis, *Pluralism of Worlds*, 2.

2. David Hume, *Dialogues Concerning Natural Religion*.

3. John Mackie, *The Miracle of Theism*.

4. Locke, *Essay Concerning Understanding*, Bk. IV, Ch. X, 2.

5. Ibid., Bk. IV, Ch. X, 5.

6. Ibid., Bk. IV, Ch. X, 6.

7. Ibid., Bk. IV, Ch. X, 10.

8. Ibid., Bk. IV, Ch. X, 15.

9. Ibid., Bk. IV, Ch. X, 16. See also paragraph 14, in which the possibility of an infinity of material beings is said to be the possibility of "an infinity of gods."

10. John Mackie, *The Miracle of Theism*, 120. This equivocation, Mackie notes, was first mentioned by Leibniz in his *New Essays Concerning Human Understanding*, Bk. IV, Ch. X.

11. Ibid., Bk. IV, Ch. X, 12.

12. For this same criticism, see Mackie, *The Miracle of Theism*: "Twentieth-century computer technology should at least make us cautious about laying down a priori what material structures could not do" (120, 121).

13. As Mackie remarks in *The Miracle of Theism*, "To develop out of this [the impossibility of a scientific explanation] a theory of a god's bare thought and intention first creating matter out of nothing, then instituting causal laws, and finally annexing animal and human consciousness to certain natural systems, is to build myth upon myth" (131, 132).

14. That a Whiteheadean system of panpsychism can be developed independently of theology is argued by Donald Sherburne in *A Whiteheadean Aesthetic*.

Chapter 7. The Religious Attitude

1. See Charles Hartshorne, *The Logic of Perfection*, 34ff.

2. Leibniz, *Monadology*, 32.

3. Ibid., 47.

4. Ibid., 76.

5. Ibid., 74.

6. Leibniz, *Discourse*, XXXV.

7. *Monadology*, 84.

8. Whitehead, *Process and Reality*, 32.

9. See *Process and Reality*, 346: "The consequent nature of God is his judgment on the world. He saves the world as it passes into the immediacy of his own life."

10. See *The Tevigga Sutta* in *Buddhist-Suttas*, ch. II, secs. 1, 8. The good man, it is said, "is compassionate and kind to all creatures that have life," and he "refrains from injuring any herb or any creature."

11. The view I outline here is similar to that developed by D. Z. Phillip in *The Concept of Prayer* and *Religion without Explanation* and defended by B. R. Tilghman, *An Introduction to Philosophy of Religion*, 211ff. It is called "religious unrealism" in Charles Taliaferro, *Contemporary Philosophy of Religion*, Ch. 2. Taliaferro contrasts it with "religious realism," which regards "God exists" as making a cognitive existential claim.

12. For the distinction between the "believe in" of faith and propositional belief see Norman Malcom, "Anselm's Ontological Argument," 41–62. Michael Hodges provides an excellent account of the believe in–believe that contrast in his "Faith: Themes from Wittgenstein, Kierkegaard and Nietzsche," unpublished manuscript.

13. See John Hick, *God and the Universe of Faith*, 24; and Roger Trigg, *Reason and Commitment*.

14. The brief sketch offered here summarizes the more complete discussion in my *Practical Inferences*, Chs. VI, VII. In this work I argue for the view that moral "ought" statements are derived within practical inferences

from expressive "we" premisses and a universalization principle. Here I simply summarize the conclusion of this argument.

15. This is the problem known as "egoist-conversion," the problem of convincing the egoist using only prudential inferences to act in ways promoting the general good. It is discussed in James Doyle's "Moral Rationalism and Moral Commitment," 1–22.

References

Alexander, Samuel. *Space, Time, and Deity*. London: Macmillan, 1920.

Aristotle. *De Anima*. In *The Basic Works of Aristotle*. Edited by R. McKeon. New York: Random House, 1941.

Bedau, Mark. "Weak Emergence." In *Mind, Causation, and World*. Edited by J. Tomberlin. Oxford: Blackwell, 1997.

Bedau, Mark and Norman Packard. "Measurement of Evolutionary Activity, Teleology, and Life." In *Artificial Life II*. Edited by C. Langton et al. Reading, CA: Addison-Wesley, 1992.

Cairns-Smith, Graham. *Genetic Takeover*. Cambridge: Cambridge University Press, 1982.

Chalmers, David. *The Conscious Mind*. Oxford: Oxford University Press, 1996.

———. "Facing Up to the Problem of Consciousness." In *Explaining Consciousness: The Hard Problem*. Edited by J. Shear. Cambridge, MA: MIT Press, 1997.

Chalmers, David and John Searle. "Consciousness and the Philosophers: An Exchange." *New York Review of Books* (15 May 1997).

Cheney, Dorothy L. and Robert M. Seyfarth. *How Monkeys See the World: Inside the Mind of Another Species*. Chicago: University of Chicago Press, 1990.

Chomsky, Noam. "Review of B. F. Skinner's *Verbal Behavior*." *Language* 35 (1959): 25–58.

Chuang Tzu, The. In *A Source Book in Chinese Philosophy.* Translated and compiled by Wing-Tsit Chan. Princeton: Princeton University Press, 1963.

Clarke, D. S. "The Addressing Function of 'I'." *Analysis* 38 (1978): 91–93.

———. *Practical Inferences.* London: Routledge and Kegan Paul, 1984.

———. "Two Aspects of Hartshorne's Metaphysics." *Semiotica* 10 (1994): 105–111.

———. *Philosophy's Second Revolution.* La Salle: Open Court, 1997.

Collins, Graham. "Fireballs of Free Quarks." *Scientific American* 282 (April, 2000): 16–17.

Dawkins, Richard. *The Blind Watchmaker.* London: Longmans, 1986.

Dennett, Daniel. *Darwin's Dangerous Idea.* New York: Simon & Schuster, 1995.

Doyle, James. "Moral Rationalism and Moral Commitment." *Philosophy and Phenomenological Research* 60 (2000): 1–22.

Dretske, Fred. *Knowledge and the Flow of Information.* Cambridge, MA: MIT Press, 1981.

———. "Misrepresentation." In *Belief: Form, Content, and Function.* Edited by R. J. Bogdan. Oxford: Clarendon Press, 1986.

———. *Explaining Behavior.* Cambridge, MA: MIT Press, 1988.

———. *Naturalizing the Mind.* Cambridge, MA: MIT Press, 1995.

Dummett, Michael. *Logical Basis of Metaphysics.* Cambridge, MA: Harvard University Press, 1991.

Edwards, Paul. "Panpsychism." In *The Encyclopedia of Philosophy*, Vol. 5. Edited by P. Edwards. New York: Macmillan, 1967.

Eigen, Manfred. *Steps Towards Life.* Oxford: Oxford University Press, 1992.

Emerson, Ralph Waldo. "The Sphinx." In *Ralph Waldo Emerson: Selected Essays, Lectures, and Poems.* Edited by R. Richardson. New York: Bantam Books, 1990.

Fechner, Gustav. *Religion of a Scientist.* Edited and translated by W. Lowrie. New York: Pantheon Books, 1946.

———. *Elements of Psychophysics*, Vol. 1. Translated by H. E. Adler. New York: Holt, Rinehart and Winston, 1966.

Fodor, Jerry. *The Language of Thought.* New York: Crowell, 1975.

———. *Psychosemantics.* Cambridge, MA: MIT Press, 1987.

Ford, Marcus. "William James: Panpsychist and Metaphysical Realist." *Transactions of the Peirce Society* 17 (1981): 158–170.

Frankfurt, Harry. "Freedom of the Will and the Concept of a Person." *Journal of Philosophy* 68 (1971): 5–20.

Gardiner, Martin. *Wheels, Life and Other Mathematical Amusements*. New York: Freeman, 1983.

Griffin, David. *Unsnarling the World-Knot*. Berkeley: University of California Press, 1998.

Hall, David. *The Civilization of Experience: A Whiteheadian Theory of Culture*. New York: Fordham University Press, 1973.

Hartshorne, Charles. *Beyond Humanism*. New York: Willett, Clark, 1937.

———. *The Logic of Perfection*. LaSalle: Open Court, 1962.

———. *Creative Synthesis and Philosophic Method*. La Salle: Open Court, 1970.

———. *Whitehead's Philosophy*. Lincoln: University of Nebraska Press, 1972.

———. "Why Psychicalism? Comments on Keeling's and Shepherd's Criticisms." *Process Studies* 6 (1976): 67–72.

———. "Physics and Psychics: The Place of Mind in Nature." In *Mind in Nature*. Edited by J. B. Cobb and D. R. Griffin. Washington, D.C.: University Press of America, 1977.

Heil, John. *The Nature of True Minds*. Cambridge: Cambridge University Press, 1992.

Hick, John. *God and the Universe of Faith*. New York: St. Martin's, 1973.

Hodges, Michael. "Faith: Themes from Wittgenstein, Kierkegaard, and Nietzsche." Unpublished manuscript.

Hume, David. *Dialogues Concerning Natural Religion*. Edited by H. D. Aiken. New York: Hafner, 1948.

Humphrey, Nicholas. *A History of the Mind: Evolution and the Birth of Consciousness*. New York: Simon & Schuster, 1992.

James, William. *The Principles of Psychology*. 2 vols. 1890. Reprint, New York: Dover, 1950.

Kim, Jaegwon. "'Downward Causation' in Emergentism and Nonreductive Physicalism." In *Emergence or Reduction? Essays on the Prospects of Nonreductive Physicalism*. Edited by A. Beckermann, H. Flohr, J. Kim. Berlin and New York: Walter de Gruyter, 1992.

Lehrer, Keith. *Metamind*. Oxford: Clarendon Press, 1990.

Leibniz, Gottfried. *New Essays Concerning Human Understanding*. Translated by P. Lucas and L. Grint. Manchester, England: Manchester University Press, 1953.

———. *Discourse on Metaphysics, Correspondence with Arnauld, and Monadology*. Translated by G. Montgomery. LaSalle: Open Court, 1962.

Lewis, David. *On the Plurality of Worlds*. Oxford: Blackwell, 1986.

Liss, Tony and Paul Tipton. "The Discovery of the Top Quark." *Scientific American* 277 (September, 1997): 54–59.

Locke, John. *Essay Concerning Human Understanding*. 2 vols. Edited by A. C. Fraser. New York: Dover, 1959.

Lycan, William. *Judgment and Justification*. Cambridge: Cambridge University Press, 1988.

Mackie, John. *The Miracle of Theism*. Oxford: Clarendon Press, 1962.

Malcom, Norman. "Anselm's Ontological Argument." *The Philosophical Review* 69 (1960): 41–62.

Malcom, Norman and D. M. Armstrong. *Consciousness and Causality: A Debate on the Nature of Mind*. Oxford: Blackwell, 1984.

Matthen, Mohan. "Intentionality and Perception: A Reply to Rosenberg." *Journal of Philosophy* 86 (89): 727–733.

Mayr, Ernst. *The Growth of Biological Thought*. Cambridge, MA: Harvard University Press, 1982.

McDowell, John. *Mind and World*. Cambridge: Harvard University Press, 1994.

McGinn, Colin. "Consciousness and Space." In *Explaining Consciousness: The Hard Problem*. Edited by J. Shear. Cambridge, MA: MIT Press, 1997.

Millikan, Ruth. "Biosemantics." *Journal of Philosophy* 86 (1989): 281–297.

———. *White Queen Psychology and Other Essays for Alice*. Cambridge, MA: MIT Press, 1993.

Nagel, Thomas. "Panpsychism." In *Mortal Questions*. Cambridge: Cambridge University Press, 1979.

Nishida, Kitaro. *A Study of Good*. Translated by V. H. Viglielmo. New York: Greenwood Press, 1988.

Paulsen, Friedrich. *Introduction to Philosophy*, 2nd edition. Translated by F. Thilly. New York: Holt, 1906.

Phillip, D. Z. *The Concept of Prayer*. London: Routledge & Kegan Paul, 1965.

———. *Religion without Explanation*. Oxford: Oxford University Press, 1976.

Popper, Karl. "Some Remarks on Panpsychism and Epiphenomenalism." *Dialectica* 31 (1977): 177–186.

Putnam, Hilary. "Other Minds." In *Mind, Language and Reality*. Cambridge: Cambridge University Press, 1975.

Quine, W. V. O. "Two Dogmas of Empiricism." In *From a Logical Point of View*. Cambridge, MA: Harvard University Press, 1953.

Rosenthal, David. "Two Concepts of Consciousness." *Philosophical Studies* 49 (1986): 329–359.

Russell, Bertrand. *A Critical Exposition of the Philosophy of Leibniz*. London: Allen & Unwin, 1937.

Ryle, Gilbert. *The Concept of Mind*. London: Hutchinson, 1949.

Schopenhauer, Arthur. *The World as Will and Representation*. 2 volumes. Translated by E. F. Payne. Indian Hills, CO: Falcon's Wing Press, 1958.

Seager, William. "Consciousness, Information and Panpsychism. " In *Explaining Consciousnes: The Hard Problem*. Edited by J. Shear. Cambridge, MA: MIT Press, 1997.

Sherburne, Donald. *A Whiteheadean Aesthetic*. New Haven: Yale University Press, 1961.

Shear, Jonathon, editor. *Explaining Consciousness: The 'Hard Problem'*. Cambridge, MA: MIT Press, 1997.

Skinner, B. F. *Verbal Behavior*. Englewood Cliffs, NJ: Prentice Hall, 1957.

Sprigge, Timothy. *The Vindication of Absolute Idealism*. Edinburgh: Edinburgh University Press, 1983.

Strawson, Peter. *Freedom and Resentment and Other Essays*. London: Methuen, 1974.

Swinburne, Richard. *The Existence of God*, revised edition. Oxford: Oxford University Press, 1991.

Taliaferro, Charles. *Contemporary Philosophy of Religion*. Oxford: Blackwell, 1998.

Tallis, Raymond. *On the Edge of Certainty*. London: Macmillan, 1999.

Tevigga Sutta, The. In *Buddhist-Suttas*. Translated by T. W. Rhys Davids. Delhi: Motilal Banarsidass, 1965.

Tilghman, B. R. *An Introduction to Philosophy of Religion*. Oxford: Blackwell, 1993.

Trigg, Roger. *Reason and Commitment*. Cambridge: Cambridge University Press, 1973.

Van Cleve, James. "Mind: Dust or Magic? Panpsychism Versus Emergence." *Philosophical Perspectives* 4 (1990): 215–245.

Waddington, C. H. *The Nature of Life*. London: Allen & Unwin, 1961.

Weinberg, Steven. *The First Three Minutes*. New York: Basic Books, 1977.

Whitehead, Alfred North. *Science and the Modern World*. Cambridge: Cambridge University Press, 1953.

———. *Process and Reality*, Corrected Edition. Edited by D. R. Griffin and D. W. Sherburne. New York: Macmillan, 1978.

Wiley, E. O. "Entropy and Evolution." In *Entropy, Information, and Evolution*. Edited by B. Weber et al. Cambridge, MA: MIT Press, 1988.

Wittgenstein, Ludwig. *Philosophical Investigations*. Translated by G. E. M. Anscombe. New York: Macmillan, 1953.

Ziff, Paul. "The Simplicity of Other Minds." *Journal of Philosophy* 72 (1965): 575–584.

Index

accountability, 57, 97–100, 124
actual entities, 32, 34–36, 152, 153
actuality, as substantial form, 21
ad ignorantium, fallacy of, 39, 82
addresses
    existential presuppositions of, 156,
        157
    means to intergenerational continuity,
        157, 158
    use in prayer, 160, 168
affective tone, 37, 38, 41
aggregates, 1, 3, 14, 26, 27, 36, 40, 41,
    115
    simple, 115, 116
    of spatial juxtaposition, 115
    structured, 115, 116
Alexander, Samuel, 119n
Alpha, as first individual with feeling,
    109–11
analogical extension, 6, 8, 11, 15, 29, 34,
    37–41, 45, 50, 59, 72, 82, 99, 138,
    171
    of mechanical models, 52, 59
analogical inference, 1, 8–17, 34, 45–49,
    52, 53, 59, 68, 85, 95, 102, 112–14,
    124, 130, 131, 136, 139, 160, 173–75
    applied to God's existence, 131, 132
    conflict with Origination Argument,
        113

    weakness of, 12, 100, 113
analytic/synthetic distinction, 16
animism, 131, 146, 168
Anselm, Saint, 132
apperception. *See* self-consciousness
Aquinas, Saint Thomas, 133
arguments for God's existence, 102, 132,
    144
    from consciousness, 139, 144, 154
    cosmological, 132, 133
    from design, 133
    Locke's, 133, 134, 137
    ontological, 132
    Swinburne's, 139
Aristotle, 5, 15, 21, 22–30, 45, 68, 72,
    150–54
Arnauld, Antoine, 24, 26, 30
artifacts, 1, 3, 50, 58
atheism, 154, 158. *See also*
    panpsychism: atheistic
Augustine, Saint, 148, 152
avowals, 75, 76, 86, 87, 95
    as expressive, 87, 88
    priority over third-person ascriptions,
        87

base of an analogy, 8, 9, 10, 12, 13, 41,
    52, 59, 82, 95, 112, 124, 139. *See*
    also relevance of base attributes